Advance Praise for *Alpha Dogs*

"A beautifully written, inspiring book from an author who has devoted her career to understanding small business excellence."

—Dr. Leonard L. Berry, Distinguished Professor of Marketing, Texas A&M University, and author of *Discovering the Soul of Service*

"*Alpha Dogs* is filled with engaging stories that provide nourishing food for thought."

—Amar Bhide, Lawrence D. Glaubinger Professor of Business at the Columbia University Graduate School of Business

"Read it! These stories will inspire and instruct any entrepreneur who wants to build a truly distinctive and durable business."

—John Case, author of *Open-Book Management*

"*Alpha Dogs* is a great resource for taking your business from the doghouse to the penthouse."

—Pat Croce, best-selling author of *I Feel Great and You Will Too!* and creator of the Pirate Soul Museum, Key West

"*Alpha Dogs* is a 'must read' book for every entrepreneur and potential entrepreneur! This excellent book spotlights leaders of the pack from ordinary businesses not just from the latest hi-tech phenomenon. Wise and practical tips for growing a company conclude each chapter. The book crystallizes the differences between businesses that lead the pack and ones that only follow."

—Marsha Firestone, PhD, president of
Women Presidents' Organization

"Donna Fenn has written a compelling book that is a must read for big company management teams who care about entrepreneurship and are struggling to grow a company and breathe new entrepreneurial life into their businesses. The riveting profiles will resonate with all struggling entrepreneurs, and the nuggets of wisdom in these real-life tales will prove to be invaluable."

—Judy George, CEO, Domain

"In a world where the big companies get bigger every year, Donna Fenn offers up this endearing and enlightening book to remind us that small can also still be beautiful. Her field guide to grassroots innovation and remarkable customer service shows companies— small, medium, and large—how to fend off commoditization and build profitable growth."

—Tom Kelley, general manager, IDEO,
and author of *The Art of Innovation*

"*Alpha Dogs* will be an essential roadmap for success for future generations of entrepreneurs."

—Steve Mariotti, president and founder, National Center
for Teaching Entrepreneurship

"Donna's book is entertaining and insightful . . . and it's an easy read. She captures the sound principles and innovative customer service strategies that raise the bar for all American entrepreneurs."

—Jack Mitchell, CEO, Mitchells/Richards,
and author of *Hug Your Customers*

"*Alpha Dogs* is a must read for everybody who yearns to start a business or already runs one. Buy every copy in town before your competitors see it. Inspiring and informative!"

—Martha Rogers, PhD, coauthor of *Return on Customer*
and co-founder of the Peppers and Rogers Group

"This book is a remarkable accomplishment. It is both the most practical and entertaining guide to how existing businesses can change course and achieve growth and strong market position. It is a book about visionaries and their concrete accomplishments. It tells how entrepreneurs remain creative and continue to push their organizations toward greatness. It is the best-written book I've read in a long time. If I could recommend only one book to someone looking to energize and transform their business, this would be it. A singular achievement."

—Carl J. Schramm, president and CEO,
Ewing Marion Kauffman Foundation

"*Alpha Dogs* has really inspired me. Now I want to be an Alpha Dog, too. This book is going to be the next *Good to Great*. It's that important."

—Pat Williams, senior vice president, Orlando Magic,
and author of *Coaching Your Kids to Be Leaders*

ALPHA DOGS

How Your Small Business Can
Become a Leader of the Pack

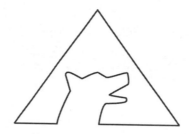

DONNA FENN

Collins

An Imprint of HarperCollinsPublishers

HarperCollins books may be purchased for educational, business, or sales promotional use. For information, please write: Special Markets Department, HarperCollins Publishers, 10 East 53rd Street, New York, NY 10022.

FIRST EDITION

Designed by Joy O'Meara

Library of Congress Cataloging-in-Publication Data has been applied for.

ISBN-10: 0-06-075867-8
ISBN-13: 978-0-06-075867-7

05 06 07 08 09 DIX/RRD 10 9 8 7 6 5 4 3 2 1

To my parents, Donald and Virginia Fenn,
with love and appreciation.

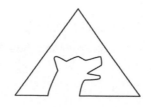

CONTENTS

FOREWORD

Will the Economy Please Come to Order!

M odern management as we know it dates back to the 1920s and the innovations of individuals such as Alfred Sloan, Frederic Taylor, J. P. Morgan, and others. Although many of the creators of the industrial economy were themselves entrepreneurs, during the following 50 years entrepreneurship was marginalized, economically and culturally. The industrial economy was shaped not by entrepreneurs, but by the large corporation and the new corporate executive.

Then, in the late 1970s, entrepreneurial hell broke loose. This economic and cultural "discovery" of entrepreneurship was a result of the convergence of two trends.

First, there was the advent of inexpensive desktop computing. This new technology was decentralized: it put into the hands of individuals—and small, emerging companies—technological capabilities that had resided in only the largest of organizations. Second, the baby boomers came of age, bringing into the marketplace values dramatically different from those of previous generations. Principal among these were a fundamental distrust of large, established organizations and a conviction that individuals could have a dramatic impact on the world at large—both legacies of the 1960s.

The rest is economic history. Start-up rates soared, from 60,000 new businesses per year in the 1960s and 1970s, to more than 600,000 in the 1980s. Today, Americans are launching new ventures at a rate of about one million each year. Even as you read this, somewhere in this country someone is launching a new venture every 30 seconds of every day.

This New Economy that has been evolving for more than two decades now is vast and complex. Nonetheless, in this context three observations about it are more important than the rest.

The Innovation Nation. The New Economy was as much a *cultural* transformation as an economic one. Young Americans coming of age in the 1980s witnessed the first significant waves of corporate downsizing, and saw their fathers and mothers, brothers and sisters, friends and neighbors lose their jobs for reasons that had nothing to do with individual performance. Twenty years later, downsizing has become a permanent feature of the marketplace. This economic reality has resulted in a wholesale redefinition of risk among younger generations. What's riskier, young people ask today, going to work for a large company only to lose one's job—often more than once—for reasons over which you have no control, or venturing into the world with the goal of creating one's own economic and professional security?

The evidence of this cultural change is apparent in the enterprise rates among young men and women between the ages of 18 and 26, who are starting businesses at twice the rate of the adult population at large. The change has even filtered down to high school students, 80% of whom reported in a Gallup poll several years ago that they were already thinking about starting a business as the preferred way to launch their adult working lives.

The traditional admonition of one generation to the next, "Go out and get a job," has been replaced by the much more bewildering mandate: "Go out and create a job for yourself."

The Last Meritocracy. The New Economy is color- and gender-blind. While historically entrepreneurship was dominated by white males, populations that lagged behind in the entrepreneurial arena recently have overtaken white guys with business plans. Consider the following data from the most recent census report. During the decade of the 1990s, the total number of businesses in the United States grew by 12%. During this same period:

- the number of women-owned businesses grew **24%**;
- the number of African American–owned businesses grew **26%**;
- the number of Hispanic-owned businesses grew **144%**; and
- the number of Asian-owned businesses grew **176%**.

With young people, women, and minorities starting new ventures at a record pace, entrepreneurship has gone mainstream.

The Execution Economy. Since 1982, *Inc.* magazine has published an annual ranking of the fastest-growing, young private companies in the United States. From its inception, the ranking has identified many of the country's entrepreneurial superstars when they were still in their infancy, including companies such as Microsoft, Oracle, Timberland, Charles Schwab, Qualcomm, Domino's, Intuit, and countless others.

In 1982, in the annual Inc. 500 survey of founders and CEOs, 75% reported that the single biggest factor leading to their success was identifying a hot, novel, proprietary idea. In the same survey conducted 15 years later, 94% of the founders and CEOs of the Inc. 500 claimed that the original idea for their business was "ordinary" or "mundane." The reason for their success: superior execution. These contemporary entrepreneurial leaders went on to explain that in today's marketplace, characterized by rapid change and intense competition, the only thing a "hot idea" guarantees is that your idea will be copied, and copied *quickly.*

During the past two decades we've witnessed the end of the era of "entrepreneurial novelty" and the dawn of the era of "entrepreneurial execution," where the only true source of sustained competitive advantage is one's entrepreneurial know-how.

The Age of the Alpha Dog

The provenance of large-company management ideas has mostly been the world of academia and strategic consulting: competitiveness and strategy (Michael Porter, Harvard), reengineering (Michael Hammer and James Champy, CSC Index), the learning organization (Peter Senge, MIT), and disruptive innovation (Clay Christensen, Harvard). If you want to learn the state of the art in corporate management thinking, visit the Harvard Business School or read the *Harvard Business Review.*

Not so for entrepreneurs. For them, just about everything worth knowing about running a small company is embedded in the social networks of successful growth companies. No ivory tower for them. They want their ideas conceived and developed in the marketplace, road tested.

That's the genius of this book. It's filled—every chapter, every page—with what we at *Inc.* magazine used to refer to as "real world entrepreneurship." This comes as no surprise to me, working as I did for so many years with Donna Fenn. From her earliest days at the magazine, she displayed an uncanny ability to sniff out the difference between what ultimately matters and what doesn't. *Alpha Dogs* has that alluring quality that's just so damned scarce these days in the management arena: authenticity. Those of you who have started something on your own, who have lived by your own wits, will know immediately what I mean.

In addition to this obsession with "real world" entrepreneurship, Donna and I share another passion: ordinary businesses. We've both long held the belief that there's often precious little to learn from businesses parked in high-growth markets. In fact, often the secret to "success" in these hot spots is simply showing up on time. And so Donna's Alpha Dogs are in such glamorous niches as selling bicycles, making ice cream, baking cookies, knitting socks. Yes, socks. It's hardly necessary to point out that businesses such as these succeed not as a result of their markets but in spite of them. And for those of us looking for best practices, ideas we can apply in our own organizations, that makes all the difference in the world. No high concept here, just world-class execution, day in and day out.

While Donna's chosen markets may be deliberately mundane, her themes are anything but: systematized innovation; high-performance workforces, over-the-top customer service, leveraging your brand. In fact, Donna's eight companies showcase the leading drivers that define what we mean when we talk about superior execution.

The Power of Poverty

I suspect that when Donna conceived this book she had the *Inc.* reader in mind—the founders and top managers of small, emerging companies. She loves this audience and has served it well for a good part of her career now. I think this book deserves, and will reach, a wider audience than that.

Ten or fifteen years ago, so many of the skirmishes that we chronicled in the pages of *Inc.* featured a young, underresourced, but agile company going head-to-head with a large, bureaucratic one. That's changed. These days, more often than not these same battles feature a young, underresourced, but agile company up against an underresourced but agile and entrepreneurial team within a large company. This book will be read and studied and discussed in companies large and small, as increasingly all competition becomes entrepreneurial competition.

I'm asked often, especially by students these days, for a clear and basic definition of entrepreneurship. My answer has been the same for more than 25 years now. Entrepreneurship is getting something new and significant done in an environment characterized by resource scarcity. It is the substitution of human capital—imagination, invention, resourcefulness—for financial capital. Looked at from this perspective, it's not only our business and financial organizations that are faced with the mandate of becoming, and remaining, entrepreneurial. The challenge is a societal one, as school systems, arts organizations, community nonprofits, and state and local governments all try to adjust to a new environment characterized by chronic resource scarcity. We are all faced with the prospect of learning how to do more with less. This pressure won't abate any time soon. And so I can easily imagine *Alpha Dogs* quickly becoming an indispensable guide to the new realities of the early days of the twenty-first century. You couldn't ask for a better companion for the days ahead.

George Gendron
Former editor in chief, Inc. *magazine*
Entrepreneur in residence, Clark University,
Worcester, Massachusetts
April 18, 2005

INTRODUCTION

I've written hundreds of stories about entrepreneurs over the past 20 years, but much of what I now know about business I might have easily learned from a man who runs a bicycle shop. I first met Chris Zane in 1995, when my friend and editor at *Inc.* magazine, Josh Hyatt, asked if I'd drive up to Branford, Connecticut, to do some reporting on a business he had heard about.

"Don Peppers and Martha Rogers really like this guy," Josh told me, referring to the Connecticut-based business gurus. "He's into one-to-one marketing in a big way."

"So what does he do?" I asked.

"Well," said Josh, "he has a bike shop."

"Oh," I said, with precious little enthusiasm.

It didn't sound like a dream assignment. *Inc.*'s readers are relatively sophisticated, and I had a hard time imagining how I might extract enough wisdom from Zane to fill up five pages in the magazine.

But Branford is a manageable drive from my home in Pelham, New York, so I agreed to visit Zane, thinking I'd politely spend an hour or so with him, then head off to Stew Leonard's in nearby Norwalk to do my grocery shopping for the week. But I never made it to Stew's.

Shortly after I sat down with Zane, I knew that Josh's instincts were right: I had a great story. Zane had applied for his first tax identification number before his voice had changed and had opened his first store when he was a junior in high school. By the time he was 30, he had mastered the kinds of sophisticated business strategies that his competitors just assumed were beyond their capability or irrelevant to their businesses: stellar customer service, one-to-one marketing, continuous learning, employee development, and cause-related marketing (see chapter 2).

Zane had done all of these things strategically—they weren't just gimmicks to lure in customers. He looked and behaved a lot more like a CEO than a shop owner. By transcending the generally perceived limitations of small business, he had moved into an altogether different stratosphere. And he did it with a bike shop!

While most of Chris Zane's competitors were cycling enthusiasts who were happy simply to sell bikes, he was busy thinking about the lifetime value of customers, employee training, inventory control, and database management. He attended business seminars that taught him, for instance, how to emulate the Ritz-Carlton's customer service program, and he tracked down industry veterans like the CEO of Raleigh, whose expertise he doggedly mined for advice on inventory management. Then he implemented every strategy that made sense to him, no matter how radical it seemed.

His programs were more L.L.Bean and Ritz-Carlton than neighborhood bike shop. Does Zane love bikes? Sure. But he loves the game of business even more. And that's why he did all of the things that his competitors could have done but didn't. He now has 65% of his local market share, only four competitors (as opposed to sixteen when he started the business), a surefire way to compete against Wal-Mart, an innovative new distribution channel for his merchandise, and $6.1 million in sales. And that's exactly what made him a "Leader of the Pack" (an Alpha Dog entrepreneur!), which was what we called the feature story that I wrote about him in the February 1996 issue of *Inc.*

There are Alpha Dogs in every sector of the economy, and I want to introduce you to some of them in this book. You'll meet entrepreneurs in a variety of industries from all over the United States whose companies appear quite ordinary, even mundane, but who have moved to the head of the pack. And I think they have more to teach us than the high-tech and high-glitz companies we so often read about in the business press. Like most businesses, they didn't have mountains of money, clever inventions, or stables of MBAs. But they did have a passion for business and a talent for seeing opportunities where others saw limitations; they grew in spite of their lackluster or, in some cases, moribund, industries. And so they illustrate one of the most important and inspiring lessons that any business owner can take to heart: it's possible to grow a great company in any industry or any economy.

It wasn't easy to choose the businesses for this book. Based upon more than 20 years of studying entrepreneurial companies, I identified a handful of growth strategies that I felt were important to emphasize:

- customer service
- employee engagement
- use of technology
- community connections
- innovation
- branding
- alliances
- reinvention

Then, keeping in mind geographic and industry diversity, I went through my own extensive database of contacts and put the word out among friends and colleagues. I was looking for:

- Companies in low-tech industries—the kinds of businesses you might find just about anywhere in the United States.
- Bootstrapped or traditionally financed companies with well under $100 million in sales, solid revenue growth, and strong histories of profitability. The companies I chose were all forthcoming with numbers, but because they are privately held, those numbers were not independently verified.
- Impeccable industry reputations as innovators or leaders.
- Companies that were great places to work, regardless of the strategy they were illustrating, because every company's lasting success rests upon its employees.
- Companies that had been around for at least 10 years because I wanted them to have experienced good economic times and bad ones; companies that don't have a few war wounds aren't terribly interesting to me.

I wanted to include some family businesses because, according to the Family Firm Institute, 80% to 90% of all businesses in North America are family owned; they contribute 64% of the GDP and employ 62% of the American workforce. Approximately 39% of those businesses will change hands within the next five years; I hope this book will be a useful resource for that next generation of managers as they seek out ways to professionalize their companies.

Manufacturing firms were high on my list of must-haves, because I believe passionately that U.S. manufacturing companies can still play a vital role in our economy, provided they pull themselves out of the commodity game.

Women play a prominent role in the book as well. According to the Center for Women's Business Research, 48% of all privately held companies are now majority owned by women; between 1997 and 2004, the number of women-owned companies grew 17%, compared with 9% for all firms.

A footnote: Back when I first joined *Inc.* in 1983 as a researcher/ reporter, a group of us were committed to tracking down female entrepreneurs to feature in the magazine. It wasn't easy. Back then, women-owned businesses seemed smaller, less visible, and less sophisticated than their male-owned counterparts. Today, that couldn't be further from the truth; female-owned Alpha Dog companies are every bit as prevalent as male-owned ones.

I think you'll learn as much from these entrepreneurs and their stories as I did, and I hope that you'll have as much fun reading about them as I did getting to know them and writing about them. But most of all, I hope you'll be enlightened with a few sparks of recognition, and inspired enough to move to the head of your own pack.

1 | Lead the Pack

If you own one of the 5.7 million small businesses in the United States, or are tempted to take the leap of faith required to start one, there's good news and bad news. Every year, 10% of small businesses—a half million or so—shut down for good; a quarter of all businesses never make it past their second year; 60% close after six years.

Today, small companies are up against an unprecedented set of challenges:

- **Consumers** are more educated, demanding, and fickle than ever before.
- **Consolidation** in nearly every imaginable industry is breeding behemoth competitors.
- **Technology** is enabling tiny competitors to look much bigger and allowing bigger competitors to forge more intimate relationships with customers—maybe *your* customers.
- **Saturation** of the marketplace by a growing number of products and services is making it even more difficult for small businesses to distinguish and differentiate themselves.

Under those circumstances, who in their right mind could expect to be a shining star in the vast entrepreneurial firmament?

You'd be surprised. According to the Global Entrepreneurship Monitor research program, established by Babson College and the London Business School, more than one in ten adult Americans is now starting or growing a new business; every year, more than 500,000 new start-up companies replace those that have gone under. In spite

of the odds, it seems that entrepreneurs are relentlessly optimistic. The
good news: they have every reason to be.

Even as small companies are facing new hurdles, they're also
being presented with a fresh set of opportunities. There's never been a
better or more exciting time to be a small business owner, or a more
critical time to begin transforming your company into a leader of the
pack. Here are seven reasons why:

1. Goliath Backlash. With 2004 revenues of $256.3 billion, Wal-
Mart Stores, Inc., now accounts for more than 5% of total U.S. retail
sales. But wherever you find one of their 3,600 stores, you're also likely
to find a heated community debate: the retailing colossus promises
low prices and jobs (albeit low-wage ones) for local residents, but will
it also threaten mom-and-pop businesses and turn downtown into a
ghost town?

Some communities have even lobbied successfully to keep Wal-
Mart out: in the spring of 2005, for example, small business owners,
City Council members, and union officials in the Rego Park neighborhood of Queens, New York, were so vocal and persistent in their op-
position to a proposed Wal-Mart (New York City's first) that the
developer scrapped the plan. Sprawl-Busters, a national organization
founded by anti-Wal-Mart activist Al Norman in 1993, lists on its Web
site 248 communities that have won battles against Wal-Mart and other
big-box retailers. Of course, they are the exception, not the rule, but
the very existence of such groups is telling.

The Wal-Marts, Home Depots, and Targets of the world are certainly here to stay for the foreseeable future, but their dominance and
prevalence have caused a backlash among a growing number of consumers who are becoming tired of their predictability and conformity.
And while these folks may not go as far as the activists who boycott
the big boxes entirely, they are more and more likely to gravitate toward the more civilized and manageable local businesses that provide
an antidote to the crowded aisles of superstores.

2. Proliferation of Small Business Alliances. All over the United
States, local small businesses are responding to Goliath backlash by

uniting to make themselves more powerful, visible, and attractive to consumers eager to support their local economies. Back in 1998, a Boulder, Colorado, bookstore owner named David Bolduc formed a local alliance of small businesses with community activists Jeff Milchen and Jennifer Rockne. Within two years, the Boulder Independent Business Alliance grew to more than 160 members, who publish a directory of locally owned businesses, form joint purchasing groups, distribute discount cards to the community, and offer one another valuable business advice.

The group attracted so much national attention that the founders also launched the American Independent Business Alliance (AMIBA) to provide advice and a template to other small business communities seeking to form similar alliances. "In our first two years, we had 120 inquiries," says Rockne. "The idea really caught fire." Since then, AMIBA has helped start twenty alliances that represent thousands of small businesses.

And in 2001, entrepreneurs Judy Wicks (founder of the White Dog Café in Philadelphia) and Laury Hammel (owner of Longfellow Clubs in the Boston area) formed another umbrella group for local alliances called the Business Alliance for Local Living Economies (BALLE). BALLE now has 19 member networks in the United States and Canada; its second annual conference, held in May 2004 in Philadelphia, attracted nearly 250 people from 25 states.

The proliferation of local alliances is great news for small business. Not only do their members pool resources and share best practices, but they often join together to brand themselves as local businesses.

3. Escalation of Consumer Rage. Consumers have never been as demanding as they are today. Whether we're picking up dry cleaning, working with a contractor, choosing a phone service, or getting a haircut, our expectations for quality and service are higher than ever before. The marketplace is so flooded with products and services that we all can afford to be picky. And high-speed Internet access, satellite television, and advanced telecommunications allow us to gather and sort through reams of information to find exactly the right company to meet our needs. Moreover, we don't hesitate to shift our loyalty if we're disappointed.

In 2004, the Customer Care Alliance, an Alexandria, Virginia–based consortium of customer service firms, partnered with Arizona State University's W. P. Carey School of Business to conduct the National Customer Rage Study. Of the 1,000 people who were surveyed about their customer service problems during the previous 12 months, 77% said their problem was caused by a large company; 73% reported being extremely or very upset; 85% shared their story with others; and 59% vowed never again to do business with the offending company.

Most striking: 56% of complainants felt they got nothing in return for their trouble, even though many of them merely wanted an explanation of the problem, assurance that it wouldn't be repeated, an apology, or simply the opportunity to vent. "There's a lot of hostility, passion, and rage associated with the services and products we use every day," says Scott Broetzmann, president of Customer Care Measurement & Consulting and a co-founder of the Customer Care Alliance. "For small companies, it represents an opportunity to cannibalize the customer base of larger ones by providing a service experience that is higher touch."

Independent pharmacies, for instance, seem to be doing just that. In October 2003, *Consumer Reports* magazine declared that "independent stores, which were edging toward extinction a few years ago, won top honors from *Consumer Reports* readers, besting the big chains by an eye-popping margin." Approximately 85% of independent drugstore customers said they were very or completely satisfied, compared with just 58% of chain store customers. The independents offered more personal attention, knowledgeable and accessible pharmacists, and the ability to track down out-of-stock drugs faster than their chain competitors. And they did it all at prices that turned out to be equal to or lower than the chains'.

4. Impending Labor Shortage. Conventional wisdom says that when the 76 million baby boomers born between 1946 and 1964 begin retiring, they'll leave behind five to ten million jobs that can't be filled by the smaller succeeding generation. "Companies are going to be competing with one another for the best workers," says Mike Chittenden, a spokesperson for Employment Policy Foundation, a Washington, DC, economic research organization. "We predict that between 2003 and 2013, there will be 30.3 million job openings for people with at least a two-year degree. But the number of people graduating from college during that same period is just 23.3 million." It's a potentially disastrous situation for employers.

Or is it an opportunity in disguise? In September 2003, the Gallup Organization's Employee Engagement Index revealed that 54% of American workers were "not engaged" at their jobs, while 17% were "actively disengaged." Human resources consulting firms like Challenger, Gray & Christmas and Towers Perrin have also reported high levels of dissatisfaction among U.S. employees. "Leaders cannot afford to ignore this wake-up call," writes Jay Jamrog, executive director of the Human Resource Institute in St. Petersburg, Florida. "Up to now, workers have stayed put because there are not many choices. That will not be true for long. Scores of recent surveys all predict the same thing: Workers will head for the door as soon as the job market improves."

So how is this good news? Because it represents an opportunity for small businesses to start implementing the kinds of workplace innovations that will make them employers of choice in the future—not just to retain current employees, but to attract top talent from companies that didn't heed the wake-up call.

5. Experience vs. Transaction. Think about what makes consumers happier at an independent pharmacy than at, say, a CVS. Even though they're probably getting the same product at a relatively similar price, the independent drugstore provides a fundamentally different experience. "The . . . offering of experiences occurs whenever a company intentionally uses services as the stage and goods as props to engage an individual," write B. Joseph Pine II and James H. Gilmore in *The Experience Economy: Work Is Theatre and Every Business a Stage.* "While commodities are fungible, goods tangible, and services intangible, experiences are *memorable*."

Anyone who has flown Virgin Atlantic or taken a child to create her own teddy bear at Build-A-Bear Workshop knows what they're talking about. These companies create value for consumers by giving them experiences that linger in their memories long after the flight has landed or the bear has lost its sheen. By focusing on experience, on the emotional connection that a consumer makes with a product or service, you not only build long-lasting brand loyalty but differentiate yourself in a way that's difficult, if not impossible, for your competitors to replicate.

6. High-Touch Technology. Amazon.com recommends books based on your past purchases, Netflix knows what kind of movies you like, and 1-800-FLOWERS reminds you that it's time to send your mom flowers for her birthday. One-to-one marketing gurus Don Peppers and Martha Rogers saw this coming years ago, and introduced the concept in their 1993 book, *The One to One Future: Building Relationships One Customer at a Time.* Back then, the idea that companies would collect so much personal information on consumers made many of us a little uncomfortable. No more. Customers have come to expect businesses not only to cater to their every need, but to anticipate those needs. Technology, of course, is the great enabler, and the good news is that no matter what size your business is, you can find the resources to collect and use data that will help you get closer to your customers.

At Mitchells/Richards, high-end clothing stores in Westport and Greenwich, Connecticut, CEO and chairman Jack Mitchell keeps a detailed database of his company's 115,000 customers. In an instant, his salespeople can access every purchase a client has ever made, not to mention the spouse's birthday, golf handicap, and the name of the family dog. "Technology helps us grow the business *and* get closer to the customer," says Mitchell. "There's a bonding effect, and that's why people come back to us." That's also how he helped transform a tiny family business into a $65 million company.

7. The Lust for Luxuries. Everyone is trading up. And why not? We've got more disposable income than ever before. According to 2003 U.S. Census Bureau figures, there are 26.1 million U.S. households with more than $75,000 in annual income and 15.1 million with more than $100,000. Of all income groups, the $100,000-and-over category saw the biggest increase over a 10-year period—up 42% from 10.6 million households in 1993. In *Trading Up: The New American Luxury*, authors Michael J. Silverstein and Neil Fiske argue persuasively that expanding incomes, as well as other social and business forces, have spawned a new category of goods they call "new luxuries." Think Starbucks, Victoria's Secret, and Panera Bread—brands that are premium when compared to others in their category, but not so wildly expensive that they're beyond the reach of the average consumer. "More and more, the middle-market consumer is a person who selectively trades up to new and better products and services, trades down in others to pay for his or her premium purchases, and, in the process, drives innovation and growth in previously stale . . . markets," write the authors.

The trend is great news for entrepreneurs who are creative and flexible enough to transform their mundane products and services into new luxury goods. Sound daunting? Just remember that it was done brilliantly with coffee and bras! And if you don't do it, your more entrepreneurial competitors most likely will.

Entrepreneurs are in fierce competition with one another. Consider that 56% of the CEOs on *Inc.* magazine's 2003 list of fastest-growing privately held companies said that the rivals they most feared were other small and midsize companies; 38% said their larger competitors made them most nervous. They know that as big companies gobble up more and more market share, the small companies that still comprise 50% of our economy are duking it out for the spoils. And it's a no-holds-barred fight.

On Main Streets all across the country, you'll find the same collection of businesses: delis, dry cleaners, florists, pizza and ice cream parlors, cycle shops, hair salons, hardware stores. Just outside of town, there's likely to be a light manufacturer, a couple of motels, and a few car dealerships. Each business attracts its own loyal following, and the occasional customer who defects to a competitor down the street is, more often than not, replaced by a new customer who defected from someplace else. Everyone operates within his or her own comfort zone. Until, that is, someone transcends the perceived limits of small business and rises to Alpha Dog status. The company ratchets up its customer service delivery or comes up with a new spin on an old product. It might find a clever way to brand its business or to engage the community. And when it does, everything changes.

The new competitive landscape will ultimately compel you to reevaluate your business. Particularly in industries where the David vs. Goliath story is played out with dramatic intensity, it's essential for small companies to find points of difference that are beyond the capabilities of their larger competitors. "Wal-Mart gives you the kick in the pants you need to get to the next level," says Chris Zane, who owns a bike shop in Branford, Connecticut (see chapter 2). "And if you don't want to get to the next level, you shouldn't be in business."

Sound harsh? Maybe, but to Zane and others like him, going to "the next level" isn't just about finding a way to beat the big boys. It's about looking at your own business through an entirely different lens. For Zane, the bikes he sold became almost secondary; the customer-service-driven manner in which he sold them became the differentiating factor that allowed him to beat out his local competitors and to survive the superstore onslaught. As a result, his business is more resilient, successful, and engaging than it ever would have been if circumstances had allowed him to remain in his comfort zone. He took himself out of the commodity game and adopted the strategy that is every successful entrepreneur's secret weapon: don't compete, differentiate.

And to do that effectively and meaningfully, companies must be strategic, not just reactionary. One of the most urgent and common utterances I've heard from entrepreneurs over the past several years is "we've got to professionalize our business." In increasing numbers, very small companies are embracing "big company" management disciplines. They're establishing quality programs, transforming their shop floors with lean manufacturing, setting up formal hiring and training regimens for employees, partnering with vendors, forging strategic alliances, and branding their products.

"Proprietors" are reinventing themselves as bona fide CEOs who are finally beginning to realize that their focus must shift away from *what* they do toward *how* they do it. Is it any wonder that Inc. 500 CEOs cited Michael E. Gerber's *The E-Myth Revisited: Why Most Small Businesses Don't Work and What to Do About It* as their favorite book? Gerber exhorts entrepreneurs to work *on* their businesses rather than *in* them. "The true product of a business is the business itself," he says. ". . . The Entrepreneurial Model has less to do with what's done in a business and more to do with how it's done. The commodity isn't what's important—the way it's delivered is."

And so, while you must make your product or service stand out in a marketplace full of commodities, you also must think about every aspect of your business as a competitive tool. The way in which you hire and retain your employees, serve your customers, gather and share information in your company, network within your industry, use technology—everything you do can and should be strategically reconceived. You just can't afford to be haphazard about anything anymore.

The entrepreneurs you'll meet in this book have mastered the art of working *on* their businesses. They are innovators, creative thinkers, mavericks one and all. But they are also deliberate and disciplined leaders who built their companies around the specific strategies they knew would take them out of the commodity game and position them as industry standouts. And they didn't do that in a vacuum. All of these entrepreneurs had a keen sense of business and social trends that had the power to either propel their companies forward or contribute to their demise. Their success is no accident, nor is it guaranteed in the future. "We're our own enemy," says Jim Throneburg, chairman of sock manufacturer THOR·LO (see chapter 6), "because we compete against ourselves to be the best every day." Then he leans back in his leather chair, folds his arms across his massive chest, and grins slyly. "And it's the best game I can think to play."

2 | Seduce Your Customers

Chris Zane.
Photograph: Tracey Kroll

Company: Zane's Cycles

Business: One retail bicycle shop and a corporate sales division

Location: Branford, Connecticut

Revenues: $6.1 million ($4.4 million corporate sales; $1.7 million retail sales)

Employees: 18 full-time; 10 to 25 part-time

Founder: Chris Zane

Year Founded: 1981

Web Site: www.zanescycles.com

Alpha Dog Credentials:

Chris Zane has leveraged a stellar reputation for customer service at a single small-town retail store to expand into the lucrative corporate sales market. He's now one of the biggest bicycle dealers in the country and the number one Trek dealer in the United States.

On February 15, 2001, Greg Ciocci, an hourly employee at Zane's Cycles in Branford, Connecticut, sat down and wrote a short note to his boss, Chris Zane. Here's what it said:

> *Dear Chris,*
>
> *On February fourteenth I dealt with a prospective "lifetime customer." In those dealings, I, as a Zane's Cycles employee, assured her that we would carry out a simple request. For whatever reason, this small request was forgotten. I realize at the moment the relationship with the customer (as well as her dozen friends) was shattered. Please consider this letter as a formal apology for any inconveniences or headaches I may have caused you or your management. Enclosed is a check for the estimated amount of rebuilding the customer relationship.*

Ciocci attached a check made out to Zane for $400; on the memo line he scrawled, "fuck-up." The poor guy must have done something dreadful. He must be terrified of losing his job. His boss must be an insufferable tyrant. No, no, and no again. Zane, a solidly built 40-year-old with a full head of silver hair, just shakes his head and laughs when he looks at the check. Of course, he never cashed it. Instead, he prominently displayed it, along with Ciocci's letter, on a bulletin board in his office. It tells him what kind of business he's created.

When Zane opened his shop in 1981, there were more than a dozen independent bicycle shops within a few miles of Branford, an upper-middle-class town just six miles from New Haven. But over the years, the competition changed tremendously. Big-box retailers and category killers like Wal-Mart and Sports Authority moved into Branford and neighboring communities, gobbled up market share, and forced the independents to duke it out for the spoils. "The number of independent bicycle stores has gone down," says Fred Clements, president of the National Bicycle Dealers Association. "But the ones that have stayed in business are bigger."

Clements says that retail bikes represent a $5.3 billion industry—a number that's remained relatively static for the past several years.

Mass retailers sell between 75% and 80% of all bicycles but account for only half of industry revenue. That's because the average bike at, say, a Wal-Mart or Toys "R" Us costs $70, compared with $360 at an independent dealer. Still, life is not easy for the smaller stores. "There are quite a few small and medium-size dealers who are in the business because they love bikes," says Clements. "And now they're struggling to develop the sophistication of someone like Zane. He's very progressive, and his store is way above average in terms of size."

The average bike shop, for example, sells 650 bikes a year and pulls in about $500,000 in revenue; its owner earns a salary of approximately $37,000. Zane sells 3,000 bicycles a year at his shop, which makes almost $2 million in revenue; he earns a "comfortable six-figure salary." He now has only four competitors and estimates that he commands 65% of market share. "When you include retail and special markets sales, he's by far our largest single-store customer," says Roger Bird, eastern regional sales manager for Trek USA & Canada. "And he's one of our top five customers in the world; the other four are all multi-store operations."

How has Zane's become an Alpha Dog when so many other companies in his industry are just barely making it or have closed up shop? The story of his "Saint Valentine's Day massacre" tells you just about everything you need to know about Zane, his employees, and the business he's built over the past 20 years.

It's Not Just the Bike

It was right before Valentine's Day, and a customer had put down a deposit on an expensive Trek bicycle for her husband. She had planned the surprise with loving attention to detail: On her way to dinner with her husband and some co-workers on February 14, she'd make a detour into Zane's parking lot. Ciocci had agreed to display the bike in the window, attach helium balloons to the handlebars, and prop up a sign that read, "Happy Valentine's Day, Bob." The customer had been saving for months to afford the bike and knew that her husband would never expect such an extravagant gift; she couldn't wait to surprise him in front of their friends. You can probably guess what happened. The bike never made it to the window, the customer was humiliated, Bob didn't go home with the bike, everyone had a lousy time at dinner, and no one had a very happy Valentine's Day.

There were tears and recriminations the next day; if Zane and his staff had publicly eviscerated Cupid, they would not have been more vilified. Still, Zane easily could have taken a "stuff happens" approach and shrugged off the incident as simple human error. No one is perfect, after all. Dry cleaning gets lost, costly restaurant food arrives cold, the car you just had serviced still knocks. Consumers expect to be abused once in while, don't they? Not at Zane's.

Ciocci, who had simply forgotten about the bike, was mortified. He immediately began fretting over the long-term ramifications of his mistake and calculating its probable cost to the business. Zane and his store manager, Tom Girard, sprang into action. Girard drove the bicycle to the customer's house and told her that the store would absorb the $200 balance. Then Zane called Cilantro's, a coffee shop in nearby Guilford, and arranged for a catered lunch to be delivered to the customer and her co-workers. Lastly, he gave the couple a gift certificate—with no spending limit specified—for dinner at Quattro's, an upscale Italian restaurant in Guilford.

"It cost us about $750 to undo what we screwed up," says Zane. "And I don't really think she expected any of it." Since then, the story has made the rounds; Girard has heard it repeated at least half a dozen times in the store. It has become one more chapter in the Zane book of urban legends. "What we did for her did not go unnoticed," says Zane. "She became an apostle rather than a terrorist."

Why is that so important? Because Zane isn't simply selling bicycles. Anyone can sell a Trek bike, and it's unlikely that a customer will be any more thrilled with the bike she buys at Zane's than the same bike she might buy down the road. A bicycle, like virtually every product, is a commodity, and if you want a customer to buy a commodity from you rather than your competitor you've got to make that commodity more valuable. Zane recognizes that the bicycle is almost secondary. What he's selling is something far more emotional.

To the Valentine's Day customer, you might say he sold an expression of love and generosity. To the father who walks in the store with a six-year-old, he may be selling a rite of passage—the first two-wheeler without training wheels. To a well-heeled baby boomer, a $2,000 titanium bike is a symbol of success, and to a recent retiree, a new bicycle may represent the hard-earned reward of more leisure time. In other words, he's selling an experience rather than just a product, and that vastly changes how he thinks about his customers. He's not just executing transactions. He's creating relationships that he hopes will last a lifetime. And those relationships all hinge on one thing: great service.

Of course, if you want your customers to stay with you for a lifetime, they must fall head over heals in love with you. And the only way that will happen is if you exceed their expectations from the moment they walk through the door. In Norwalk, Connecticut, just a few minutes down the road from Zane's, Stew Leonard's, one of the most innovative grocery chains in the country, lives by two rules that are literally set in stone—engraved in 3,000-pound hunks of granite at the entrance of each store. The inscriptions are: "Rule #1: The customer is always right"; and "Rule #2: If the customer is ever wrong, reread Rule #1." Leonard was famous for calculating the true lifetime value of a customer, and he insisted that all employees also understand the equation. The average customer, he'd tell them, spends approximately $2,500 a year. Multiplied by 10 years, that's a whopping $25,000—a huge price to pay for a disgruntled shopper.

"I always admired their business," says Zane, who counts Stew Leonard Jr. among his friends. "We walk the same path in terms of service." Zane estimates that his loyal customers might spend an average of $8,500 at his store over the course of a lifetime. That includes childhood bicycles, the last bike they'll ever ride, and everything in between. Like his role model in Norwalk, Zane is willing not only to bend over backward to correct a problem, but to delight his customers so thoroughly that they never even consider shopping at another bicycle dealer: he offers them lifetime free service and parts warranties, won't charge them for anything that costs less than a dollar, gives them free coffee at a gleaming mahogany coffee bar, sends them notes when he gets a shipment of clothing or accessories he knows they'll like, credits the full cost of the kids' bikes they bought last year toward bigger ones this year, and awards college scholarships to local high school students. You may cringe because it all sounds so frightfully expensive. But from Zane's point of view, it's far more expensive *not* to do cartwheels for your customers.

Point of Difference

Zane's Cycles is the culmination of a journey that began when Zane was a wrench-wielding 16-year-old fixing bicycles at a store called Scharf's Crafts and Hobbies. It was a traditional Main Street business, situated right in downtown Branford between Fred's Barber Shop and Mercato's Deli. Model trains dominated the floor, and the walls were lined with bins filled with balsa wood, chenille bumps, and squares of felt; the bicycle repair element almost seemed like an afterthought.

In the middle of August 1981, Tom Scharf declared that he was going out of business soon and told Chris that he probably ought to find another summer job. The kid's eyes lit up. He'd been fixing bikes for his buddies since he was 12 years old, earning as much as $400 a week by the time he was 15. His father, John Zane, a detail-oriented chemist at pharmaceutical giant Upjohn, even insisted that his son apply for a tax identification number. "No one knew how old I was because I did everything over the phone," says Zane. He was able to buy spare parts such as cables, tubes, and tires at wholesale prices from suppliers who just assumed they were dealing with, well, an adult. Even back then, his entrepreneurial nature, along with confidence that bordered on arrogance, separated him from his peers.

And so at 16, Zane was cocky enough to think that he was ready to run a real business. He cajoled his parents into letting him borrow $20,000 from his grandfather at 15% interest, which was then the going rate for a money market account. The adults would buy the business and hold the stock until Zane graduated from college; his mom would mind the store while he was at school.

Don't get the wrong impression. Patricia and John Zane weren't extravagant parents: they had given their two boys, Chris and Ken, a comfortable life in a modest Cape Cod–style house in East Haven, but there were few luxuries; buying Scharf's for their 16-year-old son was an enormous leap of faith. But they knew their boy, and they knew there was something different about him. While he seemed to have remarkable innate mechanical ability, he was not, in fact, particularly passionate about bicycles. It was *business* itself that made his adrenaline surge. "He always talked about having a business of his own," says Patricia Zane, who was a full-time homemaker until she pitched in to help her son run his store. "And if he really wanted something, he had the determination to stick with it. He wasn't a quitter."

With help from his resourceful mother, Zane liquidated the store's craft and hobby inventory within two years, earned $8,000 in cash to buy his first few bicycles, and changed the name of the business to Zane's Cycles. While he carried the same Columbia bicycles that were available at Toys "R" Us and Grant's, his prices were 30% higher. As a small, independent dealer who couldn't afford to buy in volume, he paid more for the bicycles and was forced to pass the cost on to his customers. So why would these shoppers buy from Zane and not from Toys "R" Us?

Zane enticed his customers with a longer warranty. "The first bike I ever sold came with a year's warranty on parts and labor," recalls Zane. "Everybody else was offering 30 days, and I needed a point of difference." He knew the manufacturer would guarantee the parts, so he'd be on the hook only for the labor. And since he had assembled the bikes himself in the first place, he was pretty sure his liability for repairs would also be limited. It made perfect sense, and yet Zane's competitors just didn't seem to get it. Little by little, he stole market share from them until one day they realized that the teenager they had thought harmless was actually an enormous threat.

It's All About Change

"In all honesty, I never thought this thing would be as wildly successful as it's been," says Zane. "Half a million was always my goal, so when we hit $750,000 in 1990, I really had to reevaluate." Even the biggest bicycle retailers were just barely racking up $1 million in sales. "I didn't realize I was going to hit my goal so quickly," he recalls. "I thought, if I don't show up tomorrow, this place would continue without me. And that sucks."

It's a common stage for entrepreneurs, and one that compels many to cash out and do something different. But Zane couldn't imagine what else he would do. True to his word, he had attended college, enrolling at Quinnipiac College in nearby Hamden. But he limited his course load to business classes that would help him run the store; he put off fulfilling his core requirements for so long that his frustrated parents finally realized that a degree just wasn't in the cards. Everything he did, he did with the store in mind, and now, at 27, he found himself in a premature midlife crisis. He knew instinctively that he was outgrowing his business. And so he moped. He broke up with his girlfriend, Kathleen, who had been his constant companion for five years. Then he stuffed a few clothes into a backpack and boarded a plane for Europe.

Zane had never acted so impulsively. When his peers were tramping through Europe, he was fretting over cash flow and inventory turns. But now the urge to isolate himself in unfamiliar territory was almost irresistible. It was not, however, terribly comfortable. Uncertainty about his business weighed so heavily on him that it was impossible for him to enjoy his travels. It didn't help that wherever he went, he was drawn to local bicycle shops, where he soaked up ideas, then agonized afresh over his own company. "What the hell am I doing here?" he asked himself after four days. He was ready to pack it in and head home.

One night in a Rome train station, he hit rock bottom. Exhausted and frustrated, he simply wanted to call a local pensione to reserve a room, but he had no change for the pay phone. After turning his pockets and bags inside out looking for coins, and asking every vendor in the station to change his 10,000-lira note, he collapsed in a rumpled heap on the floor, his back propped against a stone pillar. "I was freaking out," he recalls. "I thought I was going to snap."

And then a ridiculously simple solution occurred to him. He pulled the note out of his wallet, walked over to a newsstand, and bought a candy bar. The shopkeeper sneered at him, but Zane didn't care. He had change. And the coins that jingled in his hand were like a totem that revealed to him the most crucial insight of his career: spare change had rescued him in Rome and change of a different sort would rescue him back in Branford as well.

"It made me realize that there's never just one solution to a problem," he says. He felt liberated, almost invincible. For the next few days, he rented a scooter and explored Rome with the zeal of a college freshman on spring break. And when it was time to go home, he boarded the plane with a new attitude. The physical distance he had put between himself and his business had clarified his vision: it was like stepping back from an impressionist painting and watching it miraculously come into focus. He knew then that he needn't be constrained by his own assumptions or by industry convention. "To get to the next level, I knew I had to change the equation," he says. "I realized that there weren't any limits. I'd make the business bigger, better, stronger, faster, and I'd really wallop my competitors. I wanted to create an aura around the business that was unique." There wasn't any reason, he reckoned, why changing shouldn't be as easy as getting change.

Zane had never heard the phrase "game-changing innovation"—a popular business consultants' phrase. Every industry has its tried-and-true methods of selling, marketing, expanding, and competing, and most businesses play by those rules because the status quo is religiously ingrained in the way they run their companies. But as long as the game stays the same, it's tough for anyone to move to the head of the pack.

The only way to become an Alpha Dog is to change the game. That's what Stew Leonard did when he created what the *New York Times* once called the Disneyland of dairy stores. Where else can you find costumed characters, animatronics, and a petting zoo to entertain kids while parents shop? And although the store's offerings have expanded to include traditional grocery fare as well as dairy, Stew's rejects the industry model of carrying 30,000 items arranged in parallel rows that customers could easily skip. Instead, Stew's stocks 2,000 items, many of them co-branded, and designs its stores in a single meandering path so that every customer sees every product offering. The result: in 1992, Stew Leonard's won a place in the *Guinness Book of World Records* for having "the greatest sales per unit area of any single food store" in the United States—$3,470 annually compared with approximately $500 for the average grocery store. Clearly, the company had changed the game. Zane was about to follow suit with his radical new approach to customer service.

Raising the Bar

Zane had already established himself as an aggressive competitor, but when he returned from Europe, he pulled out all the stops. What choice did he have? Big retailers like Wal-Mart and Sports Authority were making it more and more difficult for small independent bicycle dealers to compete. Not only was Zane hell-bent on taking market share from his peers, he was gunning for the category killers as well. And he would do it by putting all of his eggs in the customer service basket.

That first one-year guarantee not only gave him a leg up in the marketplace, but also set the standard for almost every uncompromising competitive tactic he would conceive of in the years to come. When his competitors caught on and also began offering one-year guarantees, he upped the ante to two years. When they grudgingly followed suit, he laid down the gauntlet again and offered lifetime free service on every bicycle he sold. He even went so far as to make the policy retroactive. Sound crazy? My local bicycle shop owner certainly thought so. "I'd go broke," he scoffed, dismissing the idea out of hand. But Zane just shakes his head and grins. That's exactly what he hopes his competitors will always think.

In early 1994, he decided to move from his original 900-square-foot store to a 4,000-square-foot space in a nearby shopping center on well-traveled Route 1. He shelled out $100,000 to renovate the cavernous space—a move that some of his competitors thought would sink him for good. Indeed, he heard from customers that the new store, although spacious, lacked the intimacy of the old Zane's. But not for long.

Zane remembered a highlight of his trip to Europe: in Lucerne, Switzerland, he had visited a bicycle shop where customers lingered around a cozy coffee bar. So he paid a local cabinetmaker, who was also a former Zane's employee, $3,000 to build a mahogany coffee bar, positioning it so that customers could enjoy free coffee while watching Zane's repair staff through a large glass window. "I thought of it kind of like I think of heat," he says. "It was part of the cost of doing business, to make our customers more comfortable. People fell in love with it."

Around the same time, Zane also implemented what he calls the third leg of his grand customer service plan. He knew that some customers were suspicious of his service and parts warranties; they just assumed that he was charging higher prices to cover his costs. And so he began offering 90-day price protection. If a customer found the same bike anywhere in Connecticut for less, he'd refund them the difference plus 10%. Like his lifetime warrantee, Zane knew that only a limited number of customers would take advantage of the price protection offer; people typically don't continue to shop after they've made a major purchase. Nonetheless, the program gave customers an added level of decision-making comfort, which made the selling process easier and faster. "We spend less time with each customer because we don't have to sell them on us as well as the product," Zane says. "Because we don't have to do the hard sell, we can focus on their real needs." That year, sales increased by 54%, more than doubling Zane's normal 25% annual growth rate.

By 1995, revenues at his store were $1.2 million, making him the largest independent bicycle dealer in his market. Two years later, that number would spike to $1.6 million and Zane would be realizing margins that were at least 50% higher than the average specialty bicycle shop. How? He credits much of his financial intelligence to his mentor of 17 years, Bill Austin, the chairman and CEO of Raleigh America, whom Zane met back in 1988, when Zane was just 24 years old. Austin had just taken the helm of bicycle manufacturer Giant, and his son, Bill III, was working as a sales rep in Zane's territory. "Chris was like a sponge," recalls the elder Austin. "He'd ask penetrating questions, and he listened to advice." Austin advised Zane to drastically reduce his number of vendors so that he could not only build strong relationships, but take advantage of large-order discounts and free shipping. So Zane eventually cut his vendors down to nine; the industry standard is twenty. "He began to turn his inventory faster, improve his margins, and control his expenses," says Austin. "He learned that happiness is positive cash flow."

Life was good for Zane. He had come to his senses and married Kathleen, the girlfriend with whom he had broken up, and they had a baby son, Ian. He was driving a Porsche Boxster and was paying himself a CEO's salary. His employees were benefiting from his success as well. He had 15 full-timers, all with full health benefits, and he had even started a profit-sharing plan for his four managers, contributing the equivalent of 15% of their salary to the plan. He had taken on the patina of a CEO. Not only had he captured market share and put some of his competitors out of business, but he had raised the barrier to entry into his market. Anyone with the desire to open a bicycle shop in his territory would surely think twice; competing with Zane was not an attractive prospect.

By the Numbers

Zane's "I'll do you one better" attitude can seem arrogant, almost adolescent. He's the first to admit, in fact, that he views business as a game and that his ultimate goal is to outplay his adversaries and always, always to win. But he's far from impulsive. The idea for lifetime free service came to him at a trade show in New York, where he was chatting up other bike dealers who were beginning to offer five-year service guarantees. "I figured that for a lot of people, five years is the life of the bike, and that if they've had it for five years, they're probably not using it very much," he reasons "So if you're going to offer five years, you may as well offer life."

Percentages were the core of Zane's comfort level. Experience had taught him that most customers would take advantage of free service the first year, but that only 20% to 30% would come in the second year. He was betting that by the third and fourth years, the percentage would be minuscule. And those that did come in? They'd be the customers who were passionate about bicycles, the ones who might bring their bikes in for free service but leave the store with another

$100 worth of accessories. And they'd also be the ones that would talk up Zane's Cycles to their buddies.

Zane's competitors have actually asked him to cut a deal: if he'll drop the lifetime service guarantee, so will they. No way, he responds. He likes setting the standard, plus he knows full well that the program isn't nearly as expensive as it sounds.

When he speaks about customer service at business conferences, he uses a large bowl of quarters to illustrate that point to his audience. He walks around the room inviting people to help themselves to the coins. Most people take a few quarters and some grab a handful, but rarely does anyone demand the entire bowl. The point: people generally self-regulate their desires. Zane then explains that the total amount of money in the bowl represents how much he's willing to spend on any one customer, but since most people are reasonable, he's able to serve many for the same amount he's willing to spend on just one. Then comes the kicker. He goes back to the people who took quarters from the bowl and hands each of them a few more. They're delighted, of course, to be receiving something above and beyond what they believe is reasonable. And that's exactly how Zane wants his customers to feel.

Sometimes, he goes way over the top to exceed customer expectations. Take, for example, the man who once walked into his store with a broken bicycle pump. The pump had been expensive and he wanted it fixed.

"Did you buy it here?" asked Zane.

"Well, no," came the response.

"Let me ask you again," said Zane with a wink. "Did you buy it here?"

"Uh, sure," said the puzzled customer.

Zane took the broken pump and handed the guy a new one, free of charge. If that sounds crazy, consider Zane's logic: He knew the broken pump was a premium product. While most customers spend no more than $20 on a bike pump, this customer had probably shelled out $60, so Zane knew he was a high-end purchaser. Secondly, because he was willing to have the pump repaired rather than simply buy a new one, Zane also figured he was thrifty—the kind of customer who would be thrilled to get something for nothing. Lastly, he knew that he could send the broken pump back to the manufacturer and get a full credit, so his out-of-pocket cost would be zero. He saw an opportunity to make a customer fall in love with his store, and the cost was merely the time and effort required to send the pump back to the manufacturer. The payoff: an ecstatic customer who returned to spend more than $200 on accessories and who, Zane is betting, still spreads the Zane's gospel.

The Customer, C'est Moi

When the weather cooperates, Zane hops on his red Trek bicycle and peddles 10 miles to work from his home in Guilford, where he lives in a historic 1761 colonial house with Kathleen and their three young boys—Ian, 9; Charlie, 7; and Oliver, 5. He rides along the abandoned trolley tracks that run parallel to this part of Long Island Sound, through a forested stretch called West Woods. The trip takes about an hour and a half, provided he doesn't stop along the way. Frequently, though, he'll stretch out on the bluff that overlooks Lost Lake or linger on the causeway to gaze out at the Thimble Islands. The shop is just a 10-minute drive from his home, and if he cycled along the road, the trip would be 45 minutes. But Zane takes the long way deliberately.

No, he's not a gung-ho cycling enthusiast; he actually prefers Formula One cars. This ride, while clearly a pleasure, gives him time to think. And it keeps him in close touch with his customers and their experience with the product he sells. Like him, they're typically recreational cyclists and not hard-core enthusiasts. So the ride through the woods reminds him of their needs—comfortable seats, accessible water bottles, bright headlights for nighttime riding, lightweight clothing to shield the wind.

Zane wants his employees to think the way he does, and that's why he has people like Tom Girard working for him. Girard was 19 and working at another local bike shop when he was recruited away by Zane. "The guy I worked for nickel-and-dimed us all the time," recalls Girard. "If you made a long-distance phone call, he'd take it out of your paycheck. But Chris was really giving, and he had a lot of spark. I didn't leave my job for money, because the pay was the same. I left for Chris."

Girard now manages the store, and like most of the employees he hires, he's not a cycling enthusiast. "Enthusiasts tend to confuse the customer because they try to impress them with their knowledge of cycling," says Girard. We've all experienced information overload on the retail floor: we think we know exactly what we want until an overeager salesperson introduces half a dozen more decision-making factors that befuddle rather than enlighten us. We walk away without opening our checkbooks; it's unlikely we'll ever return.

Zane knows that most of his customers are weekend warriors who don't want to be bombarded with the intricacies of chain drives and derailleurs. So while there's always an enthusiast in the store to answer questions from the occasional serious cyclist, most salespeople have just enough bicycle knowledge to inform but not overwhelm customers.

Girard, who has been hiring all of Zane's salespeople for the past eight years, also feels that nonenthusiasts are more likely to be driven by their passion for sales and customer service rather than pure love of the product. And that makes them more motivated to close and maximize sales. To provide extra incentive, Zane gives every employee $3 for every three accessories that he or she sells along with a bicycle. Sure, the program boosts sales and compensation, but it also compels salespeople to think about what else a customer might need. "I tell the salespeople that if a customer is riding his new bike and he wants to stop for a cup of coffee, then realizes he doesn't have a lock, we haven't done him any favors. Continuing the selling process after you've sold this bike is a good thing." Since he started the program in 1999, Zane says, the store's average sale has increased from $350 to $500.

Wal-Mart Comes to Town

When Zane opened his first store, more than 20 years ago, his primary competitors were other independent bicycle dealers—people who cringed when superstores like Wal-Mart and Sports Authority came to town a few years ago. But Zane just doesn't share the classic small retailer's contempt for the big boxes. "Wal-Mart gives you the kick in the pants you need to get to the next level," he claims. "And if you don't want to get to the next level, you shouldn't be in business."

Zane knows that's a harsh assessment, but he's not apologizing. Wal-Mart, he reckons, represents a threat to independent dealers who haven't yet raised the bar, and their demise can only benefit him. Besides, he's also betting that most people who are inclined to buy a bicycle from a small, independent dealer will not be tempted by big-box retailers, which typically don't offer the same quality of merchandise or service. Just to make sure, Zane continues to ratchet up his service.

Two years after he started offering 90-day price protection, he began luring customers with a 30-day return policy. They could return any bike within 30 days of purchase for any reason and receive a store credit for the full cost of the merchandise. Zane didn't even care what kind of shape the bike was in. It was yet another aggressive tactic to close sales fast by reducing, if not completely eliminating, customer waffling. In 2004, ten customers returned their bikes and eight of them upgraded to more expensive models. And what happened to the returned bicycles? Some were sold at a discount, and some, says store manager Tom Girard, pay for themselves in goodwill.

In July 2004, one of Zane's best customers, Craig Newton, wanted to rent a couple of mountain bikes for the weekend. Girard pulled out two returned bikes and told Newton to just take them. The result: Newton, an organizational development consultant, was so impressed with Girard's generosity that when he brought back the bikes, he offered to run a free team-training session for Zane's employees. If Girard had chased the quick buck, the store may have netted $200 in rental fees. Instead, he got the promise of a consultant's undivided attention for a day—worth between $1,000 and $1,500—not to mention the potential long-term payoff the training may yield. "I try to teach customer service and I know this stuff," says Newton. "These guys are fabulous; I recommend them to everyone."

Zane always assumes that fostering goodwill among customers will pay off. First, however, you need to get them in your store. In summer 2004, he began to realize that Wal-Mart, which opened in Branford in 1996, might be a bigger threat than he had originally anticipated. Store manager Tom Girard had noted an increasing number of Schwinn bicycles in Zane's service department—bikes that had been bought at Wal-Mart. Schwinn's name evoked nostalgia among older baby boomers who recalled their own first bikes and were eager to pass on the experience to their children. But the company had gone through massive changes; it had first declared bankruptcy in 1992, was sold twice, declared bankruptcy again in 2001, and then was sold again to Pacific Cycle, Inc., which continues to market the brand. Zane had carried Schwinn briefly in the mid-1990s, but dropped the brand when he discovered that Schwinn sales reps had also signed on at least three other dealers within a five-mile radius. It wasn't the kind of treatment he had come to expect from a quality bicycle manufacturer. Today, Schwinns are sold almost exclusively in the mass market, and Zane sees that as a threat.

His response was characteristically aggressive. In November 2004, he began a trade-in policy that he knew would be irresistible to parents. Buy a 12- or 16-inch bicycle from Zane's, he told them, and trade it in for full credit on a bigger bike in a year or two. Again, he made the policy retroactive, using his extensive customer database to send postcards to everyone who had bought a small bicycle within the past few years. With an offer like that on the table, choosing a Schwinn from Wal-Mart just wouldn't make sense, he wagered.

But how can he justify the cost of such a wildly generous program? First of all, just as with his lifetime free service and price guarantees, only a limited number of customers actually take advantage of the offer. Last year, for instance, just 10% of children's bikes came back to the store; Zane thinks that's because they're being passed down within families. Secondly, every returned bicycle is given away to a needy child at Christmastime via a highly publicized in-store event. Zane gets press coverage, community goodwill, and a tax write-off. But more importantly, he's buying customers for life. "We won't make money until they buy their second bike from us at full price," he says. And what makes him so certain that they'll stay with him for that long? Zane predicts that he'll see those customers several times a year as they come in for service or accessories for their growing kids. By the time they need a 20-inch bicycle at full price, he predicts, they will have experienced enough extreme customer service that going to a competitor will be out of the question.

Taking Service to a New Market

While Zane had built a company that was far bigger and more sophisticated than your average Main Street cycle shop, he knew there was a limit to how much he could grow. He had opened a second shop in 1986 and lost a whopping $100,000 in 10 weeks; a 1994 attempt to expand his current business by adding high-priced treadmills was equally unsuccessful. But in 1998, he set his sights on the $23 billion premiums and incentives market and hit pay dirt. The industry, also called "special markets," serves large companies such as American Express and Citigroup that offer incentives or rewards to their customers or employees, often through a catalogue filled with merchandise that can be purchased with "points." It's a quirky business, but the prospect of selling, say, a hundred bicycles to a single corporate customer was too enticing for Zane to pass up.

Unfortunately, Zane found that most corporations had little interest in including bicycles in their incentive programs. Nor did most bicycle dealers go after the market because it was such a hassle. The bikes had to be partially assembled and shipped by the dealer to people who invariably had trouble finishing the assembly or who had chosen the wrong size bike. Delight gave way to frustration, creating ill will between the employee or customer who received the incentive and the company that awarded it. To Zane, that slippery slope was a challenge he couldn't resist; he felt sure he could succeed in the industry if he simply employed the same exacting customer service values that had worked so well at the store.

It took him eight years to gain the trust and respect of corporate customers, but the special markets part of his business now accounts for 70% of revenue and he's Trek's exclusive supplier to that industry. Recently, Zane's won top honors as a stellar supplier from two customers—Hinda Incentives and BI, firms that manage award and incentive programs for large companies. "I don't look at him as a bike company," says Michael Arkes, CEO of Hinda. "He's selling us service that happens to be paired with a bike, and he's by far one of the most customer-focused companies we do business with."

Zane now has 6,000 Trek bicycles in a new 23,000-square-foot warehouse, and they're ready to be shipped out, one at a time, at a moment's notice. To each recipient, he first sends a questionnaire asking for height, inseam measurement, and cycling style. The information helps his staff choose the right bike among the thousands that are stored in the warehouse unassembled. Zane's mechanics fully assemble the bikes, check them for defects, and test ride them around the warehouse. They're then partially disassembled, reboxed, and shipped directly to the award recipient with a full set of instructions. Recipients are also given access to a webcam with live feed directly to Zane's warehouse, where a mechanic will walk them through the assembly process. It's a systems-driven process that depends 100% on great service, and that's something that Zane knows a great deal about.

Still, he's not complacent. A few months ago, Zane was talking to a customer who buys large numbers of bicycles from him—the president of a company that runs incentive and recognition programs for major corporations. For Zane, every customer conversation is an opportunity to deepen the relationship, so he began quizzing the fellow on how Zane's might better serve the company. "Listen," the president told him, "think of [our business] as an annuity. Just don't screw up and don't break what's already working."

Most CEOs would take that as a cue to relax a little. Not Zane. "That's uncomfortable for me," he says. "Because they don't even know that they need something better, but I want to give them something better." There's a little voice inside his head that's calculating the lifetime value of this customer. It's in the millions, and that's a lot to lose. And so Zane won't relax, won't ever take a customer for granted, won't stop raising the bar. He can't afford to. Neither can you.

"Seduce Your Customers" Tips from Zane's Cycles

1. **Use Service to Compete.** Your customers expect the moon; you need to give them the universe. Zane, for instance, offers customers lifetime free service and a 90-day price guarantee. He invites everyone who walks though his door to sit down at his coffee bar for a free cup of joe, and gives away any item in the store that costs less than a dollar. Nuts, bolts, master links, and spokes—bicycle parts that are inexpensive but essential—are free.

2. **Keep Raising the Bar.** Keep a close eye on what your competitors, both large and small, are offering in terms of service, and be willing to ratchet up your own programs. Zane ups the service ante consistently. For example, the full cost of every 12- to 16-inch child's bicycle is credited toward a new, bigger bicycle a year or two down the road. Zane thinks the program prevents parents from buying bikes at Wal-Mart.

3. **Turn Terrorists into Apostles.** Like Zane, you're going to screw things up once in a while. But if you're skillful, you can turn a bad situation around. First, fess up. Nothing deflates an angry customer more quickly than your honest and heartfelt admission of guilt. Follow up with a detailed plan for making things right; make sure to include a little something extra (a small gift or a discount certificate) that will leave your customer feeling ahead of the game.

4. **Hire Customer-Focused Employees.** Think about who your customers are, and hire salespeople who can relate to them. Most of Zane's customers are recreational cyclists, not enthusiasts who ride 50 miles every weekend. So he doesn't hire enthusiasts, who he thinks are inclined to confuse and oversell consumers. He knows it's easier to educate a good salesperson about bikes than it is to teach a dedicated cyclist to sell.

5. **Calculate the Real Cost of Service.** How much will it cost you to become a customer service Alpha Dog? Not as much as you think. Yes, a computer system that captures customer informa-

tion will require a significant cash outlay, but don't forget that it may also help you manage inventory and speed the checkout process. You may balk at the kind of lifetime guarantee Chris Zane offers, but consider that only a small percentage of customers will ever take advantage of your offer.

. . . And from Others

6. **Pamper Your Best Customers.** The 80/20 rule is as relevant to small businesses as it is to big ones: 20% of your customers account for approximately 80% of your profits, so why would you treat them like the patron who walks through your door only occasionally? At **Dorothy Lane Market** in Dayton, Ohio (see chapter 3), CEO Norman Mayne diverted his advertising dollars from traditional circulars to a loyalty program called Club Dorothy Lane, which tracks customer spending with a plastic card. Discounts and specials, customized to individual shopping habits, go only to club members, who are so heavily courted that they get monthly newsletters, free flowers, concert tickets, and a turkey at Thanksgiving. The result, says Mayne, is "an extra three points of gross margin to give back to our best customers."

7. **Watch Your Customers Use Your Product.** If you rely solely on what your customers tell you they need, you might be missing the boat. Scott Cook, co-founder and chairman of the executive committee at **Intuit, Inc.,** frequently tells the story of Quicken's initial entry into the marketplace. Determined to uncover any difficulties that consumers might have with the personal finance software, Cook initiated the Follow Me Home research program, where Intuit reps prowled the aisles of local office supply stores and asked Quicken buyers if they could follow them home to watch them install and use the program. The result: pages of notes that revealed sticking points that customers may not have been able to articulate on a survey.

8. **Create a Community of Customers.** At Joe Fulmer's Dayton,

Ohio, sewing store, the **Stitching Post,** customers drop in for more than just a few yards of fabric or a spool of thread. Fulmer invites them in eight times a month for coffee hours, during which they socialize and chat about their latest projects. He also gathers them together to sew cancer caps for chemotherapy patients and sleeping bags for homeless kids. The events help forge social and emotional connections between the store and its customers.

9. **Exceed Expectations.** In some industries, consumers just expect shoddy treatment. Think general contractors, dry cleaners, auto mechanics—they're not known for great service. But at **Direct Tire & Auto Service** in Watertown, Massachusetts, customers are pleasantly surprised. Drop off your car in the morning and CEO Barry Steinberg will get you a ride to work. If you prefer to linger, his waiting room is filled with over 90 different magazines, and there's always a pot of fresh gourmet coffee on the burner and some pastries to nibble. The restrooms will remind you of the ones at your doctor's office. "I knew I didn't want a vanilla tire company, with prices in the gutter and guys wearing jeans and t-shirts giving lousy service," says Steinberg. "I wanted to deliver the product in a way that people didn't expect. I wanted to wow them when they walked in and wow them when they walked out."

10. **Treat Your Business-to-Business Customers Like Partners.** It must be tough to differentiate yourself to customers when you're selling them soil, mulch, and manure, right? Not for **Banfe Products, Inc.,** which sells its high-end products to independent garden centers, hardware stores, and golf courses. CEO Dan Banfe says "no thanks" to mass retailers like Home Depot because he wants to earn loyalty from independents by offering them products that aren't available to their larger competitors. So he pulls out all the stops with attractive, brightly colored packaging and gives his lawn products clever names like Premium No. 2, Turf 4 Tots, and Magical Mushroom.

He helps his customers pay for storage bins, gives them a nine-second dealer tagline on every radio ad he runs, and even has a loyalty program that rewards his best customers with a weeklong group trip. Last year, he took several customers to Curaçao.

3 | Convert Your Employees into True Believers

Company: Dorothy Lane Market, Inc.

Business: Three grocery stores

Location: Dayton, Ohio

Revenues: $60 million

Employees: 250 full-time; 457 part-time

Founders: Calvin Mayne, Frank Sakada

CEO: Norman Mayne

Year Founded: 1948

Web Site: www.dorothylane.com

Calvin and Norman Mayne at Dorothy Lane Market.
Photograph: Nick Nawroth

Alpha Dog Credentials:

Independent grocery stores are a dying breed, but Norman Mayne has kept his family-owned company growing and vibrant not only by offering great products and service, but by regarding his employees as his most effective secret weapon. He's converted them into true believers—people whose words and deeds thoroughly and consistently reflect his long-term vision.

"For how many of you is this your first job?" asks Norman Mayne with a glint of mischief in his eye. The 61-year-old CEO of Dorothy Lane Market is talking to 15 new employees, most of them high school or college students who were recently hired as part-time cashiers or baggers. They fidget in their seats around a large conference table, and about half of them raise their hands. Mayne raises his hand as well. "Mine too," he answers humbly.

Mayne's monogrammed dress shirt, silk tie, custom-fitting suit, and Italian loafers make him look more like an investment banker than the grocer he has been for most of his life. And as he speaks to the young people in the company's Dayton, Ohio, corporate offices, just upstairs from Dorothy Lane's Washington Square market, he is every inch a company president. But at most companies, the president doesn't spend an hour talking to each and every new entry-level employee about company culture, industry margins, customer retention, demographics, and the competition. Mayne has been doing that for the past 20 years—a practice that was based upon a suggestion from a 16-year-old cashier.

Mayne spends $25,000 annually on this training program, which he conducts several times a year because he wants to keep the number of people in the room well under 20. Dorothy Lane's human resources manager (and Mayne's nephew), Matthew Hieb, estimates that turnover among part-timers runs between 20% and 30%—far below the industry average, which is typically around 100%. So Mayne usually speaks to 90 to 135 new part-timers and a handful of new full-timers every year. There's no question in his mind that it pays off.

Customer service was Mayne's mantra for years. And then, he says, it dawned on him one day that "the person at 7-Eleven who doesn't treat me right is just treating me the way his boss treats him." Great service begins with great employees, and great employees don't just walk through your door ready to treat your customers like gold. You can break the bank on training programs and seminars that preach the customer service gospel, but the bottom line is that your employees' first and most effective teacher is you. And it's not just about pay and benefits and an occasional pat on the back. How you hire, train, promote, share information, and interact with your employees on a day-to-day basis will drive their performance and, hence, your bottom line.

If you doubt the connection between a great work environment and financial performance, you should check in with the Great Place to Work Institute, which creates the 100 Best Companies to Work For list with *Fortune* magazine every year. When an independent investment adviser "looked at those companies as if they were a stock portfolio," says Great Place to Work Institute co-founder Robert Levering, "they found that if someone had invested in the companies we listed in 1997, they would have beaten the S&P 500 by a factor of three. If they had sold the portfolio every year and reinvested in the current year's list, they would have done five to six times better than the S&P." Consider that the institute doesn't use financial criteria at all when choosing its 100 Best; the list is based entirely on employee surveys and analysis of employment practices. To Levering, the results told a revealing story: "There was a clear correlation between the level of trust employees had in an organization and financial performance."

Mayne, however, doesn't need those numbers to tell him he's on the right track. These new employees sitting around his conference table are his front line—the people who will have the most direct contact with the customers at his three stores and who hold the company's reputation in their inexperienced hands. They are important and he wants them to know it. "One of the things you're going to find out here is that we feel an obligation to treat you right," he tells them in his typically soft-spoken, avuncular manner. "We need you more than you need us, and if we're not decent to you, then you can tell us to take this job and shove it. You may never hear that again from an employer. In my heart of hearts, I don't believe the customer is the most important person. The most important people are the people who work here." And with that statement, he hopes he is on his way to converting at least some of them from mere hourly employees into true believers.

A Different Path

Between 1992 and 2003, thirteen thousand five hundred grocery stores went out of business, most of them small, independent companies like Dorothy Lane. According to *Supermarket News,* an industry trade magazine that recently ranked companies according to revenues, total U.S. grocery store sales are $775 billion, with Wal-Mart Stores' Supercenters (which carry groceries as well as general merchandise) accounting for a whopping $118 billion. As of October 2004, eight Wal-Mart stores were situated within ten miles of Mayne's three markets, and their number is almost certain to increase. The next largest company, Cincinnati-based Kroger Company, has $56.2 billion in revenues and five stores in Dorothy Lane's backyard.

"I wake up every morning afraid," admits Mayne. "I'm afraid of Kroger because they offer more private label merchandise, and they sell lawn chairs and motor oil and cosmetics. And Wal-Mart is so big and powerful that they can offer huge cost advantages over the independents."

Still, Mayne has an effective slingshot to wield against these Goliaths. "We focus on creating faster than the competition can steal," he says. To do that, he relies upon the loyalty, ingenuity, and flexibility of his employees. They, in turn, count on him to create an environment where they feel appreciated, stimulated, and proud. Both have held up their end of the bargain over the years, and as a result, Dorothy Lane has earned Alpha Dog status. Profits have run as high as 4%, which is more than double the industry average; revenues have increased from $18 million in 1992 to $60 million in 2004; and turnover is well below the industry average. And in September 2004, the *Gourmet Retailer,* an industry publication, placed Dorothy Lane among the 25 most important specialty food stores in the country, along with Balducci's, Dean & DeLuca, Trader Joe's, Stew Leonard's, and Whole Foods Market. "I travel all over the world talking to people about supermarkets," says Howard Solganik, an international supermarket consultant based in Dayton. "And I always use Dorothy Lane as an example. You can name just about any category—employee programs, merchandising, customer relations, technology—and they're a leader in it."

Walk into any of Dorothy Lane's three markets, and you'll see what he means. Customers can order up lattes and cappuccinos from a skilled barista at a full-fledged coffee bar before they begin shopping. Just around the corner, there's a bakery, where they can savor the aroma of artisanal breads being baked in the French hearth oven. In the center, there's a wine store and tasting bar with a sophisticated enough inventory to please the pickiest oenophile. Young, fresh-faced cashiers in crisp white shirts and bow ties stand at attention at the end of their stations, personally greeting customers who are ready to check out. The look and feel of the stores, particularly the newest store in Springboro, is European. That's not surprising since Norman's 42-year-old son, Calvin, took the designer on a research trip to France and Italy. Calvin is the oldest of Mayne's six children, the planned successor, and the company's COO, but he is also a passionate foodie who loves talking about the brix (sugar) level in peaches or the lingering flavor of Hoch Ybrig alpine cheese. With his wide grin and boyish cowlick, he's affable and always eager to strike up conversations with customers, often trying out his fluent French, Spanish, and Italian. The Springboro store is his baby, but all three markets reflect his father's—and grandfather's—mission. "With great intention," says Calvin, "they wanted to build an atmosphere where people are excited about food." And that starts with employees.

Out of the Ashes

Norman Mayne was just a few years younger than his newest group of employees when he first started working at Dorothy Lane Market. The company was founded in 1948 by Mayne's father, Calvin, and an equal partner, Frank Sakada. Loath to put their own names on the business, they named it after the street on which it was situated. In his teenage years, Norman Mayne swept floors, stocked shelves, worked the register, carried out groceries, and trimmed vegetables. But he secretly dreamed of leaving Dayton and pursuing an acting career in New York. One of his most wistful memories, in fact, is of a young Dayton resident, Ramon Estevez, who read a poem in a talent show that was sponsored by Dorothy Lane Market. Mayne's father was so impressed that he lent the fellow $3,000 to cover living expenses in Manhattan while he studied at the Lincoln Center Repertory Company. Estevez vowed to pay him back and kept his promise a couple of years later—when he returned to Dayton with a new name: Martin Sheen.

But Norman Mayne never made it to New York. Instead, he fell in love with his high school sweetheart, Terry Dalton, married her, and started a family. And in 1966, Norman was thrust into the role of successor when his father, who had bought out his partner in 1958, suddenly suffered a stroke. Calvin's illness put an abrupt end to his career; he died six years later.

"Before his dad got sick, Norman was just the boss's kid," recalls Wayne Chrisman, who has been with the company since 1960 and now manages the Oakwood store. "And he didn't appear very interested in making a career of it." But that changed quickly. "The family came to me and said, 'You have to do what it takes to save the business,'" recalls Mayne. "So I went from driving a truck and working in the produce department to having the job I have today." That transition could not have come at a worse time.

The company, which was posting $3.6 million in revenues, had two grocery stores and two 100,000-square-foot discount stores, which sold clothing, furniture, and appliances as well as groceries. But it was in deep financial trouble; by May 1967, Dorothy Lane had filed for bankruptcy under Chapter 11. "We went to the creditors, and they had no reason to let a 22-year-old stay in business," Mayne recalls. So he sought help from a family friend, Jack Pickrel, who was also a respected attorney. Pickrel came up with a 10-year plan for the banks: the company would close all of its operations except one grocery store, and Norman would bring in a senior executive to help him run the company. And Dorothy Lane would pay its debt in full—100 cents on the dollar. The creditors agreed and Mayne was back in business.

Most of the management staff was let go, but Mayne retained sixty employees, five of whom are still with him today. "We were completely humbled," he says. "We were so down that we just really appreciated those associates who stayed with us. Together, we started building customer confidence back; we never took a customer for granted. If they had a request, we did somersaults." Case in point: During the blizzard of 1978, when nearly every other grocery store in Dayton was closed, Mayne insisted that Dorothy Lane remain open. He ferried employees to work in four-wheel-drive vehicles and on snowmobiles, and he sent them out to deliver groceries to customers who were stranded at home.

Mayne's concept of customer service was uncompromising, and so were his ideas about how his children should be raised. In the late 1960s, he and Terry moved their young family to a farm in Waynesville, Ohio, 17 miles from Dayton. "We raised sheep, fed some hogs, and milked a goat and a cow," says Mayne. "We thought it would help the kids appreciate creation, nature, and hard work." It did. "As a kid, I had two hours of chores a day," recalls Mayne's son Calvin. "I was raised to work." The Maynes moved their family, which would eventually include six children, back to Dayton several years later.

By that time, the business was healthy again. In fact, eight years after filing for bankruptcy, Dorothy Lane's debt was paid in full—two years ahead of schedule—and the company was solidly profitable with revenues of $12 million. In 1976, the 31-year-old Mayne was filled with confidence and couldn't resist the opportunity to jump on some cheap real estate and open a second store in a location left vacant by Kroger. "It was in a run-down shopping center and people said it wouldn't work, but I knew it would," he recalls. "I was eager to provide opportunities to some really great people, and I thought if I didn't grow, I'd lose them." But the naysayers were right: the store was a dismal failure. Mayne closed it a mere six months after the grand opening.

Staying the Course

Mayne had learned his lesson: he wouldn't let his desire for growth cloud his judgment; next time, he'd wait patiently for the right location. He absorbed the failed store's employees into his original operation and resolved to remain focused on building a local reputation for a unique product mix and great service. There's a story—now part of Dorothy Lane legend—about meat cutter Regan Ross, who still works the third shift at the company's Oakwood store. He received a call at 11:30 p.m. from a panicked customer who had bought a leg of lamb that day, only to discover too late that the meat was not boneless. She had planned to put it in the oven that night, but the bone needed to be removed. "So he went to her house at midnight and boned her leg of lamb on her kitchen table," recalls Mayne. "And that's an example of the kind of thing that goes on all the time here."

Mayne stayed the course for nearly 15 years. "It was a great time," he recalls. "We remodeled the store and we treated it like a laboratory." The Oakwood store, like the two other stores he would eventually open, was situated in an affluent suburb of Dayton, home to dual-income families and executives from companies like General Motors, LexisNexis, and NRC, a leading maker of automated teller machines. And so he filled his store with fine wines, exotic cheeses, and a new line of prepared foods that would appeal to people whose time was more precious than money. The store's bakery experimented with baking its own bread and developed Dorothy Lane's signature Killer Brownie, now a trademarked product that can be ordered online; Mayne ships them nationwide.

By 1990, Mayne was finally ready to open a second store. His revenues had grown to almost $18 million, and he felt that he had his systems down pat. But drastic changes were afoot in the grocery industry. "When Wal-Mart started opening supermarkets everywhere, people in the trade said they were going to put a lot of people out of business," he says. "I knew that if we stayed in the middle of the market, they were going to take us out."

The world, he reckoned, needed Days Inn and it also needed the Ritz-Carlton. "And so we decided to be the Ritz," he says. He also took a cue from Whole Foods Market, Inc., a chain with no stores in Ohio, but one that Mayne had been watching carefully for years. Whole Foods, he noted, had carved out a niche for itself with organic fare, but had lately begun adding more upscale and gourmet goods to its product mix. It struck Mayne as a winning combination. So he decided to emulate the strategy in reverse: Dorothy Lane, which had made a name for itself with its gourmet offerings, would begin carrying more healthy and organic products. It turned out to be a great competitive tactic.

In February 1991, the same month that Dorothy Lane opened its new Washington Square store, Meijer, a Grand Rapids, Michigan-based chain of grocery and general merchandise stores, came to town with a supercenter store. "They came in fighting Kroger and Cub Foods for market share, and we got in the middle of it," recalls Tom Winter, who has been with Dorothy Lane since 1967 and is now the marketing manager. "The economy was down, and this store was surrounded by four Krogers." Mayne estimates that 30 independent Dayton grocery stores shut down between 1991 and 1997. But Dorothy Lane held on by aggressively positioning itself as Dayton's premier market—a place where customers came not just to shop, but to be pampered with superior service and to sample the latest gourmet products. By 1995, revenues were $35 million.

The Secret Weapon

The employee practices that have evolved at Dorothy Lane over the past 15 years could easily come out of a Management 101 textbook, but if you mention the buzz words—learning organization, career coaching, intrapreneurship, open-book management, empowerment— Mayne looks a little confused, as if he's surprised that the things he's been doing for so long are the stuff that business school case studies are made of. To him, Dorothy Lane's uncommon work environment is just common sense, and maybe that's why it has served him so well for so long as his most effective competitive tool. He's not just creating a great place to work; he's training frontline soldiers for a cutthroat market-share battle, and he wants them to feel highly invested in the outcome. His most successful strategies involve:

Hiring

At Dorothy Lane, 90% of the company's 75 managers are homegrown, and nearly every full-time job is filled internally by a part-timer. Because Mayne relishes the thought that today's cashier may blossom into tomorrow's department manager, he puts every job applicant, "whether they're 16 or 60," through the same rigorous process.

The first interview, which is typically conducted by a store manager or assistant manager, is just a few minutes long. "It's a two-minute attitude check," says HR manager Matthew Hieb. "We want to see if they're smiling and outgoing." If an applicant is lucky enough to make a good first impression, he or she comes back for an initial formal interview with a department manager, and then returns again to take a 40-minute personality test with questions that Hieb says are designed to gauge integrity (Would you steal to feed your starving family? "No" is the answer Hieb is looking for). If the test looks good and the applicant passes a background check, he or she will come back yet again for a final interview with the assistant store director. New hires, both part-time and full-time, are assigned a trainer/mentor to familiarize them not only with the mechanics of the job, but with the Dorothy Lane culture.

"For every person we hire, we turn down five," says Mayne. And that's true in good economic times and in bad ones as well. "Dorothy Lane has always been at the top of all the independent grocery stores," says Dan Lucas, the grocery manager at the company's Oakwood store. "If you could get a job here, you were privileged." The pay at Dorothy Lane is a bit above average and the company offers a good health care plan, hands out annual bonuses, and contributes an average of 10% of profits to a 401(k) plan. There's also vacation pay for part-timers. But there's more to being an employer of choice than just compensation. "One of the big perks is the training," says Lucas. And that begins by sitting around the conference room table with Mayne and ends, well, never.

Orientation

Within six weeks of being hired, new employees meet in small groups with Mayne for a formal introduction to the grocery industry and Dorothy Lane. "Ozzie and Harriet don't live here anymore," Mayne tells his new trainees. "Ozzie Osbourne is the new family. When Ozzie and Harriet were around, 15 cents out of every food dollar went to restaurants, and now it's 50 cents. Restaurants are our competition." Maybe that explains Dorothy Lane's staff uniform: black trousers, crisp white button-down shirts, and black bow ties. The staff all look as if they're ready to serve you chateaubriand and a fine cabernet in one of Dayton's toniest restaurants. In fact, Mayne prepares them to do just that. At Dorothy Lane's Springboro store, the meat department will custom grill your meat or fish (at no charge), which you can then either take home or enjoy in the store's community room with a glass of wine served in Riedel crystal. It's not your typical trip to the corner market, and Mayne wants his new employees to understand that on every level.

"Let's talk about pricing," he says to his new employees. "Lots of people don't shop here because they say it's too expensive. Actually, we price the same as Kroger, but we don't get credit for it." He knows this because Dorothy Lane employees check 400 prices every other week by stalking competitors' aisles and writing down observations. They used to dictate into tape recorders, a practice that once got Mayne into hot water with a competitor.

Nonetheless, Dorothy Lane is not the cheapest store in Dayton (Meijer beats them on price), and Mayne makes no apologies for that. "As you go through life," he tells his young charges, "businesses will tell you that they'll give you three things: the cheapest price, the best service, and the best quality. And when they tell you that, they're lying because you can only do two out of three." Dorothy Lane is all about service and quality, and over the course of the next hour, he makes that point again and again. He tells them about the $60,000 French oven that was purchased for the bakery on the advice of a customer, the store's policy against antibiotics and hormones in its meat, the exorbitantly expensive balsamic vinegar that customers sample with an eyedropper.

There's a bit of Finance 101 as well. "On a $25 grocery order, how much profit do you think we make?" he asks them. "Is it $12.50, $7.50, $2.50, or 75 cents?" He goes around the room and asks for educated guesses, and it's clear that most of these kids don't have a clue about the grocery industry's notoriously thin margins; they're genuinely flabbergasted when he tells them the answer: 75 cents.

After speaking to them for an hour or so, he turns them over to David Andrews, his son-in-law, who teaches for both the Dayton school system and nearby Sinclair Community College. Andrews uses a customer-service training program called Feelings, which he's customized for Dorothy Lane, to bring home some basic customer service tenets. But he also breaks it up with in-the-trenches exercises that send the group downstairs to the store, where they scramble in teams to hunt down 23 items on a grocery list that includes such foreign-sounding items as mascarpone, aceto balsamico, and Oregon Chai. "I want you to find these items in 10 minutes without asking anyone for help," he tells them. "It'll help you understand how customers feel." Later, they'll be asked to approach customers and offer to help them find an item on their grocery list.

Opening the Books

Dorothy Lane has an intranet that Mayne thinks is "the best in the industry." Every employee can log on and get a good look at the company's key numbers, which are compared with the previous year every week: total sales, revenue by department, sales per hour, labor dollars, and wages as a percentage of sales. "If you're a delivery guy in the back room, you probably know what our revenues are," says Kent Dimbath, Dorothy Lane's CFO. And if you're a bakery manager, you might even place a friendly wager with your counterpart in the meat department—a sawbuck to whoever had the greatest sales increase over the prior year for the week. "It gets very competitive within stores," says one employee.

"Information is power, so I want the people who work here to know as much as they can," says Mayne. "Everyone needs to know the score of the game." But he doesn't just post the information on the intranet and hope that his employees find the time to read it. Every 13 weeks, Norman, Calvin, and Dimbath meet with the company's managers and department heads, in groups of half a dozen or so, to go over Dorothy Lane's entire income statement. And twice a year, they hold similar sessions for all full-time employees. During a two-week period, Mayne might run 15 meetings, giving his staff an update on the state of the industry and analyzing the most important items that affect Dorothy Lane's bottom line.

Profits, for instance, have been a big topic of discussion. Dorothy Lane's newest store, which opened in March 2002, put the company in the red until September 2004. And health insurance costs have also battered the bottom line. "From 2001 to 2003, our health care expenses went from $400,000 to $800,000 to $1.4 million," explains Mayne. Profits, which ran as high as 6% prior to 2002, are now more in line with the industry average of 2% to 3%. And so the company had to reduce some of its health coverage and ask employees to foot the bill for a greater percentage. No one welcomed that news, but, says Mayne, because his employees had access to the company's financials, they understood why the decision was made. "People don't mind the word *no*," he says. "What they do mind is not being told why."

Mayne also hopes that sharing information, particularly about company expenses, will give employees an incentive to be more efficient and less wasteful in their own departments. John Izzo, a workplace consultant and co-author of *Awakening Corporate Soul: Four Paths to Unleash the Power of People at Work,* thinks that's a reasonable expectation. "If you've got people fully engaged at your company, it creates a cycle of profitability," he says. That's partly because one of the bottom-line benefits of a highly engaged and informed workforce is that "people will work harder to cut costs." He points to Southwest Airlines, which appealed to its employees to come up with expense-cutting ideas after the airline industry was decimated after 9-11. While other carriers faltered, Southwest remained profitable, says Izzo. "And that's a kudos to having an engaged staff," he says. "There's a level of trust, and people say, okay, we really need to cut costs—we know you're not lying to us."

Continuous Learning

"Dad is never content to rest on his laurels," says Calvin Mayne. "He's always a student." Even when he's on vacation, Mayne takes note of every venue where food is the centerpiece and looks for great ideas that he might take home to Dayton. In 2002, he was strolling down a narrow street in Arezzo, Italy, when a butcher shop caught his eye. "The Italians combine different meats in creative ways," he explains, "and at this shop, I saw a beautiful presentation of products."

The next day, he called his meat and seafood director, Jack Gridley, and asked him to book a flight to Italy with his wife, Judy. "I want you to work in a meat shop over here," he told him. Mayne contacted an Italian consultant he had known for years, and she agreed to make the arrangements.

"Within a month," recalls Gridley, "I was in Tuscany working in a fifth-generation butcher shop. They spoke no English." Despite the language barrier, Gridley came back a week later with a dazzling array of new skills. His customers were treated to such delicacies as boneless chicken stuffed with ground pork and veal, seasoned with garlic and rosemary and topped with pancetta bacon. "They were a little intimidated at first, so there was a learning process," said Gridley. He suggested to Norman and Calvin that his department start doing cooking demonstrations all day long to give customers a little hand-holding. "It wasn't a hard sell because they're innovators," says Gridley. Soon after he started the demos, his department revenues began growing at twice the store's overall rate.

Gridley's experience is by no means unusual; Mayne is famous for sending his employees into the trenches to learn new skills, to observe best practices at other companies, and to apply them back at Dorothy Lane. There are a handful of high-end supermarket chains that he admires and tries to emulate: Andronico's Market in the San Francisco Bay area; Metropolitan Market in Seattle; AJ's Fine Foods in Phoenix; Lunds in Minnesota; West Point Market in Akron; and his all-time favorite, Wegmans in Rochester. He's forged friendships with some of their CEOs, including Danny Wegman, and he's not shy about asking for advice.

Back in 1990, for instance, when he was getting ready to open the Washington Square store, he sent 18 managers to Queen Anne Thriftway (now Metropolitan Market), Larry's Markets in Seattle, and West Point Market in Akron to do some research on store floor plans. His employees spent several days studying the markets and came back with some strong opinions about store layout, including a plan to open up the bakery's production area so that customers could watch (and smell) the bread being baked. Several years later, a similar trip to Andronico's would result in an unconventional decision to put a "hall of wine" and a wine bar smack in the middle of the newest store in Springboro, where it would become an upscale venue for weekly wine-tasting events.

That's Todd Templin's department. He started working at Dorothy Lane in 1987 while still in high school, and by 1992, he was a second-shift store manager and a college senior. By then, he had fallen in love with the wine business. Mayne was quick to capitalize on that passion. He moved Templin into the wine department and sent him to a Miami University of Ohio wine appreciation course for two semesters. He's now the director of beer and wine sales for Dorothy Lane—a position that comes with some very attractive fringe benefits. Templin has traveled to the major growing regions in France and makes regular pilgrimages to Napa Valley, where he meets winegrowers, strolls through vineyards, and, of course, samples some of the best wines that California has to offer. He has even worked with one small vineyard—Havens Wine Cellars—to create a private label wine just for Dorothy Lane. Mayne playfully named it Todd Norman Napa Valley Merlot.

As a manager, it's Templin's responsibility to make sure his 14 employees are as well educated about wine as he is, so he sends them to Napa Valley as well. When we spoke in July 2004, two wine department managers and two assistant managers had just returned from California. "We try to get as many people out there as possible," says Templin. "It makes them more aware of what's going on in the wine world, and that gives them a lot of credibility with customers."

Isn't it all prohibitively expensive? "We spend an enormous amount of money on travel and education," says Calvin. "Accountants were always questioning that item." In 1997, in fact, Calvin announced to his father that he wanted to take the ultimate field trip: a leave of absence to attend a 10-week course at Le Cordon Bleu in Paris. An extravagance? Maybe it seemed that way at the time. But both Calvin and Norman knew that more and more of their business was coming from the sale of prepared foods, and it made sense for the heir apparent to have some gourmet cooking skills under his belt. "It trained my palate," says Calvin, who his father says will most likely succeed him within five years. "I know that our bakery makes baguettes better than 90% of the ones I've had in France." But the real proof is in the numbers. "We sold more baguettes last year than Wonder Bread," says Mayne, "and I don't think there's another supermarket that can say that." That's a testament to his philosophy that educated consumers will factor quality into the value equation.

Mayne's employees regard his commitment to continuous learning as a fringe benefit that helps define the company as an employer of choice. But for Mayne, there's return on investment to consider as well. By regularly sending his employees out into the world beyond Dorothy Lane—a practice that typically costs $150,000 a year—he's inoculating his company against a disease that's common and insidious among small, local companies: organizational myopia. CEOs of entrepreneurial companies are notoriously isolated, often by choice as well as by necessity. They're too busy to spend much time focusing on anything beyond day-to-day operations, but they're also paralyzed by fear that any attempt to seek out advice, ideas, or solutions to thorny problems will be seen as a sign of weakness.

Intrapreneurship

"You're a mini-celebrity wherever you go," says Ed Flohre, who runs the store in Springboro and has been with Dorothy Lane since 1969. "It's because we're so knowledgeable—Norman and Calvin let us become the experts." Even outside of Dayton, Dorothy Lane has gained a reputation as a store to emulate. Dennis Chrisman, the Washington Square store director and Wayne's son, attended an executive leadership program at Cornell University and found himself in the company of CEOs and marketing heads of much larger grocery store chains. "I was the only store-level person among those 28 people," he recalls. "And you know what? A lot of them knew about Dorothy Lane, and everyone wanted to talk to me. As the week went on, I didn't feel intimidated; I felt important."

For Mayne, one of the key measures of success is the extent to which his employees feel like vital cogs in the wheel. He wants them to treat his business as if it were their own, using newly acquired knowledge, or simply their own passion for a particular discipline, to come up with innovative ideas for their own departments. He's never been tempted, he says, to put his own name on the business because that might undermine the contributions of his employees. "Everyone has to own something, and it so happens that I own this company," he says. "But there's such a thing as emotional ownership as well."

In 1995, Patrick Arnold was a college student majoring in computer science and working part-time in the Oakwood store's produce department. He thought Dorothy Lane's Web site could use a facelift, so he e-mailed Jack Gridley, then the company's de facto technology honcho, with a few suggestions. Gridley told him to go ahead. So Arnold went to work on the project, and within two months, he was yanked from the produce department and given an upstairs office. He was 19 years old, and he cringes at the recollection of his first Web site. "It was pathetic," he says sheepishly. But Arnold learned a lot about Web development, and Mayne, who was skeptical of e-mail but is now joined at the hip with his BlackBerry, learned how technology could help grow his business. The company now has an e-commerce-enabled Web site, which it hosts with an on-site server, sends electronic newsletters to 8,000 customers a week, electronically manages a complex loyalty program, and gives customers the option of ordering and paying for their groceries online, then picking them up at Springboro or Washington Square for a flat fee of $6.95. "I was given a tremendous amount of autonomy," says Arnold.

The same goes for Lori Kelch, a certified nutrition educator who co-manages Dorothy Lane's healthy living departments. Just eight months after she was hired in 2002, she insisted on conducting a store seminar on natural products for hormone replacement. "It was right after we were hearing about the dangers of hormone replacement therapy," she says. "So I really didn't even ask anyone if I could do it—I just went for it." She enlisted help designing the poster, commandeered the kitchen staff to cook up some healthy snacks, and *then* checked in with Calvin to make sure it was all okay. Now Kelch does about nine seminars a year, many of them outside the store at local community organizations. "It's all my initiative," she says. "But Calvin and Norman see it as really benefiting the store."

But just because Mayne gives his employees autonomy doesn't mean he's a hands-off manager. "No matter what job you have, you can always go to Norman," says store manager Wayne Chrisman. "His door is always open." Chrisman, who has been with Dorothy Lane since 1960, recalls that about 25 years ago, back when he was a second-shift store manager, Mayne called him into his office and gave him a stern reprimand. "Wayne," he said, "you're doing a good job, but we're hearing from the people that you're driving them too hard and you've got to let up a little." Bakery director Scott Fox had a similar experience. "It can be hard to work here as a manager because of the way Norman and Calvin feel about all their employees," says Fox. "I'd been working here less than a year, and I thought I was doing a pretty good job. But Norm told me, 'We like what you're doing in the bakery, but we're getting a lot of complaints from our associates. My dad didn't build this company on good bread, he built it on good people.' " Fox got the message and softened his approach; like all the company's managers, he knows that Mayne won't hesitate to step in to protect his employees when he feels he must. He's not a command-and-control CEO, and he won't tolerate that approach from his managers.

Community Building

As Dorothy Lane grows, more and more of Mayne's employees develop specialties of their own, immersing themselves in projects and departments that give them "emotional ownership" in the company. It's a stimulating environment, but one that can spawn little fiefdoms, where employees are so focused on their own interests that they lose sight of the larger community. To prevent that from happening at any growing company, a CEO must build community among his or her staff. Mayne does that in several ways.

- **Company Newsletter.** Mayne makes sure that his employees hear about one another's accomplishments through a quarterly newsletter that he calls "The Legend Letter." It was Regan Ross's midnight leg-of-lamb story that first sparked the idea—a publication that would celebrate "legendary" customer service. Mayne insists that the newsletter remain within the company; customers don't see it and it's not accessible on the company's Web site. "Customers would see it as a marketing tool, and that's not the point," he says.

- **Group Entertainment.** Throughout the year, there are interstore tournaments in softball, volleyball, bowling, and basketball; Dorothy Lane even hires professional referees. In November, Mayne closes the stores one evening at 7:00 p.m. so that all employees and their spouses can attend a companywide staff party. There's a DJ, a movie, and a raffle where Mayne gives away bicycles, televisions, radios, and other treasures.

- **Community Events.** In September, Mayne asks employees to participate in the Dorothy Lane Umbrella Brigade, which marches every year in the local Labor Day parade. The group puts in hours of practice (Mayne pays them $50 each for their time) to learn a highly choreographed routine with large red-and-white-striped umbrellas—the company's local trademark.

- **Perks for All.** Managers get free use of Mayne's condominium in Sarasota, Florida; part-timers earn an hour of paid vacation for every 45-hour period worked; female employees have enjoyed free on-site mini-spa treatments from Mayne's daughter Chimene Ross; students get a one-time 20-cents-an-hour raise if they make the dean's list or honor roll; college students get a bonus of 75 cents an hour for every hour they work at Dorothy Lane during a grading period, provided their GPA is 2.75 or better and that they're signed up for at least six credit hours.

"Whatever is rightly done, however humble, is noble." The quote, from Sir Henry Royce of Rolls-Royce, is prominently displayed in Dorothy Lane's stores, and Mayne fervently hopes that his customers and his employees believe it. If employee tenure is any indication, the message seems to be sinking in. Typically, when businesses grow significantly, owners discover that the managers who helped fuel that growth aren't always prepared to take on the responsibility of managing a larger and more sophisticated company. But at Dorothy Lane, that's the exception rather than the rule.

Produce director Jose Manzano joined the company in 1962, and his wife, Patty, was hired in 1967 and runs the floral department at the Springboro store. Ed Flohre and Wayne Chrisman, who manage the Springboro and Oakwood stores, have been with Dorothy Lane since 1969 and 1960, respectively; HR director Matt Hieb has been with the company since 1971. Meat and seafood director Jack Gridley has been around since 1976, and vice president of marketing Tom Winter started in 1967. Every key manager, in fact, has been with Dorothy Lane for at least 10 years. And when it's time for their jobs to be filled once again, Mayne is convinced that the next generation of homegrown managers will be up to the task.

That includes his son, Calvin, who started out sweeping the Oakwood store's basement floor when he was 12 years old. He also stocked shelves on the night shift and managed the second shift before he became a bona fide foodie and took on the role of specialty food buyer in the mid-1990s. He's been general manager since 1996, COO for the past five years, and feels he's earned his stripes. "Dad and I never had the conversation, but it was understood that I would have to prove myself," he says. And in that respect, he's really no different from any other employee at Dorothy Lane. So in a few years, when Norman Mayne passes the torch to Calvin, he'll do it with confidence that he's not just passing on a business. He's passing on a community of true believers.

"Convert Your Employees" Tips from Dorothy Lane

1. **Hire the Right Employees.** You may think that's a no-brainer, especially in a labor market filled with downsized overqualified workers desperate for jobs. But be careful: A bad hire can cost you up to 200% of an employee's compensation. And more often than not, a bad hire isn't someone with lousy skills—it's someone who just doesn't fit into your organization. Education and skills are important, but it's even more critical to hire employees with the right attitude and work ethic. Skills can be taught; attitude can't.

2. **Invest in Your Employees' Professional Development.** Cultivate an environment of continuous learning. Start by assigning every new employee a seasoned company mentor for at least two weeks; then make training an ongoing part of the job. Training not only insures that your people are constantly up to speed, but it sends them the message that their future and your company's success are intimately linked.

3. **Share Information with Your Employees.** Let them know where you stand in the marketplace, the challenges your industry faces, and what your short- and long-term business goals are. Consider sharing financial information and educating your employees so that they understand the key numbers that make your business tick. Even if they're not owners, you need to make them feel as if they have a stake in your company.

4. **Impart Your Mission to Employees.** Your mission may be to provide the best service, the fastest delivery, or the most error-free product, but if your employees don't know that, they have no way of helping you succeed. Articulate your vision every day so that employees never forget why they're coming to work in the morning. If it's just for the paycheck, you're in trouble.

5. **Build Community.** Company newsletters, outings, parties, and sports competitions aren't just perks. They're community-

building opportunities that should be an integral part of your company. Employees who both work and play together will develop stronger relationships with one another and with your company.

. . . And from Others

6. **Recruit Creatively.** When Deb Weidenhamer, CEO of **Auction Systems Auctioneers & Appraisers** (see chapter 4) was trying to fill two positions in 2004, she used her customer database to send out 6,000 e-mails with an invitation to "join our Auction Systems team." Her rationale: traditional ads attract people who don't know a thing about auctions, while her customer base is filled with knowledgeable, passionate people. Weidenhamer filled both positions within two weeks of sending out the e-mail.

7. **Interview for Behavior, Not Just Skills.** Barry Steinberg, owner of Watertown, Massachusetts, **Direct Tire & Auto Service** has used headhunters to track down potential employees who are unhappy with their current jobs. Then he interviews them three times, often scheduling the first appointment for 7:00 a.m. because he wants to find out if the candidate makes a great impression early in the morning—the time of day when most customers will drop off their cars. Is the prospective employee on time and well-groomed? Is his shirt neatly pressed? Does he need to slug down two cups of coffee before he can speak articulately? Steinberg is interviewing as much for behavior as he is for skills, and so should you.

8. **Hire Outside Your Industry.** Everyone can benefit from an outside perspective. Peter Metcalf, CEO and co-founder of **Black Diamond Equipment,** a maker of mountaineering and backcountry ski equipment in Salt Lake City, Utah, recalls receiving an out-of-the-blue e-mail a few years ago from a toy industry executive who was also a climbing enthusiast. "He was head of their new product engineering department, and he had an idea for how we could improve one of our ice-climbing products," says Metcalf. "I thought he had skills that we could re-

ally use." Metcalf called the fellow to thank him; a year and a half later, the man came to Black Diamond as head of R & D. The lesson: think in terms of skills, not job description, and you'll vastly expand your recruiting frame of reference.

9. **Tailor Incentives to Individuals.** Some employees are motivated by bonuses, others crave flexibility, and still others thrive on increasing levels of responsibility. Meet with them individually once a quarter to discuss goals and how they can achieve what's most important to them. That's what George Johnson, CEO of **Cosmi Corporation,** does, and it's paid off. His $25 million Carson, California, software company boasts 0% turnover among salaried staff.

10. **Take a Contrarian Approach to Managing.** In the building maintenance industry, says **Harvard Maintenance**'s president and CEO Stanley Doobin, company owners typically try to drive employee performance "by discipline, particularly if they're in a union environment." Not so at his New York City–based company, which has grown from $10 million in 1995 to $135 million in 2004. Doobin attributes that to his "inverted pyramid" style of management, which puts employees at the top. "It's really simple," says Doobin. "We go out into the field and ask them what they need, listen to them, let them gripe, then take action." Every quarter, the company gives out a Crown Award to the building team that provides the best quality service, gets the least number of complaints, takes the best care of its equipment, and receives the most thank-yous from tenants. Each building maintenance employee receives a $100 bonus. "They're union people, so we're under no obligation to give them additional money," says Doobin. "But it works wonders. They care about one another and that builds teamwork."

4 | Transform with Technology

Company: Auction Systems Auctioneers & Appraisers

Business: Auction house; appraisal services

Location: Phoenix, Arizona

Revenues: $11.5 million

Employees: 27 full-time; 9 part-time

Founder: Deb Weidenhamer

Year Founded: 1995

Web Site: www.auctionandappraise.com

Deb Weidenhamer in Auction Systems' warehouse with Spot and Sage.
Photograph: Cameron Burns

Alpha Dog Credentials:

Deb Weidenhamer was an early adopter of technology in an old-line industry that has a reputation for clinging to the status quo. By approaching eBay and other Internet auctions as opportunities rather than threats, she has grown exponentially, earning a place on *Inc.* magazine's annual list of the 500 fastest-growing privately held companies three years in a row.

D eb Weidenhamer likes to say that she's a member of the world's oldest profession. It isn't what you think. As CEO of Phoenix-based Auction Systems Auctioneers & Appraisers, Weidenhamer is well schooled in the history of her industry, which dates back to before 500 BC, when comely maidens were auctioned off for marriage. Of course, the industry has come a long way since then. Or has it?

"Ten years ago, when I first began to look at what auction companies were doing, I found that most of them were still very mom-and-pop," says Weidenhamer, an attractive blond in her thirties with the authoritative presence of an opera diva. "My industry was so antiquated; I knew there was room for someone to kick it up a notch." And she has.

Weidenhamer has grown Auction Systems to $11.5 million in annual revenues, earning the company three-time inclusion on both *Inc.* magazine's list of the 500 fastest-growing privately held companies and its list of the 100 fastest-growing inner-city companies (compiled with Michael Porter's Initiative for a Competitive Inner City). Those distinctions alone make her unique in her industry. So how has she done it? "You can't think like an auction company," she claims. "You have to think like a technology company."

Given eBay's prominence, you may think that sounds obvious. Think again. "This industry is very slow to embrace new technology," says Robert A. Shively, chief executive of the National Auctioneers Association (NAA) in Overland Park, Kansas. He says the $217 billion industry is comprised of approximately 25,000 companies, only 13% of which offer online bidding. Roughly 48% are sole proprietorships, and only 38% reported *gross* revenues of more than $1 million (that includes revenues that passed through the companies from buyers to sellers). By comparison, Weidenhamer's clicks-and-bricks strategy puts her at the top of the industry food chain. She was an early and enthusiastic user of eBay; she integrated spreadsheet and bar-code technology into her company back in the late '90s; and she was one of the first traditional auction companies to offer her clients online bidding and then simulcast Internet auctions, which allowed bidders to participate in live auctions via the Internet in real time.

Despite the technological advances, Weidenhamer's company

hasn't lost the look and feel of a traditional auction house. Two or three times a week, she runs live auctions in her warehouses, and those events attract lively and diverse crowds. Auctions are "show day" at the company, and even employees who aren't scheduled to work often show up for the fun.

Levi Jordan, who was the 2004 Arizona State Champion Auctioneer, typically runs the show, and his presence at the podium is pure entertainment. Sporting an impressive mustache and a cowboy hat, he can chant for four hours straight, revving up the buyers so they'll bid higher on everything from a collection of bar stools to an avocado green refrigerator. ("C'mon, you can't get this at Wal-Mart," he teases. "It doesn't get better than this.") An Auction Systems "ring person" helps him out by walking the floor and reading the crowd, egging on individual buyers and encouraging friendly competition. Internet participants are competing at the same time. Auction Systems employee Shannon Flowers sits on a stage in front of the crowd, her eyes glued to the laptop that's processing live bids from the Internet as well as proxy bids that were entered online during the previous week. Whenever the Internet outbids the live auction, she calls out the bid to Jordan and he goes back to the crowd for a higher price. It's a system that seamlessly merges man and machine, one that took years to develop and has propelled Auction Systems into the realm of Alpha Dogs.

From her earliest days, Weidenhamer understood that technology is a great enabler for small businesses that want to look and act much bigger than they actually are. But entrepreneurs who throw money into information technology without fully understanding the potential return on investment will ultimately look a lot like the venture capitalists who plowed money indiscriminately into dot-com start-ups: eventually, they'll be caught with their pants down. Main Street businesses can transform themselves into Alpha Dogs through the use of technology, but the business model has to make sense to begin with.

Take, for instance, Pets.com, a company that shut down in 2000, the same year it went public. Did it ever make economic sense for consumers to buy pet food and supplies over the Internet, paying a fortune on shipping, as opposed to a local supermarket or pet store? Well, no. In the end, Pets.com even attempted to compete on price, slashing its already slender margins in a desperate attempt to entice customers. And then it rolled over and died.

Your investment in technology should streamline your operation and eventually cut your costs, better serve your existing customers, and make it easier and more efficient to drum up new business. If your information technology efforts don't pass that simple test, then you've merely been seduced by the bells and whistles. Are you mastering your technology, or is it mastering you? In Weidenhamer's case, it's most certainly the former. She's an early adopter—someone who embraces new technology and leverages it not only to create a competitive advantage in the marketplace, but to entirely change the playing field for competitors. That she's done this in an industry that has embraced the status quo for centuries makes the strategy all the more successful.

Unlikely Player

Before eBay put *auction* back into our everyday lexicon, the word typically conjured up images of Sotheby's and Christie's, the blue-blooded auction houses whose most visible stock in trade is art and antiquities. But the vast majority of companies in this $217 billion industry are small family businesses that are far more likely to sell used farm equipment and household goods than Louis XIV armoires.

Stroll through Auction Systems' two cavernous warehouses in downtown Phoenix and you'll find big-screen televisions, cash registers, hospital beds, bicycles, slot machines, tools, tires, stereo systems, guns (locked up, of course), jewelry, and antique coins. The stuff is often piled high on metal shelves and wooden pallets or wrapped in plastic sheeting. Weidenhamer's staff knows where everything is, down to the last iPod. But to an outsider, the eclectic collection of goods looks haphazard and disorganized: it's like Costco run amok. In May 2004, the inventory even included two life-size plastic statues of Mary and Joseph and a 600-year-old samurai sword. There's very little, in fact, that Weidenhamer doesn't sell. On the short list: people, such as eligible bachelors; pornography; and livestock. Just about everything else is fair game.

At first blush, Weidenhamer (née Ludden) is an unlikely inhabitant of the auction world. She grew up in Galveston, Texas, the youngest of five children in a household that welcomed everyone from migrant farm workers to gypsies. "My father had a tender heart," recalls Weidenhamer, who idolized her dad, Richard Clark Ludden. She was precocious and willful, demanding classical sheet music for the piano before she even began elementary school. A gifted student, she was graduated from high school at age 14, then indulged her passion for piano and voice training for a couple of years. Eventually, she enrolled in Asbury College in Wilmore, Kentucky, a small and prestigious Christian liberal arts college where her father, who was an evangelical Methodist minister as well as an inventor, attended seminary. Three of her four siblings also attended Asbury, where Weidenhamer earned a BA in business.

"Then I got this wild idea that I wanted to live on a farm," she recalls. In 1987, her parents had moved to Nebraska to be near her recently widowed grandmother, so Weidenhamer followed them. She leased 80 acres of land and sublet 70 of them; on the remainder, she grew tomatoes, corn, green beans, and cucumbers, which she packaged in baskets lined with gingham cloth and sold at a local farmer's market. "I made more money than I'd ever made," she says. "And I worked from the moment the sun came up until it went down." When the growing and harvesting season was finished, she worked as a salesperson for her father, who had founded a company that specialized in etching bar codes into metal objects, such as medical instruments. "Even though he was a minister, he was always active in the business world," says Weidenhamer. In Nebraska, she met her future husband, Bruce Weidenhamer, who also worked for her father. She accepted his marriage proposal on one condition: "I didn't want to stay in Nebraska because it was boring," she recalls. "So I gave him a list of three places: Boulder, Phoenix, or anywhere in Texas." He agreed.

Weidenhamer, who was then in her early twenties, landed a job in Phoenix with a bar-code technology firm that was in friendly competition with her father's company. But by the time the young couple moved, the position had disappeared. "We were both out of work for four months," says Weidenhamer. Eventually, Bruce was hired by American Express as a computer programmer. And Weidenhamer leveraged her experience with her father's company, as well as a short but successful stint selling computer keyboards for Rowland Automation, Ltd., while she was in college to talk her way into a job as an entry-level business analyst with the George S. May International Company in San Francisco. "I had an apartment in Redwood City, and I commuted between San Francisco and Phoenix for five years," she recalls. She rose through the ranks, but she was miserable. "It had reached the point where I'd start to cry every Sunday morning because I knew I had to leave that day." And that's exactly when a chance meeting changed the path of her life.

It was on a flight home to Phoenix in the summer of 1995 when the auction industry first hit Weidenhamer's radar screen. Her seatmate was an auctioneer in his late eighties, and he regaled her with war stories that sparked her imagination. "It was business and it was sales, but there was also the stage and an audience," she recalls. "And the idea that I could be working with a guy who sold petroleum one day and with a restaurateur the next really intrigued me."

Eager to end her interstate commute, she quit her job a month later and enrolled in a Phoenix auction school, where she learned the industry basics, including how to coax her expertly trained singing voice into the auctioneer's chant. "There were 10 people in my class," she recalls, "and all of them except me were there to learn the family business. It was taught by a man in his eighties, and he told us that very few people make it." Weidenhamer was determined to count herself among the successful. But Bruce, she recalls, "thought I was insane. And to have someone who knows you so well wonder if you've gone off the deep end makes you wonder if you really *have* gone off the deep end."

The New Girl in Town

In November 1995, Weidenhamer plunked down $5,000 and started her auction company in a rented run-down building between a soup kitchen and a homeless shelter in a crime-ridden downtown Phoenix neighborhood. "I had never been around homeless people," she says, "and it changed how I felt about material things—they became less important. I went to work in the morning grateful for ambition." The local police suggested that she might want to consider coming to work armed, so Weidenhamer, who was taught gun safety at an early age, started carrying a .38 revolver. "I'd walk out of my office door every night with my gun in my hand," she says. On nights when she worked very late, she often called the police and asked them to drive by her building. "I had a very good relationship with them because I let them use my building for stakeouts," she says.

Her first task was to find sellers willing to let her auction off their products, so she began by bidding on local government contracts for small municipal auctions. "With the first few that I bid on, I had the procurement officers tell me that it was the first time they had received a typewritten [as opposed to a handwritten] proposal," she recalls. But that wasn't the only way she differentiated herself from the competition. "This was a dirty little industry," she says. "There was a lot of dishonesty. A government agency might deliver 20 pallets of surplus, and the auction house would break it into 30 pallets. Ten would be sold for the house, and 20 would be for the government. It was a common practice, and I was very vocal that I didn't want to be part of that kind of business." Weidenhamer started placing ads in the local newspaper. "Do you hire auctioneers?" the ad read. "Are you sure you're being paid for everything you sent to the auction house?"

Those in-your-face ads made her extraordinarily unpopular with her competitors. "She was not very well liked," recalls Paul Ramirez, a contract auctioneer who calls auctions for a number of companies, including Auction Systems. "There were old, established businesses, and suddenly, this young lady began showing up on the bid lists." Weidenhamer recalls that within her first few weeks in business, "almost every auctioneer in town dropped by to tell me I'd be out of business within a few months. But it just fired me up because I wanted to prove them wrong."

Weidenhamer plowed another $20,000 of her own savings into her fledgling company "just to stay alive." For the first year and a half, she worked alone, occasionally enlisting her sister and her friends to help her sort through the products in her warehouse. She kept the company afloat by selling government surplus such as desks, chairs, telephone systems, computers, and heavy equipment, taking commissions from 5% (on, say, a bulldozer) to 60% (on an estate sale that required extensive pre-auction organization). She learned how to drive a forklift and how to deal with the quirky and often unpredictable customers who populated the auction world. "You might see a guy pull up in a beat-up pickup truck from the fifties, and he'd haul several thousand dollars out of his overalls to pay a bill," she says. Often, she arrived home at 10:00 p.m. and collapsed on her bed while Bruce, who was supporting them on his salary, cooked dinner. "Then I'd wake her up and keep her awake so she could eat and go back to sleep," he says.

Weidenhamer landed 18 government contracts that first year by bidding low, which did not add to her popularity among her peers. And to develop a buyer base, she placed clever ads in newspapers, sent out direct mail, and searched for offbeat items that would entice customers to brave her dicey location. She even put a collection of love letters on the block as part of an estate auction. As business steadily increased, she hired a warehouse manager, who was followed by two additional employees six months later. Weidenhamer didn't pay herself a dime for three years. Her most important "employee" was probably Spot, a Saint Bernard–bull terrier mutt and a reject from police-dog training, who had, at least, learned how to attack on command. He's still alive and a constant presence at the company, along with his successor-in-training, Sage. Weidenhamer credits them with protecting her and her business, where transactions are often made in cash. "I think if it hadn't been for Spot, something bad would have happened to Deb," says Bruce. "It was not a good neighborhood."

Auction Systems grew steadily, increasing revenues from

$176,800 in 1996 to $246,000 the following year. The vast majority of Weidenhamer's clients were government agencies, but she also began actively marketing her services to corporations and estates. "I looked for buyers in places where other auctioneers were not looking," she says. "If we were having a jewelry auction, for example, I'd send flyers to real estate offices because there were lots of women who were brokers and sales agents. It worked."

The eBay Disruption

But it was in the late 1990s that Auction Systems' biggest growth opportunity came out of the blue, from a source that many in the industry regarded as a mortal threat: eBay, Inc. In 1998, Meg Whitman took over as president and CEO of the company that Pierre Omidyar started in 1995, ostensibly so his girlfriend could trade Pez dispensers online. Whitman had just begun to transform eBay from an online marketplace for quirky collectibles to one of the most successful Internet companies in the world.

Traditional auctioneers, like retailers who feared that consumers would abandon bricks-and-mortar stores for the world of "e-tailing," suddenly felt vulnerable and defenseless. "I remember at the first national convention I went to after eBay had become well-known," recalls Weidenhamer. "I heard several speakers say that as a group we ought to do everything we could to kill this evil beast before it ruined everything." Others simply dismissed eBay as a shooting star that would crash and burn before it could do much damage to the industry. As far as Weidenhamer was concerned, both attitudes were off the mark. Always a contrarian, she reckoned that "anything that scared my industry so much must be a good thing."

Weidenhamer's reaction to eBay was classic Alpha Dog: where others saw an emerging threat, she perceived an enticing opportunity, and she began to think about how her company might profit from eBay's disruptive presence in the industry. On a good day, a live auction might attract 250 participants, she reasoned, while the Internet would provide her with thousands of potential buyers who might drive the price of goods higher with their competitive bidding. And higher selling prices meant higher commissions. It wasn't the right venue for all of her clients, but for those who had specialty items that were sought after by collectors, eBay might be just the ticket. By that time, she had grown Auction Systems to $350,000 in revenue and eight employees.

Weidenhamer's first foray into the Internet auction world was in October 1998 with a collection of 50,000 Cabbage Patch dolls, which an eccentric client had collected over a period of several years and needed to sell in order to finance her mother's nursing home care. Weidenhamer decided to sell the dolls on eBay one at a time—a process that took three months and which required her and her staff to acquire more Cabbage Patch knowledge than seems appropriate for any right-minded adult. How much, for example, should a 1986 Freddie Korie doll with a pacifier and a pink Xavier Roberts signature fetch? What about a 1984 Libby Laurel with a blue signature that was missing her original birth certificate? "And I hate dolls," sneers Weidenhamer. After a while, so did her staff. One key employee, she says, quit because he had chronic nightmares about removing Cabbage Patch dolls' bloomers to examine the color of the signatures on their bottoms.

Despite the fallout, the experiment was a grand success. "Had I sold the dolls in a traditional auction, they would have brought $20,000," she says. "On eBay, they sold for $300,000. We were shipping those dolls to China, Australia, even Guam." That year, Weidenhamer finally began drawing a modest salary. A whole new world had opened up for Auction Systems, but Weidenhamer knew that she had to tread cautiously. She had her core business to consider, and she carefully weighed the effect of her eBay experiment on the company.

Weidenhamer didn't advertise her use of eBay, and she used the online auction house only when she thought it would best serve her clients. Running the auctions online, while continuing to maintain and grow the traditional side of her business, was time-consuming and exhausting. She was always on the lookout for hot products and hit pay dirt when she started auctioning guns on eBay. "I wanted to do it right and make sure that auctions weren't a place where criminals were coming to buy guns," she says. So she became a Federal Firearms Licensed dealer, which meant that everyone who bought a gun from her at auction had to go through a Brady background check by the FBI.

In the true spirit of eBay fever, she even went out and bought guns at pawn shops so that she could sell them online; it was the first time that Weidenhamer had ever purchased inventory. Her husband, Bruce, helped her identify and grade the guns. "We had a ton of guns that were being used for cowboy competitions that were becoming more popular on the East Coast," she says, estimating that she sold nearly 800 guns on eBay between November 1998 and February 1999.

And then eBay pulled the rug out from under her and declared that it would no longer allow firearms to be auctioned on the site. Its exit from the gun business in February 1999 opened the door for scores of independent online gun dealers to grab market share, and Weidenhamer briefly began using them to sell her gun inventory. But the experience of having a reliable source of income disappear overnight taught her a lesson: she didn't want to hitch her star to eBay or any other online auction company, for that matter. So she decided to take her company to new levels by building her own online auction site.

A Technology of Her Own

It wouldn't have taken much for Weidenhamer to get ahead of the industry curve in terms of technology use. The procedures that most auction houses use to keep track of inventory and run their auctions look a lot like they might have a century ago. Buyers' items come in the door, often in big plastic bags or buckets, and are sorted and tagged by hand. Before the auction, each lot is slapped with a numbered perforated ticket, which is ripped in half as the items are sold. "As you auction each item, someone writes down the item number, the buyer number, and the price," says Bruce Weidenhamer, who frequently helps his wife research the industry. "And that's how the whole thing is recorded—with someone writing as fast as they can, and someone else pulling off tags and sorting them by buyer number.

In the end, the buyer's record of what they bought is a handful of tags and a receipt from an adding machine."

Weidenhamer, however, was already doing things differently. From the beginning, she had used an Excel spreadsheet to keep track of who bought what on auction day. It was a system that allowed her to quickly tally buyers' purchases and provide them with printed, item-ized receipts at the end of an auction. It sounds like common sense, but most smaller auction houses do all the tallying by hand. And for the most part, their inventory systems are equally antiquated. Weiden-hamer, however, knew that she needed a better way to keep track of goods in her warehouse, especially if she planned to grow the busi-ness. So shortly after she started selling on eBay, she used the expertise she had developed working at her father's company to purchase a $7,000 bar-code system. It allowed her to tag every item in her ware-houses, scan them with handheld devices, and monitor inventory elec-tronically to create a comprehensive database. "The effect was almost immediate," she recalls. "We cut out 80 man-hours the first month." Again, Weidenhamer was ahead of her time; even today, very few auc-tion houses have bar-code systems.

But Weidenhamer had something in mind that would raise the bar even further. She began reading about Visual Basic, a programming language that would be the cornerstone for any software that helped display Auction Systems' goods online. Then she took a stab at writing the program herself, an unlikely endeavor for a CEO. Weidenhamer, though, is loaded with steely self-confidence, and she's always been convinced that she could learn to do just about anything as long as she could read a decent training manual.

"Deb reads very little for recreation," says her husband, Bruce. "A book is like a tool to her; she learns what she needs and then she sets it down. She's not an intellectual, but she's got laserlike intelligence." For eight months, she worked at cobbling together some off-the-shelf soft-ware, and she concedes that the results were "sketchy at best." Nonetheless, she was able to create a company Web site where buyers could leave bids for items that were to be auctioned off at her ware-house the following week. "All the items would be on the Internet for a week, and bidding would close at midnight the night before the auction," says Weidenhamer. "Someone would leave an opening bid and a high bid, and we'd represent that at the live auction." It was the beginning of a clicks-and-bricks system that would integrate Internet bidding with live auctions.

She sent faxes to her database of sellers and buyers, telling them about the site, but her marketing efforts were only moderately successful. While she managed to increase the number of auction participants, the proxy bidding did little to capture the excitement of an eBay-style auction. The ticket to that, Weidenhamer knew, was to create simulcast auctions, where Internet participants could bid against live auction attendees in real time.

A New Playing Field

By that time, in November 1999, several high-tech start-up companies were beginning to develop software for the auction industry, so Weidenhamer thought she'd give one of them a try. Seattle-based Bidpath Corp. worked with Weidenhamer to develop the right simulcast program for Auction Systems. But there were a multitude of problems.

The software was often too slow, making it hard for the program to keep up with the fast pace of bidding. And sometimes it crashed completely. When Weidenhamer was finally convinced that the kinks were worked out, she invited some key clients from a local government agency to attend one of her first simulcast auctions, hoping that the experience would convince them to award her a $300,000 contract that was currently up for bid. "If we had done well, we would have gotten that contract," says Weidenhamer. "But when it came down to it, the software failed. I think that was the first time that my employees ever heard me yell."

Despite the failure, Weidenhamer continued to work with Bidpath, which paid her to beta test its product. "I learned a lot and I gave them a lot of corrections," she says. "And as I became more familiar with the technology, I just decided to do it myself." From her experience with Bidpath, Weidenhamer learned that the worst possible thing she could do was to make a huge investment in technology that was more complicated than she required. "The biggest thing I learned was to keep it simple," she says. "As it turned out, there were some off-the-shelf software building tools that worked just as well as what they were investing hundreds of thousands of dollars in." In fact, Bidpath fell off the radar screen in 2002.

By the end of 1999, Auction Systems' sales had skyrocketed to $2.9 million, despite only limited success with Internet auctions. However, Weidenhamer was still convinced that simulcast auctions were the road to even more robust growth. Using what she had learned on her own and from Bidpath, she once again developed her own software.

Seven months later, she was ready to go live with the technology, but she was still skeptical that it would actually work. So she ran her first three auctions at her warehouse on two separate systems, entering the same bidding information on both systems so that she would be sure to have a backup. But while the auctions went relatively smoothly, Internet bidders didn't flock to Auction Systems' site. "Our first auction was very small," says Weidenhamer. "I think we only had 17 online bidders. But I knew it would take a while for us to gain the trust of the online community." Her goal: within a year, she wanted 25% of her company's revenue to come from the Internet. Nine months later, she was there.

Weidenhamer's new technology, combined with growing consumer awareness of both traditional and online auctions, boosted Auction Systems' revenues. By the end of 2000, the company was solidly profitable for the first time and had racked up $4.2 million in revenue. Heartier cash flow also meant that Weidenhamer could finally afford to move her company to a better neighborhood. She had reached a critical turning point. "The Internet became part of our pitch to our clients," says Weidenhamer. "We were no longer an apples-to-apples comparison with other auction companies."

Today, Auction Systems' Web site gets 1.5 million hits a month, says Weidenhamer. Eighty percent of its auctions are now simulcast online, and close to 70% of its products are sold to online buyers. Typically, a live auction might attract 200 or so participants, while another 4,000 to 5,000 are bidding online. Since auction items are listed online a week before the live auction, Internet bidders drive up the starting prices before the auctioneer even starts calling out the items.

"We just sold some motor scooters for an average price of $1,100 each," says Weidenhamer. "At a traditional auction, they might go for $520." The higher prices have allowed Weidenhamer to raise her commissions, which typically increase 2% a year, without cutting into her sellers' profits. In 2004, for instance, her average commission was 37%, compared with 24% in 1998. In fact, in 2000 she raised commissions 5% hoping to winnow down her customer base. "I was trying to control growth," says Weidenhamer. "And raising commissions seemed like the best way to get rid of some of the less desirable business. But it was a shock because we didn't lose anyone, and that confirmed to me that we were setting ourselves apart in the market. We weren't competing on price anymore."

Weidenhamer had succeeded in setting Auction Systems apart from its competitors not by changing or reinventing the products she had to offer, but by immensely improving the system for selling her clients' wares. But the new technology on its own would not have driven Auction Systems' exponential revenue growth if Weidenhamer had not been attuned to the profound effect the technology would have on every other aspect of her company.

The Right Team

At a live auction, the buyer is responsible for previewing the items on sale, but Internet participants must rely on photographs and accurate written descriptions. So Auction Systems' warehouse employees, whose job it had been simply to lot the items and stack them on shelves, were suddenly required to take digital photographs of every item in the warehouse, write physical descriptions, and upload both into the company's computer system. Levi Jordan, who is both head auctioneer and warehouse manager, learned how to take pictures and match them with their correct descriptions when Auction Systems was working with Bidpath, and then taught his two warehouse employees to do the same. Now when Jordan interviews candidates for a warehouse job, he hands them a basket filled with auction items—a drill, a car stereo, a collection of CDs, and a cut-glass bowl, for instance—and asks them to write descriptions. "It's sometimes tough to find people talented enough to do that," he says.

But Weidenhamer is looking for more than just skills when she interviews employees. Because her company is so different from others in her industry, she's not as concerned about hiring people with auction experience as she is with getting the right kinds of people on her team. "We look for people who have passion and who are not afraid of change," says Weidenhamer. "If we find the right attitude, we can train for skills." Often, she says, she will create a position for someone she thinks is a great fit for the company.

That's exactly what happened with Jacque Weiner, who found her way to Auction Systems as a customer in 2002. Weiner had spent 15 years as a business service analyst at American Express, had owned her own graphic design business, and was an avid eBay seller, hawking everything from Russian samovars to her father's antique law books. "In my quest to buy low and sell high, I came across Deb's business," she recalls. She became curious about the company, did a bit of research on it, and liked what she found. "The company had a lot of integrity," Weiner says. So when she came to collect the goods she had bought in an Auction Systems online auction, she sought out Weidenhamer and told her she wanted a job.

There were no openings, but Weidenhamer was impressed with Weiner's enthusiasm, her corporate and entrepreneurial background, and her knowledge of eBay. So Weidenhamer hired Weiner, who quickly took on responsibilities that ranged from learning how to appraise jewelry, to designing online advertising graphics, to helping devise a new computerized inventory control system.

Like Weiner, most of Auction Systems' employees are excellent at multitasking. Weidenhamer knows that some people thrive in that kind of atmosphere, while others wither. "We spend a lot of time talking to people about our culture," she says. "We know not everyone is going to love who we are."

She insists, for example, that everyone in the company work at the company's auctions, which are often held on weekends. Upper-level employees may find themselves working side by side with line-level staff, often taking orders from people whom they regard as lower on the food chain. For instance, Betsy Brewster, who started out tagging items in the warehouse and is now in an administrative position, is also a self-schooled antiques expert. So when interesting pieces come into the company, she takes the lead in identifying and valuing the items. "It's been a really good way to hire upper-level candidates," says Weidenhamer. "Because if they're uncomfortable with that, we know they're not a good fit."

Conspicuously absent at Auction Systems: an IT manager. And that's deliberate. Weidenhamer wants to hire people who are technology savvy and willing to learn new skills, but seasoned IT professionals with little experience or interest in the auction business "aren't right for us," she says. "Good technology comes from the people who are the end users or who truly understand the end user." She'd rather send her auction-savvy employees to seminars where they can learn specific computer programs and hone the technical skills that her company needs than hire an IT manager with broader but less applicable knowledge. She still serves as the company's webmaster.

Marketing with Technology

Weidenhamer has always worked diligently to market Auction Systems to new buyers and sellers; she thinks of her business as "a marketing company with a little inventory control in the middle." In the beginning of 1999—a year she describes as "pivotal" in terms of strategic thinking—she made a big push to wean her company from dependence on government contracts, which frequently accounted for 75% of revenue. Weidenhamer wanted to shrink that percentage to 50%, so she identified several sellers' markets to pursue aggressively: retailers who had overstock or were going out of business; corporations that were upgrading technology and looking to unload their outdated machines; entrepreneurs who were selling their companies; trust offi-

cers, bankers, and lawyers who were liquidating estates; firearms dealers who might be persuaded to consign some of their inventory. She
even brought in an instructor from a local community college two
days a week to teach an entire semester's worth of Spanish to her employees in order to help them court Phoenix's burgeoning Hispanic
population.

Weidenhamer knew that she could introduce those new sellers
to an expanding world of potential buyers because "eBay created new
clients for us. People were looking for something to buy at auction so
they would have something to turn around and sell on eBay." The
company's database, which helps Auction Systems keep track of its individual customers' participation patterns, was its most powerful tool
for bringing buyers and sellers together. To participate in Auction Systems' online auctions, all bidders must register with the site, at which
time they provide an e-mail address plus a street address and a phone
number. The information is then stored in the company's database and
used for future marketing efforts. Registrants typically receive e-mail
reminders of upcoming auctions at least once a week. If they agree to
be called, their phone numbers are passed on to Auction Systems' call
center in Nebraska, which is run by Weidenhamer's brother Don Ludden.

Ludden's staff of four, who might make as many as 2,000 calls a
week, uses the database to ferret out specific customer information.
For instance, they might extract the names of customers who have
participated in coin auctions and then call those people to remind
them of a similar upcoming event. The four telemarketers might also
offer promotions, such as a code that will give buyers $10 off the final
auction tab. That isn't a standard practice among auction houses, and
Weidenhamer was initially skeptical of it. But Ludden, who had also
created a weekly radio show for Auction Systems, convinced his sister
to give it a try. As it turned out, the telemarketing program yielded a
5%-to-7% increase in online attendance and a 12% revenue boost—
numbers that proved the program's worth and that landed Ludden a
full-time job with Auction Systems.

Weidenhamer's technology not only allows her to extract data
about her customers, but it enables her to keep track of products and

how they sell from year to year. "We can tell you, for example, that three years ago we could sell a Sony Walkman for $17.50, but that today we'd need to put 10 together to get the same amount," says Weidenhamer. The data is used to discourage sellers from attempting to unload dud products that do little except occupy valuable real estate in Auction Systems' warehouse. Conversely, the numbers also tell Weidenhamer what products hold their value over the years. On the hot list right now: tools, computer components, and jewelry.

Refining the System

Like all Alpha Dog CEOs, Weidenhamer is perennially restless in her quest to make Auction Systems bigger, better, and more efficient. In the summer of 2003, she added an audio component to her Web site so that online participants can now listen to live auctions in real time as they sit in front of their computers and watch a slide show of items for sale. "After three months of audio feed, the average time spent on the site went from an hour and forty minutes to three hours and twelve minutes, and our number of registered users increased 416%," says Weidenhamer. "We've actually got more people listening than bidding," she adds. "So we know that for lots of people, it's entertainment. It's created what we always wanted, which is a community on the Internet."

The audio component was designed by Ludden, who also created Auction Systems Radio Network, a streaming Internet radio station that plays adult contemporary music 24/7. Like Mike's Famous Radio (see chapter 9), it's a branding tool for the company, but it also strives to educate potential customers. Between cuts, Weidenhamer offers prerecorded tips for bidding at auction. And to further market the company on air, Auction Systems Radio runs a Saturday morning "new to auction" program, where listeners can get their feet wet in the auction world by bidding on 10 or so items—such as a pedometer from the Sharper Image or an iPod—either online or by calling in. "I'm sure we lose money on it," says Weidenhamer, "but it's for education and entertainment purposes. We consider it an advertising cost."

"I think the next thing will be video streaming our auctions on the Internet," says Weidenhamer. "And I think that after that, the trend will be an auctioneer in a ballroom with a big screen behind him with a slide show of items, and everything will stay with the sellers until it is sold. We'll have virtual inventory."

They may be a long way off, but Weidenhamer is already preparing buyers for the changes she perceives down the road. If you attend a live auction at Auction Systems today, the items you're bidding on will be physically present, but Weidenhamer also might run a slide show on a large projection screen behind the auctioneer. "We want to get buyers used to buying from photographs, to gradually get them accustomed to not physically seeing the product." Trust plays a big part in that transition. Buyers need to know that if there's a crack in a piece of glassware, for instance, that Auction Systems is going to tell them about it.

Leading the Way

"Deb is definitely a leader," says auctioneer Paul Ramirez. "She's been changing the industry." And that has been one of Weidenhamer's goals from the very start. It was never her sole intention to grow and capture market share simply by employing technology and management techniques that few others in her industry were using, although that's certainly been the effect of her innovative practices. She was also hoping to play a significant role in bringing a relatively unsophisticated industry into the 21st century.

To that end, she's been involved with her state auctioneers association, of which she was president for a year, and she was instrumental in lobbying for state legislation requiring licensing for auctioneers. For several years, she's written a column for *Auction World,* a monthly publication that's published by the National Auctioneers Association. In it, Weidenhamer voices strong opinions and gives solid advice about the use of technology, hiring, how to land government contracts, and why the industry should cater to the Hispanic market. Why not keep the good ideas to herself? "I'd like to see some people copy what we do," she says. "Having good competitors is important because it helps you build up the market. My goal is to see the auction industry full of professional, ethical people."

It's getting there. In 2004 and 2005, the National Auctioneers Association conducted the largest independent research study of the auction industry, and as it turns out, eBay wasn't the grim reaper after all: the industry grew 4% in 2003 and 7.1% in 2004. "Today, there's a positive relationship between what eBay is doing and the live auction industry," says the NAA's chief executive Bob Shively. "People go on eBay and say, 'Hey, this is fun; I want to go to a live auction,' and as a result, we've seen growth."

But while eBay has apparently driven more and more auction-crazed customers to live auctions, traditional auction houses have not exactly responded in kind by flocking to the Internet. While use of the Internet has become more widespread among auction houses, there are still only a handful (13%, says NAA's study) that offer online bidding, let alone the simulcast system that puts Auction Systems at the head of the pack. Shively sees that as a potential problem. "In three to five years, if auctioneers don't embrace that technology, they will probably be competitively disadvantaged," he says. Weidenhamer hopes they see the light. But she's also confident that by the time her peers catch up to her, she'll be onto something altogether different.

"Transform with Technology" Tips
from Auction Systems Auctioneers & Appraisers

1. **Be a Techie.** Research the technology that's currently being made for and marketed to companies in your industry. Find out how it works and if it can be tweaked for your purposes before you reinvent the wheel with a custom-made solution.

2. **Be an Early Adopter.** What new technology is being used in related industries that may ultimately impact how you operate? Weidenhamer, for example, adopted bar coding long before her competitors. Now she has her eye on RFID (radio frequency identification) tags, which are becoming more and more popular among large retailers.

3. **Support Continuous Learning.** A company that uses technology to challenge the status quo must have employees who aren't intimidated by change. Encourage employees to learn new technology skills and put them to work in innovative ways at your company. Accept occasional failure as a natural by-product of creativity and experimentation.

4. **Be Patient but Persistent.** It may take time for your customers to get comfortable with new technology, so don't panic if they're slow to embrace your new toy. But *do* make sure that their reticence isn't the result of glitches in your technology.

5. **Upgrade Wisely.** As your business becomes more sophisticated, your technology needs will change. But don't be seduced by bells and whistles. Think about the return on investment for every new purchase and upgrade in concrete terms: will it increase revenue and/or profits, improve efficiency, reduce labor hours? If not, save your money.

. . . And from Others

6. **Use Technology to Share Information.** At Staunton, Virginia–based **Specialty Blades, Inc.,** a manufacturer of cutting blades for industrial and medical use, chairman Martin Lightsey provides his 70 employees with all the information they need to

run his $13 million company with a minimum of supervisors. On the company's intranet, workers can check individual and team job performance, and track production, shipments, and orders with actual month-to-date and quarter-to-date numbers compared with budget. Weekly scorecards show margin improvements on repeat jobs, and a forecast shows predicted business volume for the next three months. "The biggest advantage," says Lightsey, "is that the information is extremely timely and accessible to everyone without a chain of meetings. Now, in meetings, we don't need to talk about the minutiae of data; we can talk about more important things, like trends and strategic issues."

7. **Build an Online Community.** The **King Arthur Flour Company,** based in Norwich, Vermont, created an online community called the Baking Circle, where members post messages, trade recipes, get coupons, and purchase online. There are now 100,000 members, who help drive demand for the brand and provide the $35 million company with a highly accessible focus group for new products. The site helps King Arthur compete for market share with flour giants like Gold Medal and Pillsbury. While it's now number three in the marketplace, revenues are growing at a time when U.S. flour consumption is actually decreasing.

8. **Support Customer Service with Technology.** The more you know about your customers, the better you can serve them. Jack Mitchell, CEO and chairman of **Mitchells/Richards** clothing stores and author of *Hug Your Customers: The Proven Way to Personalize Sales and Achieve Astounding Results,* maintains database profiles of 115,000 customers. His salespeople not only have access to every purchase a customer has made, but know his or her size, color preferences, birthday, anniversary, kids' names, hobbies, and any other piece of information a customer happens to share.

9. **Steal Great Ideas.** Wherever he goes, Mike Schwartz of Mike's Famous **Harley-Davidson** is on the lookout for ideas that he can apply to his business. As a Hertz customer, he was

always impressed with the company's method of using hand-held scanners to keep track of its inventory. So in 2003, he asked his information technology manager, Bob Patch, to develop a similar system for the dealership. Now employees scan $12 million in motorcycle inventory every day and can instantly check the location of every bike in stock. Customers can check the inventory online.

10. **Use the Web to Wow Your Customers.** "We take on technology and master it," says Eric Ersher, co-founder of **Zoup! Fresh Soup Company,** a Southfield, Michigan–based franchise company with 12 restaurants featuring homemade soup. The company also serves up a very impressive Web site. Customers can log on and find out which of the company's 12 rotating soups (like Thai Vegetable or Ginger Butternut Squash) are being served at each store, order, and pay online while also specifying a pickup time, print a menu/order form that can be filled out and faxed back to the store, and request a daily e-mail that includes promotions and discounts. The site also allows customers to look up nutritional information on selected items, so that those who are watching the scale know to forgo the Roadhouse Sirloin Chili (26 grams of fat) in favor of the Vegetarian Split Pea (0.5 grams of fat and 0 Weight Watchers points!).

5 | Stake a Hometown Claim

Company: Amy's Ice Creams

Business: 12 ice cream parlors, all in Texas

Location: Austin, Texas

Revenues: $5.3 million

Employees: 20 full-time; 155 part-time

Founder: Amy Simmons

Year Founded: 1984

Web Site: www.amysicecreams.com

Amy and Steve Simmons with baby Henry.
Photograph: fagan.com

Alpha Dog Credentials:

Amy's has thrived even as chains like Ben & Jerry's and Cold Stone Creamery have moved into its territory. That's because Amy Simmons has solidly established herself as a quintessentially Austin company, embracing the local culture and community to give herself a killer competitive advantage that the chains can't touch.

On a steamy Austin afternoon in May 2004, Amy Simmons, her husband, Steve, and fellow business owner Daryl Kunik stand in an empty lot of scrubby grass sorely in need of mowing. Just to the right is the Trek Motel, a low-slung, 1950s-style building that looks as if it could be home to a few down-on-their-luck roadies. And to the left, there's an uninhabited ramshackle house. But Amy, Steve, and Daryl, a local entrepreneur dabbling in real-estate development, see grand possibilities in this rather forlorn site. Simmons, who wears chunky platform sandals, a flowing skirt, and a simple t-shirt, envisions a sparkling new production facility churning out more than 200 flavors of ice cream for her 11 stores. And maybe, she muses, she'll even take a page from Napa Valley and offer tours and a tasting bar to the public. Kunik sees her wheels turning and goes along for the ride. He hasn't even bought the property yet, let alone developed it, but the prospect of nailing down Amy's Ice Creams as a prospective tenant/partner just about makes his day. "I thought of you guys first when I began looking at this property," he gushes. "Thinking of you being down here gives me goose bumps. Really."

The meeting alone tells you something vitally important about Amy's Ice Creams, even though the deal will not come to fruition exactly as the three imagine. Amy's stores are famous in Austin not only for their eclectic selection of ice cream (like Simmons's all-time personal favorite—Belgian Chocolate with Reese's Peanut Butter Cups crushed in), but for their wild antics (think flying scoops of ice cream, tossed overhead and caught on paddlelike scoops), original architecture and design, and commitment to community. Kunik, who owns five custom tailor shops and a couple of Austin restaurants, thinks Amy's is the perfect tenant for the development that he hopes will help transform this run-down section of South Congress Street. "What I'm looking for is an eclectic mix of locally owned businesses that are in keeping with the character of Austin," he says. "And Amy's epitomizes that character; it's homegrown and it's an Austin tradition." Amy's presence, he reckons, could draw other similar businesses, such as a locally owned toy store or a small, funky restaurant. Big chains need not apply. "If Starbucks came to me, I'd say no," Kunik claims. "I'd take less money to not have them here." The "think locally, buy locally" movement is flourishing in Austin, and Kunik is an enthusiastic supporter.

Of course, not every developer nor every consumer feels the way Kunik does. But in Austin, where local pride is as prevalent as tattoos and multiple body piercings, Amy's link to the city's culture and gestalt gives her a distinct hometown advantage, and makes her company an undisputed local Alpha Dog. Sometimes, the word even spreads beyond Texas borders. In fall 2004, for instance, Al Roker visited Austin for his Food Network show, *Roker on the Road,* and declared Amy's "the best ice cream in Austin."

That's high praise considering the competition. Five years ago, Amy's had Austin's ice cream scene pretty much wrapped up. There were a few Baskin-Robbins stores and a handful of other independent shops, but Simmons was the dominant player in the premium ice cream market. Today, there's the "highly predatory" (Simmons's description) Ben & Jerry's; a Houston-based company called Marble Slab Creamery, Inc.; a feisty young Scottsdale, Arizona–based chain called Cold Stone Creamery; and MaggieMoo's, which operates out of Columbia, Maryland. All of them are franchise companies and have stores in Austin, and the latter three feature mix-in ingredients and encourage their employees to entertain customers as they scoop. Those are Amy's trademarks too. Plus, many of her competitors have something she lacks: deep pockets. Ben & Jerry's has Unilever's vast resources, Cold Stone Creamery racks up in excess of $150 million in annual revenues, and Marble Slab now has more than 400 stores either open or in the works.

It's a familiar story—the one where the 800-pound gorilla moves in next door and proceeds to eat your lunch—and Simmons might worry a lot more if she had built her business solely around the uniqueness of her product. All products, even key lime pie ice cream, eventually become commodities, and commodities are easily copied. "The initial reaction to competition is fear," she says. "But competition is good; it makes us sharpen our sword." Besides, Simmons is betting that what she has built is not so easily replicated.

Hometown Advantage

It's one thing to merely set up shop in your hometown and quite another to become a real hometown business, like Amy's. While Simmons is from Ann Arbor, Michigan, her business is pure Austin. Today, that kind of local identity matters more than ever. After years of superstore homogeneity, a growing number of consumers are gravitating to local companies and businesses that have long-standing connections to their communities. In Austin, there are two highly visible small-business groups: the Austin Independent Business Alliance was formed in 2002 by Steve Bercu and John Kunz, the owners of BookPeople and Waterloo Records & Video, respectively, to protest city incentives for a major real-estate development project that included a Borders; and Choose Austin First, a smaller and less political group, was spearheaded by Simmons in the spring of 2003. Both groups embrace the city's unofficial motto, "Keep Austin Weird," a slogan you'll see on bumper stickers and t-shirts all over the city. It reminds Austinites that the funky vibe they so cherish is intimately linked to the colorful, local businesses whose own cultures reflect their city.

Amy's is an established member of the club, and that has helped drive its growth over the years. Total revenue for Simmons's 11 stores now stands at $5.3 million, and profitability has been 10% to 15% in 17 out of 20 years. Growth is deliberately slow and controlled; Simmons staunchly rejects the currently popular "are you going to be the next Starbucks?" model of success. If you don't live in Texas or travel to Austin frequently, chances are you've never heard of Amy's. And that's perfectly okay with Simmons, who rejects pleas for franchises almost daily. "Our model is the old model," she says. "I want to be a 100-year-old company. If my kids want the business, I'd like to pass it down to them, but if not, I want someone who loves it to take it over."

The 45-year-old Simmons has two girls, Emma, nine, and Olivia, seven, from a marriage that ended in 2000. In March 2001, she married Steve Simmons, a local entrepreneur and real-estate salesman. Three years later, she gave birth to their son, Henry, who accompanied his mom to the office every day for the first six months of his life. Steve

Simmons now puts nearly all of his energy into his wife's business—
he's as comfortable negotiating real-estate deals as he is dressing up in
a cow costume to hand out free ice cream. He describes himself as "a
fix-it man," but Amy says that a more accurate description is "marketing
animal." They have a nice life, and it would be easy to misjudge Amy
Simmons, with a baby slung over her shoulder and her free-flowing
brown hair with thick blond streaks. She looks like a laid-back earth
mother. Don't be fooled. Her sword is battle ready every day.

We All Scream for Ice Cream

First, there were Howard Johnson, Dairy Queen, Friendly's, and
Carvel—chains that transformed ice cream from a local soda-fountain
treat to a roadside destination that was often the culmination of a Sunday drive with Mom and Dad. Those iconic institutions did for ice
cream what McDonald's would do for the hamburger 20 years later:
they offered families a predictable experience, and what they lacked
in imagination they made up for in consistency.

But in 1959, Reuben Mattus changed all that. He single-handedly
transformed the face of the ice cream industry by concocting a product that was higher in butterfat, lower in overrun (or air), and that
tasted far superior to anything on the market. The clever Bronx entrepreneur christened his new "premium" ice cream with a name that
sounded foreign and exotic and sold it to high-end specialty food
shops in New York. The marketplace went nuts, and the Häagen-Dazs
legend was born.

Mattus paved the way for other ice cream entrepreneurs, like
Ben Cohen and Jerry Greenfield, who renovated a Burlington, Vermont, gas station in 1978 and opened the first Ben & Jerry's Homemade scoop shop. The two quickly extended their reach by selling
franchises, first in Vermont, then nationwide. And then there was
Steve Herrell, whose tiny shop in Somerville, Massachusetts, Steve's
Ice Cream, attracted hoards of loyal customers with the promise of a
customized treat: he'd slap their favorite ice cream down on the
counter and mix in bits of crushed candy or chocolate chunks. In

1976, Herrell sold his business to serial entrepreneur Joey Crugnale, who saw mix-ins as more than just a cool way to attract a bunch of MIT students. So he took Herrell's concept, ratcheted it up with eye-catching store design and goofy scooping theatrics, and grew the business to 26 nationwide locations, most of them franchises. And it was at Steve's that Amy Simmons (then Miller), a pre-med student at Tufts University, got a job scooping ice cream "for fun and money," but ended up discovering her true passion. For ice cream? Well, yes. But more importantly, for business.

"With any business, as long as it has the basics well in hand, you take the common and make it uncommon," Crugnale was fond of saying. And that's exactly what he did. "Joey realized that you find good people and you let them run," recalls Simmons. "He provided support when you needed it, but he gave you freedom. He had people from Harvard and MIT not taking professional jobs and coming to work for him at Steve's for $15,000 a year." For her part, Simmons pushed aside her dream of becoming a doctor to help Crugnale grow the company. She thrived under his mentorship. In her early twenties, she was responsible not only for opening up new Steve's franchises, but for helping Crugnale launch yet another company, a pizzeria chain called Bertucci's. It was a heady time. "I was 21, with absolutely no experience, but he let me do everything," she says. "It felt like my success." She took that experience to heart and remembers it now when she's hiring, training, and developing managers at her own company.

Crugnale sold Steve's to a large publicly traded firm in 1983, and that was the beginning of the end of Simmons's career at the company. She and another Steve's employee, Scott Shaw, decided to open their own ice cream store. Over the next several months, the two would capitalize on Simmons's reputation in the ice cream industry and the people she had met "over the counter at Steve's" to sell 45% of their fledgling enterprise to 22 equity investors for a total of $100,000. Their lead investor was Gus Rancatore, whom Simmons had met "when he was a janitor at Steve's" but who had gone on to start his own ice business, Toscanini's, now a Cambridge favorite. Simmons later bought back some of the stock, including Rancatore's; she now has 32% of the stock and is the company's largest shareholder.

Location, Location, Location

But Simmons still had a lot to learn, and she needed to learn fast, so she signed up for an accelerated two-week dairy science program at Rutgers University—a course that was a breeze for her, given her background in chemistry and biology. The partners made a commitment to using only the finest ingredients, including real lemon juice, pure vanilla, and the best Belgian chocolate. And while they did intend to emulate Steve's method of crushing in ingredients, they planned to use a different type of ice cream maker and to develop their own recipes.

On a whim, they considered London as the site for their new venture, but an exploratory visit quickly changed their minds. The dreary weather (and economy) turned them off, as did the stark realization that they'd need to pay up front for a 10-year lease in order to set up shop across the pond. They were at loose ends, and then Simmons just happened to pick up the May 26, 1984, issue of the *Economist;* an article about Austin caught her eye.

The iconoclastic Texas capital, nestled in hill country and surrounded by lakes and forests, was "becoming a magnet for high-tech industry," and was now home to more than 150 computer companies. Among them, by the way, was a tiny start-up called Dell Computer Corporation, which would one day become Austin's largest private employer. "The combination of Sunbelt weather and Texas's unabashed nonunion ways is a natural attraction to out-of-state business," gushed the article. Plus, it was home to half a dozen colleges and universities—a population that was a likely source of both customers and employees, and one that reminded Simmons of her hometown, Ann Arbor. Itching to get started and lacking other alternatives, Simmons and Shaw set out for Austin.

"The first thing about Austin that struck me was the number of locally founded businesses that were just incredible," Simmons says. There was the Good Eats Café, which served fresh grilled fish; Texas French Bread; and the Uptown Enchilada Bar. The city was free-spirited and bohemian—a quirky liberal enclave where aging hippies, cowboys, college students, and high-tech executives sat side by side at music clubs on the Strip, listening for the next Willie Nelson. It felt absolutely right to Simmons and Shaw. They decided to stake their claim in Austin and spent the following weeks scoping out the city for the perfect location for their premium ice cream parlor.

"We were looking at a location across from the University of Texas," recalls Simmons. "It's called the Drag because that's where all the bars are." But some newly befriended local entrepreneurs waved the red flag. "They told me it would be a mistake," Simmons recalls. Being close to the university would mean lots of foot traffic, but the customers would be students and tourists—a transient customer base that would force Amy's to constantly re-earn loyalty. True Austinites tended to stay away from the area because it was too crowded and parking was a nightmare. If you care about repeat business, her new pals told her, look at the more established inner-city communities.

Simmons heeded the advice and opted instead for a location on Guadalupe Street, in Austin's more established North University neighborhood. "The building was very art deco, and they were in the process of redoing it," recalls Simmons. "We knew that it would be stunning and attract a lot of attention." But when Simmons first approached landlord Roger Joseph about renting space in the building, there were no streetfront locations available. So Simmons sweet-talked another tenant into taking an interior space so that she could get the frontage she wanted. "I knew right then that she was going to be successful," says Joseph. And so Simmons and Shaw wrote a check for $800 to cover the first month's rent (it bounced, she admits sheepishly) and got to work.

She hired Joseph's designer, who brought the art deco theme to her interior with clean, sharp lines and glass-block walls. While a crew of contractors transformed the space, Simmons and Shaw greedily tapped every intellectual resource they could unearth.

Joseph graciously forgave them for the hot check and introduced them to the local business community. They knocked on doors at the University of Texas, where the MBA program was just beginning to recognize entrepreneurship as an honorable career choice, and they chatted up professors and students for advice and ideas. Likewise, they visited UT's law school and wangled some free legal counsel. Three months and $30,000 later, the contractors put the final touches on the store, and Simmons and Shaw threw a pre-opening bash for all of their new friends in October 1984.

A few days later, they opened their doors to the public, relying entirely on word of mouth. The promise of free ice cream on opening day (a treat that Simmons still offers whenever she opens a new store; she still doesn't advertise) drew crowds lined up around the block. And the next day? "We figured that our break even was $350 a day, and from the beginning, we broke even," says Simmons. "That allowed us to survive and not be afraid." Austin had given her a big Texas welcome, and she would respond by keeping Amy's a quintessentially Austin company.

Growing It Slowly

Simmons never really had a grand plan for Amy's. Instead, she has allowed the company to evolve and grow organically, using the talents and inspiration of her friends, employees, and community to help define the business. For example, before she left Austin to visit her family in Michigan in the winter of 1985, she asked her friend John Henry Green (for whom baby Henry is named) to paint the store while she was gone. "He painted the ceiling with cow spots," recalls Simmons. "And that's where our cow theme came from. All my good ideas come from letting other people do their thing."

That's also how Amy's became the most entertaining ice cream parlor in town. One day, Amy's 10th employee, Ira Major, stood on a milk crate and got everyone in line to do the hokey pokey. "And that was the beginning," says Amy. Now her "scoops" (behind-the-counter employees) are famous for stunts such as tossing ice cream up to the ceiling and catching it on their foreheads. Amy's personal style is more reserved, although she's been known to step into a cow costume. "I'm not really an antics person," she concedes. But Austin—where a homeless cross-dresser named Leslie Cochran has run for mayor several times—is an antics town. And so Simmons lets her company reflect the character of her city, her employees, and the neighborhoods it serves.

It never occurred to Simmons and Shaw that they might eventually have more than one shop, but the business took on a life of its own. Customers lined up in droves, sometimes waiting 20 minutes for their turn at the counter as they eagerly anticipated not only the ice cream but the entertainment. "Do you want 'em dead or alive?" Amy's scoops might ask a customer, referring to the approximate level of pulverization a handful of M&M's should receive as it is crushed into a flattened scoop of Mexican Vanilla.

It was partly because of those loyal employees that Simmons and Shaw began, after about six months, to consider opening up another store. One store meant limited opportunity for employee growth; a second would open up more management positions and a clear career path. But there were financial considerations as well. Simmons and Shaw felt that a single location left the company uncomfortably vulnerable. A second store, they reckoned, would give Amy's "legs to stand on" if revenue at the original location should decline. "You can break even with one store," Simmons says. "But that's not what you want to do for a long time." The first store, in fact, was bringing in $250,000 and was profitable in its first year.

So in 1985, Simmons and Shaw opened a second store in the northwest section of Austin called the Arboretum, a high-income neighborhood populated by technology companies. "I remember going out there and saying, 'It's a mud hole; nothing is out here,' " says Simmons. "But it was where the high-tech companies were going." With a $90,000 bank loan at 18% interest and guaranteed by three of her original investors at another 2% each, Simmons and Shaw rented a 600-square-foot space. They knew they'd be catering to a different kind of customer, so they hired an architect to design an interior that was far more conservative than the Guadalupe store. "Our design in Central Austin is very eclectic, but North Austin is a little afraid of that," says Simmons. And so she played to the crowd, employing sleeker, less cluttered design elements, and instructed her staff to tone down the theatrics a bit. "It established us as a neighborhood business," she says.

One Neighborhood at a Time

Two years after co-founding the company, Simmons's partner, Scott Shaw, left to pursue other business interests in Florida, but Simmons continued to broaden Amy's reach on her own, with production manager Phil Clay as her "right-hand dude." She recalls that she received "an embarrassing amount of press" in those first few years. She was even named Young Entrepreneur of the Year by the Austin Chamber of Commerce and Entrepreneur of the Year by the *Austin Business Journal.* There was intense pressure from consumers to add new locations and to expand into more far-flung markets; Simmons responded by opening a store in Dallas in 1986. It was a huge mistake.

She had situated her store in a new development called West End Marketplace, a Dallas version of Boston's Faneuil Hall. But the area, which floundered with the Texas economy, drew a tourist crowd, and the out-of-towners were often befuddled by Amy's crushin's system. Her scoops spent more time explaining than scooping and entertaining; even though the store was financially successful, employee morale deteriorated.

When the lease was up three years later, she closed up shop and moved the equipment to Austin, where she opened two more stores. She had learned a critically important lesson: "In Dallas, we were earning our customers every day, and it was exhausting. I learned that I really valued ongoing relationships with my customers."

From then on, she was more cautious. By 1990, she had four stores—all in Austin—and in 1993, she ventured into Houston, where she would open a second store in 2004. She chose her neighborhoods carefully, always opting for locations with a steady flow of local traffic. But she stayed away from high-rent districts, often scoping out the seedier, up-and-coming parts of town. Take, for example, her South Congress Street location, a walk-up window in a building that looks like a tiny turquoise jewel-box with jauntily dressed cows frolicking along the roof. Opened in January 2003, it's not in the trendiest part of Austin. That would be Congress Street, where posh boutiques sidle up to live music clubs and fashionable eateries. But SoCo is home to funky antique stores, taco joints, and tattoo parlors; Amy's fits right in.

Back when Simmons first decided to open more stores, she knew that she had no interest in creating cookie-cutter replicas of her Guadalupe location. While there are some predictable design elements at every Amy's—old-fashioned photo booths, cow spots, green checkerboards, blue waves, purple stripes, and a bit of neon signage—Simmons wanted each store to reflect its neighborhood. So she used different architects, giving them the freedom to incorporate creative and original design, but cautioning them to always keep in mind local sensibilities. The Westgate store, for instance, is situated in a suburban-style shopping center and attracts lots of families with small children. So Simmons made the counters lower and decorated the walls with kids' artwork. The 6th Street store is funkier, with neon cows and music from local bands playing in the background. The Arboretum, now Amy's most profitable store, has a fountain and cow sculptures and caters to the high-tech crowd; Westgate is known for having a very high ceiling, which is perfect for dramatic ice cream tossing. The eclectic feel of the stores sends an important message to customers: Amy's isn't a national chain where everything from the table and chairs to the clock on the wall is standard issue and chosen by someone at corporate headquarters. Simmons is living in a city of individualists, and she wants her business to reflect that.

Playing to the Crowd

Employees play a big part in Simmons's mission, which, she says, is "to make people's day." So she gives her store managers the freedom to read the crowd so that they can play to it accordingly. There are no uniforms at Amy's, and scoops cover their hair with a vast array of offbeat headgear such as cowboy hats, bandanas, Ninja Turtle headgear, jester caps, and the latest favorite—mesh-backed trucker's caps.

Store managers also decide what music to play—a privilege they take seriously, given Austin's obsession with music. "Say you've got a bunch of suits at the Arboretum store," poses 6th Street store manager Matthew Swift. "It's got to be Willie Nelson, not Slayer." Swift's store attracts a younger crowd, and he's known for giving Austin bands generous airtime at Amy's. A couple of years ago, he also hosted a Kiss theme night at the store, with all scoops in full makeup and regalia. His customers loved it, but it might not have played well in the North Austin stores. "We just all have to remember that even though we get to pick the music, the music isn't for us," he says. "It's to enhance the customer's experience." According to Steve Simmons, Amy's actually hires lots of young musicians as scoops because they "love the flexible schedule that allows for gigs and tours." And sometimes, employees' bands even play at the stores.

Managers are free to let their creative juices flow without always having to first check in with the boss. Simmons recalls an incident that's now an Amy's urban legend. Early on in the company's history, a manager at the Guadalupe store started locking in lingering customers at closing time and refusing to let them go home until they danced the "Time Warp" from *The Rocky Horror Picture Show.* Simmons got wind of his exploits when she was out late with friends one evening and one of them suggested that they all race to Amy's Guadalupe store to get locked in. The ritual had earned a cult following; that night, Simmons learned the true value of theatrics. Recently, the manager at the newest Amy's, in Houston, revived the "Time Warp" tradition for the next generation of Amy's customers.

Of course, giving managers that kind of freedom can backfire. When Amy's opened in San Antonio, the manager was so impressed with the lock-in idea that he decided to copy it. But Simmons soon began receiving complaints from customers that the dancing was "lewd" and that the manager was far too assertive with customers who didn't particularly want to learn the "Time Warp." "He just took things a little too far," says Simmons. And then there was the time she actually lost her lease at her Highland Mall location in Austin. Employees took the fun factor to extremes when they began tossing scoops of ice cream from their second-level space down to the first. "One of our employees would go down there and catch it in a bowl," recalls Simmons.

"We tried to reel them in, but in retrospect, I wasn't tough enough. I lost the lease and they put in a Swenson's."

The Paper Bag Test

As her former boss Joey Crugnale did for her, Simmons gives her managers as much freedom as she dares. And her trust threshold runs high because she goes to a great deal of trouble to hire and train them. Most (75%) of the company's managers have risen through the ranks, from scoop to shift supervisor to assistant manager to manager. New managers spend time joined at the hip with veterans, among them Matthew Swift, who has been a manager for 10 of his 13 years with Amy's. "I give them a play-by-play of everything I do," says Swift, who sports a ponytail, goatee, and several earrings. "They learn how to schedule, do bank runs, inventory, and put together a good staff." That last one is always the most difficult. "I always remind new managers that the mechanics of the job are pretty simple," he says. "What's difficult and challenging is the element of theater. We need to know if job applicants understand the concept of having fun and being creative."

And how do you get a handle on someone's creativity? Simmons thinks she's hit upon a pretty accurate, albeit unconventional, test—one that she came up with serendipitously. Years ago, one of her stores ran out of job applications, so she handed a job seeker a white paper bag instead. The bag, recalls Simmons, came back as a basket attached to a helium balloon. "She sent it floating in with her Girl Scout badge, a picture of her dog, fortunes that she had saved from fortune cookies—all things that said something about her," says Simmons. She got the job, and Simmons has been using the paper-bag test ever since. The bags come back as masks or puppets, inscribed with witty poems, or as cleverly invented board games, folded into intricate origami shapes, or even fashioned into a banana split. But while creativity gets you an interview, it doesn't always get you the job. Westgate store manager Mark Banks laments that he had high hopes for an applicant who presented him with a whimsically painted papier-mâché cow. Alas, he says, "we loved the art, but we didn't like the guy."

Every new scoop goes through a two-day training camp, kicked off by Simmons with a four-hour presentation on the company's history and its commitment to customer service. There are field trips too. New hires act as secret shoppers at Amy's, and they also drop in on the competition for comparison's sake. On the second day of training, Matthew Swift takes new hires under his wing to teach Scooping 101—a crash course in crushin's, shakes, portion size, and ergonomic exercises designed to prevent carpal tunnel syndrome, an occupational hazard.

Trainees are also made aware of the security webcams in every store, which Banks says are "a necessary evil." With a heavy heart, Simmons installed them in 2002, after a handful of employees stole $75,000 from her registers over the course of several months. While not everyone is thrilled with the cameras, Amy thinks her managers accept them as "a tool that helps them manage." Banks says there's "no doubt in my mind that having cameras has reduced theft. One thing about Amy," he adds, "is that she only puts in a rule when it's absolutely necessary."

The cameras certainly don't inhibit employees when it comes to having fun. During training, newbies practice tossing scoops in the air with a ball of Grape-Nuts cereal wrapped with cellophane and duct tape so they master the art of entertaining before going live. And if they really want to see how it's done, they can visit the 6th Street store on Thursday nights. That's when Pete Kelly takes a break from his grown-up job at Freescale Semiconductor, one of Austin's largest employers, and resumes his place behind the counter at Amy's. He's a former full-time Amy's manager who just can't seem to let go. "He's the ultimate scooper," says Matthew Swift with admiration. "He'll toss the ice cream over his shoulder and catch it behind his back or under his leg. He's got a loyal following." And that, Swift tells the new kids, is what Amy's is all about.

The result is that Simmons has her own loyal following of current and former employees who are encouraged to think of themselves as members of an exclusive club. In November 2004, in fact, Simmons threw a gala 20th anniversary reunion for over 500 members of the Amy's cult. It was a three-day bash, starting out with a party at Club

DeVille, a nightclub owned by an Amy's alumnus, where revelers watched a 20th anniversary film produced by Rick Redmann, the legendary time-warp employee. Redmann, who now lives in New Orleans and has worked in television production, came to Austin in October 2004 and interviewed more than 50 of Amy's customers, employees, and alumni to create the film. "People told stories I had never heard before," says Simmons. "We were all ecstatic and crying. I think it was the nicest gift I've ever received." The next day, everyone pitched in at a street fair, where Amy Simmons joined in an ice cream–tossing contest, Steve Simmons sat in the dunking booth, and employees decorated wacky hats to wear at work. The event raised about $2,000 for a new children's hospital in Austin. The festivities spilled over into a dance party that night and a barbecue on Sunday. How much did it all cost? "Lots," says Simmons. "But we got 15 to 20 stories in the local papers and tons of local television coverage. It reaffirmed us as a favorite and got us in the forefront of people's minds and that's important."

Good Citizen

Fans who have moved out of Austin, like many of Simmons's former employees, often beg for Amy's franchises in other parts of the country. She flatly refuses. It may seem as if she's deliberately limiting her company's potential for growth, and that's true to an extent. But running her company on her own terms has given her the kind of freedom that she has always valued. "For most people, business is the pursuit of the dollar, which holds no value in and of itself for me," she wrote in *Inc.* magazine back in 1995. "But I've discovered . . . that business can be an effective vehicle for making the contributions that I think are more worthy." Simmons will tell you that one of the most significant measures of success is what she does for her community. Amy's sponsors at least one community event every week, and that can involve anything from donating ice cream to an elementary school fund-raiser, to running a blood drive. And while Simmons can't say exactly how much that amounts to, it's roughly the equivalent of 5% of revenues—what a "normal" company would allocate to an advertising budget.

But whatever you do, don't call it altruistic. "It's symbiotic," says Simmons. Amy's has never had an advertising or marketing budget. Instead, that money is earmarked for the kinds of community events that not only generate publicity, but create positive buzz and goodwill toward the company. Amy's has a long history, for instance, of supporting the Austin Museum of Art. An avid runner and former triathlete, Simmons sponsors Amy's Cattle Drive, a 10-mile run that raised $10,000 for the museum in 2003. The funds were used for a program called Seeing Special Things, which sent arts educators into low income–area schools, heavily populated with at-risk kids. She's also a faithful sponsor of the arts festival held every year in downtown Austin. "But Amy goes above and beyond what the majority of our food vendors do," says Jamie Carpenter, former executive director of the Austin Fine Arts Alliance. Amy's created a special flavor for the festival—Artist's Ambrosia—and gave all customers who purchased it a discount coupon for the festival. "She's also allowed us to hang our banners outside her stores and posters inside," says Carpenter, who also worked for Amy's as operations manager in 2002. "The employees are excited about the event, so they're talking about it to the customers. It's a dream come true to have a partner like that in the community."

Just as Simmons allows employees to set the tone within their individual stores, she also encourages them to come up with their own meaningful ways to serve the community. The grand opening of a new store, for example, always has a philanthropic theme, and Simmons asks the managers to choose their pet causes. That was an easy choice for Mark Banks, manager of the Westgate store, which opened in 2000 with a fund-raiser for the Heart Hospital of Austin. "I had open-heart surgery as a child, and it was partially funded by a hospital," says Banks. "So it was natural for me to want to make that kind of thing possible for another unfortunate child." Simmons, who also had a heart problem and has a pacemaker, loved the idea. So Banks and Simmons organized an event: he gave out free ice cream to everyone who made an in-store donation to the hospital, and he recruited the doctors to do the scooping. By the end of the day, the donations totaled $3,500.

United They Stand

One of Simmons's most passionate community projects is Choose Austin First, a coalition of Austin-based small company owners who have banded together to encourage Austinites to patronize local businesses. Amy and Steve Simmons organized the group in 2004. "What makes Austin special is that there are still a lot of locally owned businesses," says Steve. "But businesses often don't look like they're small and local. Our goal was to put faces on those businesses."

The idea was to gather local business owners together to support and promote one another by making themselves more visible in the community. It's worked for Amy's, and now she's hoping it will work for Choose Austin First's 120 members—a diverse group of business owners that includes retailers, restaurateurs, architects, dog groomers, massage therapists, and cell phone shops. "Chains are moving into Austin fairly strongly," says Mark Negro, co-owner of Mangia Chicago Stuffed Pizza, a Choose Austin First member and Amy's neighbor on Guadalupe Street. "With more businesses taking up slices of the pie, you have to use your resources more creatively." So the group spreads the "buy local" gospel to the public through banners, community events, and their Web site.

For instance, Choose Austin First just sponsored a .2K Run, Walk Crawl, which Simmons says is "about as far as you can run without spilling your beer or dripping your ice cream." Participants paid $15 and "ran" to about 50 different booths to get a quick look at—and sometimes a free sample of—what local businesses had to offer. The event, which included live music from local bands, was also a fundraiser for the SIMS Foundation, a local nonprofit that provides low-cost mental health services to Austin musicians and their families. In 2004, the .2K event raised $3,500 for SIMS.

An equally important part of the group's mission is to get to know, trust, and do business with one another; some members offer discounts to other members, and a few are talking about doing cooperative advertising via local media during the holiday season. The group has grown into a tight, supportive community. In September 2004, for example, vandals destroyed Mangia Pizza's beloved mascot, Mangiasaurus rex, by pushing the 10-foot, 500-pound plastic foam T. rex from the restaurant's roof, breaking the dinosaur into more than 100 pieces. To co-owner Mark Negro's delight, the Texas Memorial Museum offered to rally its team of sculptors and paleontologists to restore Mangiasaurus at no charge.

A month later, Choose Austin First members gathered together at the unveiling event, also attended by Austin mayor Will Wynn, state representative Elliott Naishtat, museum director Ed Theriot, and local radio personality Bama Brown. Mangia Pizza served free pizza, and Amy's offered free scoops of Mangiasaurus Mint to celebrate Mangiasaurus's rooftop homecoming. Choose Austin First, says Negro, "has helped us go from a group of businesses that just happen to do business in the same community to being like a family. It's tied us together with a common thread." He credits Simmons with bringing the group together. "A number of us had been talking about it, but she's the one who took action and pulled everyone together," says Negro. "She's a very strong and loved character—an Austin icon."

Time to Grow, Again

As it turns out, Daryl Kunik will get his wish. He's the entrepreneur-cum-developer who was champing at the bit to land Amy's as a tenant. He bought half the property that he, Amy, and Steve were looking at back in May 2004 and, at this writing, had signed on Amy's, a toy shop called Toy Joy, and ThunderCloud Subs. They are all locally owned businesses.

Since the property wasn't big enough for both a store and a new production facility for Amy's, Steve Simmons continued to scour the city for other possibilities, often approaching landowners whose property wasn't even listed for sale. He struck pay dirt on Burnet Road, in an industrial area filled with used car lots and small strip malls, but bordering several established neighborhoods. And so he and Amy bought two tracts of land totaling an acre, property that's currently home to a former post office and a 1940s Humble gas station, which will be incorporated into the new building's design. There's enough room not only for a 5,000-square-foot production facility, but for an ice cream shop and an icehouse-style restaurant, which Simmons will call Phil's Ice House, after her longtime production manager, Phil Clay, who died in a motorcycle accident in 2003. "I'm so excited about Phil's that I can barely contain myself," says Simmons, who holds a blood drive in Clay's memory every year.

By the summer of 2005, the production facility was up and running, and Simmons was working full-tilt to get her newest store and Phil's ready for an August grand opening. The plan, as always, was free ice cream for all. "It will be massive chaos," says Simmons. "But that's what we're trying to create." With 20 years of practice under her Western-style belt, you get the feeling that the hometown girl will pull it off.

"Stake a Hometown Claim" Tips from Amy's Ice Creams

1. **Choose a Killer Location.** That doesn't necessarily mean the most heavily trafficked neighborhood. If it's local loyalty you're after, don't put down roots in an area that's a tourist magnet. Instead, seek out neighborhoods with local character and stability.

2. **Focus on Experience.** Remember that it's not just your product or service that attracts customers. Everything from your decor to the music you play to your employees' uniforms (or lack thereof) has the potential to draw people in or drive them away. Amy's use of theater to entertain and engage customers is every bit as important as the ice cream she serves.

3. **Grow It Slowly.** If one store is good, two must be better, right? Not necessarily. Simmons might have had twice as many shops as she does now, but she was conservative about expanding, making certain that her production facility and her management staff could handle growth. The result: whenever she does open a new store, there's an enormous amount of local excitement and press because Austin knows that every new Amy's is unique and painstakingly conceived.

4. **Be a Good Citizen.** What kind of entrepreneurs give away their products or services? Smart ones. Amy's giveaways and community events may sound expensive, but consider that she has no advertising budget. The freebies not only attract a crowd, but they build goodwill in the community.

5. **Tap Local Intelligence.** When Simmons first came to Austin, she immediately began networking with local businesspeople, academics, and lawyers. She wasn't shy about asking for—and taking—advice from people who knew the lay of the land. Later, she helped form a small business alliance of companies that continues to support one another with fresh ideas and advice. The group also gives its members brandable local identity.

. . . And from Others

6. **Support Your Community's Youth.** Chris Zane at **Zane's Cycles** (see chapter 2) gives out five $1,000 scholarships to Branford High School's top five graduating seniors each year. "We give it away at an awards night, where there are probably 125 organizations giving away $70,000," says Zane. "It's our opportunity to get in front of 350 kids and their parents, and it positions us as a business that gives back to the community." An unexpected benefit: August has become the store's second largest revenue month, with sales driven primarily by those graduating seniors heading off to college.

7. **Protect Your Turf.** In 2000, Steve Bercu and John Kunz, owners of **BookPeople** and **Waterloo Records & Video,** respectively, learned that the city of Austin was providing a real-estate company with hefty public incentives to build a complex in their neighborhood that would include a Borders. "I got offended that I was paying with my city tax dollars to build a building for someone whose purpose was to drive me out of business," says Bercu. He and Kunz launched a grassroots campaign, starting with e-mails to their customers, who in turn sent e-mails to the Austin city council. "Thousands of people sent e-mails," says Bercu. "Within five days, I was getting my own e-mails back from other lists. It galvanized our customer base and public opinion." The upshot: in spring 2003, Borders withdrew. BookPeople and Waterloo Records remain Austin icons.

8. **Use Community Resources.** Since her company's early days, Trish Karter at **Dancing Deer Baking Company** (see chapter 7) has used local nonprofit groups in Roxbury, Massachusetts, to recruit new employees. The practice helps her find workers who live in Dancing Deer's neighborhood, but it also contributes to her reputation as an inner-city entrepreneur who is invested in her community. That has earned Dancing Deer a place three years in a row on the Inner City 100, a list of the fastest-growing inner-city companies compiled by the Initiative for a Competitive Inner City (ICIC) and *Inc.* magazine.

9. **Encourage Employee Volunteerism. Green Mountain Coffee Roasters, Inc.,** in Waterbury, Vermont, encourages its employees to volunteer in the local community—on the company clock. The program, called CAFE (Community Action for Employees) gives employees the equivalent of 6.5 workdays a year to volunteer wherever they choose; in 2003, they logged 1,270 hours at schools, volunteer fire departments, the March of Dimes, Habitat for Humanity, and other grateful organizations. But it's not all altruistic. Volunteering also helps build employee morale.

10. **Be a Hub in Your Community.** Susan and Matthew Sheehan, owners of **Oswego Wine Company** in Lake Oswego, Oregon, don't just own a wine shop, they've created a "social and education destination." In order to compete with big retailers, the Sheehans began hosting weekly wine-tasting events with West Coast wine makers. Consumers demanded more events, so they converted half the shop into a weekend wine bar, with Susan Sheehan preparing and serving country-style snacks, like panini, fresh salads, and fondue, made with regional ingredients. The shop became such an attractive gathering place that customers now use it during the week for school fundraisers, fashion shows, investment meetings, and cooking classes. "We offer something our competitors never could," says Susan Sheehan. "Hospitality."

6 | Innovate the Mundane

Jim Throneburg with Thorlos.
Photograph: Dan Routh

Company: THOR·LO, Inc.

Business: Manufacturer of Thorlos® sport-specific socks

Location: Statesville, North Carolina

Revenues: $40 million

Employees: 360 full-time; 4 part-time

Founder: Lewis Thorneburg

Chairman: Jim Throneburg

Year Founded: 1951

Web Site: www.thorlo.com

Alpha Dog Credentials:

Jim Throneburg applied the principles of innovation to a commodity product, creating a whole new category of socks. As a result, this family-owned company has grown, thrived, and continued to manufacture in the United States while many other sock companies have gone belly-up or moved their manufacturing operations overseas.

A sock is just a sock, right? Don't ever suggest that to Jim Throne-burg, a 68-year-old, six-foot-four-inch, 250-pound bear of a man, otherwise known as Big Thunder. "I've been given the opportunity to be known as the caretaker of your feet," says Throneburg in a deep North Carolina drawl that makes him sound like an evangelical preacher. The owner and chairman of THOR·LO, Inc., a Statesville, North Carolina, manufacturer of high-end sport-specific socks, is so passionate about his mission that he actually trademarked the phrase "preventive foot health."

Throneburg's socks, called Thorlos, are made with proprietary yarns, and they are specially padded to absorb, say, the pounding a foot takes when it's running on pavement or the chafe of a ski boot against a shin. Thorlos customers spend $11 for a pair of socks, when generic brands go for about $3.50. Throneburg has spent millions on the technology to produce them, and he owns 50 trademarks and 20 patents that prevent competitors from copying everything from the colored yarn on the heel and ball of a pair of Thorlos, to the way in which they're packaged. Throneburg has innovated himself out of the commodity game that has pummeled so many other U.S. hosiery companies.

While domestic sock manufacturers still own a far greater percentage of the U.S. market than their peers in other apparel sectors, their share of the $3 billion U.S. sock market has been decimated over the past several years. Between 1999 and 2003, their piece of the pie has declined from 76.13% to 43.6%. According to the Domestic Manufacturers Committee of the Hosiery Association, sock imports from China have burgeoned from close to 1 million dozen pair in 2001 to 42 million dozen pair in the 12 months ending in August 2004. Between 2001 and 2003, domestic sock production fell from 207 million dozen pair to 166 million dozen pair, and the average market price of socks plummeted from $9 a dozen pair to $4.15 a dozen pair. And in 2002 and 2003, due to plant closings and layoffs 3,717 U.S. sock industry employees lost their jobs. With panicked eyes on the January 2005 expiration of textile import quotas, the Domestic Manufacturers Committee petitioned the U.S. Commerce Department in June 2004 for limits on Chinese sock imports. Commerce responded by limiting

2005 Chinese imports to 7.5% more than 2004's imports—a quota that was close to being met back in April 2005. But what happens after 2005 is still unclear.

Jim Throneburg would be foolish if he didn't have his eye on China, but he's in a far better position than most of his peers. In fact, THOR·LO actually *exports* socks; sales to 29 different countries, including Italy, France, Germany, the United Kingdom, New Zealand, and Australia, account for 12% of revenues. "THOR·LO is not competing against China because Jim has built a reputation around a high-end, high-quality product, and they don't scrimp," says Dan St. Louis of the Hosiery Technology Center in Hickory, North Carolina. "They've got real brand loyalty." They had better, because China isn't the only threat. THOR·LO may have given birth to the specialty sock industry, but it's not alone in the category anymore. There's SmartWool, for instance, which now has more market share than THOR·LO in the outdoor market. And brands like Wigwam and Wrightsock, which both make high-quality athletic socks that appeal to gear-hungry baby boomers with plenty of disposable income, now appear next to Thorlos at many sporting goods retailers.

But Throneburg still thinks he has something that they don't. And it begins with the THOR·LO story. "In the beginning, there was the foot," says Rick Mathena, THOR·LO's knitting-manufacturing director, with a raised index finger. Fit and trim with a tidy beard and mustache, he is accompanying a visitor on a tour of the company's 45,000-square-foot Statesville plant, where 200 knitting machines produce 13,000 to 15,000 dozen pair socks each week. The socks then go to a second plant in nearby Rockwell, where they are finished, dyed, packaged, and shipped. Mathena, who has been with the company since 1991, wears a polo shirt, khaki shorts, new athletic shoes, and of course Thorlos socks. He speaks just above the constant hum of the knitting machines, stopping frequently to chat with machine operators, to inspect a cone of acrylic yarn, or to watch a sock or two being churned out. "As a child, the fatty pads on the bottoms of your feet are prominent, but as you get older, they get worn down," he says. "With different activities, the foot is subject to different pressures. So we look at where the shoes get worn out, ask if the sock should be warm, how much pressure the foot has to handle and where. We're the premier foot-health product in the world." Mathena is preaching the THOR·LO gospel; Throneburg would love it if every employee followed suit.

Throneburg's office is just down the road from the company's manufacturing plant, in a modest trailer with a screen porch that overlooks a wooded lot. On a temperate fall day, he settles his impressive frame in a mahogany rocker and tells the THOR·LO tale; it seems he never tires of talking about his business and the journey that led him out of the commodity world. He likes to say that he lives in "the aha space," and describes himself as "an experimenter in a laboratory," "an old dog desperately trying to learn new tricks," and "not a sock man anymore, but a doctor." In the industry, he's a legend—a colorful, opinionated, fervent, sometimes volatile man who embraces his role as the first industry maverick and has spent his life trying to live up to that distinction. "THOR·LO revolutionized the sock business," says Denise Friend, women's footwear and sock product manager at Recreational Equipment, Inc. (REI), the Sumner, Washington–based outdoor retailer. "And they raised the bar for everyone else."

How did Throneburg build a 360-employee, $40 million company around a product that no right-minded individual would ever associate with innovation? The word makes us think of Edison, Ford, Gutenberg, and Gates. And yet, most innovation occurs when someone looks at an existing product or service in a new way. Ray Kroc didn't invent the hamburger, but he did conceive a radically innovative system that gave birth to one of the most significant entrepreneurial successes of the twentieth century. Likewise, Charles Schwab transformed the brokerage industry, and Howard Schultz's Starbucks Corp. changed the way we feel about—not to mention how much we'll pay for—a simple cup of coffee.

As management guru Peter F. Drucker tells us in *Innovation and Entrepreneurship,* innovation is rarely sparked by a "flash of genius," but is more often the product of "organized, systematic, rational work" performed by entrepreneurs who have developed the habit of seeing the world through the lens of opportunity. They refuse to be constrained or limited by the products they sell, the services they offer, or the industry they're in. So if innovation is possible with coffee and hamburgers, then why not with socks?

Life in the Commodity Zone

THOR·LO started out as Thorneburg Hosiery Mill, a "greige goods operator" founded in 1951 by former hosiery mill workers Lewis and Mattie Thorneburg, Jim's parents. Mattie was a knitter, and Lewis, a "fixer," or mechanic, and they saved scrupulously for years until they could afford to start their own knitting operation, which produced unfinished socks that were then sent off to a separate finishing plant. They built a concrete block extension onto their modest home and enlisted help from their sizable North Carolina clan to set up and run the company. It was "a way of escaping the corporate world," according to Jim, who changed his name from *Thorneburg* to *Throneburg* after family research revealed the original spelling.

The mill was a subcontractor, knitting socks for a Philadelphia company that had landed a lucrative government contract for dress hosiery. When the government business dried up in the mid-1950s, the company jumped on the bobby socks bandwagon, only to return to government work five years later when that trend petered out. This time, they manufactured a military boot sock with a cushioned sole, a product that they would perfect over the next 10 years. It would teach them important lessons about the use of padding.

Jim, an only child, started operating a knitting machine at his parents' company when he was 13, and with the exception of a two-year tour of duty on an experimental navy submarine in the mid-1950s ("my college," he says), the mill is where he has spent the bulk of his life. Shortly after he was discharged from the Navy, his parents incorporated the mill, which had been operating as a proprietorship, and made Jim an equal partner. Back then, 70% of all hosiery production took place within 50 miles of Statesville, a modest city in the foothills of North Carolina, with hundreds of small companies competing with one another to make a few pennies on the dollar. Lewis Thorneburg, however, staked his claim on quality, not price, and earned customer loyalty with the same devotion to excellence that he would pass on to his son.

By the mid-1960s, Jim was growing restless and eager to make his mark on the business. "I saw early on that in order to escape the rat race of being in a commodity business, I needed a brand that would be so good that people would ask for it by name," he says. He had an idea for a man's golf sock, which he decided to bring to market with a partner, a semipro golfer named Lowell Lyles. The sock would be made by Thorneburg Hosiery Mill, but marketed and sold by a new company started by Throneburg and Lyles, with Throneburg's mother as an equal partner; they christened that entity THOR·LO, a combination of *Thorneburg* and *Lowell*.

Like future iterations of Thorlos, the golf sock was designed with great attention to function. What part of a golfer's foot would require the most padding? How would the fit of a golf shoe affect the sock's design? The product enjoyed some modest success in the marketplace, but things really began to cook after the two partners met golf pro Cynthia Sullivan, who was the buyer at a South Carolina country club. She implored them to make her a heavy sock like the man's sock, but with a short roll-top that wouldn't cover her ankles or slip down into her shoe. So Throneburg went home to Statesville and began tweaking the knitting machines.

A year later, in 1966, he had patented a heavy roll-top ladies' sock. "We went to Izod with it, and they put it out in 18 to 20 colors, and they set the world on fire with it," says Throneburg. Izod, which would be acquired by Phillips–Van Heusen in 1995, was then an independently owned U.S. company that had earned brand cachet by partnering with tennis player René Lacoste to produce the now-famous alligator shirt. Throneburg benefited hugely from the relationship. The mill, which contract-manufactured socks for Izod, went from producing around 7,000 dozen pair military boot socks with a profit of 35 cents a dozen pair, to making an additional 5,000 dozen pair roll-top socks with a profit of five dollars a dozen pair. Revenue doubled three years in a row. And Sullivan, by the way, eventually became the president of the Ladies Professional Golfers Association.

Throneburg's partnership with Lyles had fizzled out in 1967, but he had made new inroads on his own. Between the time the roll-top was first launched, in 1966, and the early 1970s, when Throneburg bought out his parents, the mill had grown from about $2 million to almost $6 million in revenue, was earning $1 million in profit, and was producing more than 400,000 dozen pairs of socks. In 1976, Throneburg even took the concept of sport-specific socks to a chain of westernwear stores in Knoxville, Kentucky, where he convinced the owner that he could design a sock with an extra thick heel to prevent a western boot from slipping. "I think we increased sales by a million with just that one company," says Throneburg.

By the late 1970s, though, the patent on his roll-top sock had run out, and domestic competitors began flooding the marketplace. His big customers, like Izod, Bonnie Doon, and Woolworth Corp., were pressuring him to lower prices, and he was faced with the prospect of his margins shrinking from a hefty 50% to 20%, which was then the industry standard. He refused to do it. Instead, he put all his eggs into the innovation basket once again.

The Aha Moment

Throneburg has always struggled with his weight, and back in 1978, at age 41, he finally decided he needed help getting it under control. So he booked a stay at Structure House, a residential weight-loss program in Durham, North Carolina, where he was compelled to walk up to eight miles a day. "My feet were killing me," he recalls. "So I called my R & D guy, Marvin, and I said, 'Make me the thickest-soled sock you can.' " Marvin complied, but when Throneburg tried the socks, he discovered that while the heel and ball of his size 13 foot felt fine, his arch began to hurt. So Marvin went back to the drawing board and removed some of the padding, but Throneburg complained that while his arch had stopped bothering him, his heel was sore once again. "So I called him and I said, 'Just take the padding out of the arch and leave it in the heel and ball.' Well, my feet quit hurting and I could walk 10 miles a day. That was my aha moment."

Throneburg had stumbled upon an opportunity to innovate a thoroughly common product in a way that addressed a consumer need—a need that most people weren't even aware they had. "Innovation begins with an eye," says Tom Kelley in *The Art of Innovation: Lessons in Creativity from IDEO, America's Leading Design Firm.* As general manager of IDEO, one of the world's best-known product development companies, Kelley knows that innovation typically happens when you habitually look at the world in terms of problems that are crying out to be solved. "You watch where people have trouble," says Kelley. "And where there's trouble in the status quo, that's where your opportunity is." Throneburg's trouble was all in his feet, and he assumed that if his uniquely padded socks could solve his problem, they could help others as well.

He rushed to patent his design, which consisted of extra terry padding in the heel and ball of the sock, and the absence of padding in the arch. Next, he had the mill's machines reengineered to "make them do things they were never intended to do" because he was determined to handle all of his production in-house. Years later, he would even forge strong partnerships with local yarn-spinning companies, one of which would work with him to develop a trademarked acrylic yarn called Thorlon, which was softer and more moisture resistant than the cotton and wool fibers that other sock makers were still wedded to.

To Market, To Market

While Throneburg was busy developing Thorlos sport-specific socks, the athletic shoe industry was already in the process of its own sweeping transformation. One morning in 1970, Nike, Inc., co-founder Bill Bowerman poured rubber into his wife's waffle iron, creating the first prototype for what would become the Nike Waffle Trainer, a shoe designed to give runners superior traction. Podiatrists began putting in their two cents as well, advising major shoe companies with brands like Nike, Adidas, and ASICS on the use of wedges and arch supports to enhance comfort and performance. The upshot: generic sneakers like

PF Flyers and Converse's Chucks were becoming obsolete, squeezed out of the marketplace by running, tennis, and basketball shoes that were suddenly being endorsed by professional athletes. It was spot-on timing for Throneburg. His sport-specific socks, which entered the market under the brand name Thorlos in 1979, were the perfect high-end companion to the new athletic shoes. And because they were far pricier than 10-to-a-bag tube socks, margin-hungry retailers snapped them up. At the time, the going rate for the best pair of athletic socks was $2.50; Thorlos sold for $4.50.

THOR·LO first approached the specialty stores—small outdoor and sporting goods retailers that were constantly on the lookout for new products that would give them an edge over their larger competitors. "I remember seeing the first Thorlos and being amazed," says REI's sock product manager Denise Friend. "The beautiful cushioning, the thought process that went into the different zones, and the packaging— I thought, 'Wow, this is fabulous.' Customers responded wildly."

But as important as retailers like REI were, Throneburg prided himself on being more concerned with sell-through than sell-in, meaning that he valued the consumer even more than the retailer. "We want to own the consumer before the retailer owns the consumer," he says. "This forces all the channels to have our brand whether they want it or not." And eventually, everyone did want the brand. "For the first time, people would come in, ask for Thorlos by name, and refuse an alternative at any price," he says. That brand loyalty would be even more important when Throneburg's patents expired and competitors began trying to copy his designs.

Out of the Socks Box

It was loyal customers, in fact, who sparked a major change in the way Throneburg viewed his company and how he would eventually define its mission. Around 1985, he began getting letters from doctors— cardiologists and podiatrists—who told him that Thorlos socks were enabling their patients to exercise more. At the same time, consumers began writing to the company, praising the socks for their ability to re-

duce blisters and increase walking time. Throneburg gathered his management team and made a pronouncement: "If all this is true and we
could prove it, we'd be in the health business, and that's a huge
growth area."

And so Throneburg spent several million dollars to fund medical
research, using his powers of persuasion to convince a handful of doctors to put Thorlos socks to the test with their patients. "We supported
the fellows that did the research, but they made it very clear that we
couldn't control the protocol," says Throneburg. "So I perceived that
there was a risk, but I still wanted to know the truth." The result: half a
dozen peer-reviewed articles that gave scientific credence to the anecdotal evidence. "We got one that said we reduce blisters for long-
distance runners, another that we improve circulation in feet and legs
and relieve pressure on diabetic feet," says Throneburg. "And one that
said we reduce foot pain for arthritics by 50%." For Throneburg, the research results, which are posted on his Web site, didn't just change the
way he thought about the product; they changed the way he saw himself. "I'm not a sock man anymore," he says. "I'm more like a foot
doctor."

"Before that research, we were making educated guesses when it
came to product design," says Richard Oliver, who has been with
THOR·LO since 1992 in a variety of roles and is now the company's
president. "But the research gave us a scientific understanding of what
we were doing, and we built that into our design criteria." THOR·LO
started using a technology called F-Scan, a computerized device that
measures the force and pressure points on a foot in motion by using
paper-thin sensors and a 3-D monitor. It's a machine more commonly
found in a podiatrist's office than at a sock manufacturing company,
but remember that Throneburg wasn't thinking of himself as "a sock
man" anymore. He told himself, his employees, and his customers that
he was in the foot protection business, and that shift not only set the
company on a new course of innovation, it infused Throneburg's job
with the deeper meaning and broader significance that he seemed to
crave.

Changing the Game

Today, sport-specific socks are a $250 million industry—up from just $50 million five years ago. The niche is, in fact, an anomaly in an industry that's been declining steadily for the past 15 years. Sally Kay, president of the Hosiery Association in Charlotte, North Carolina, estimates that there are now just 240 domestic hosiery companies, down from 345 in 1990. "There's been a lot of consolidation in the commodity sock market," she says. "Other countries are becoming more competitive with both production and access to raw materials." According to industry statistics, the number of socks imported from China increased 373% between 2002 and 2003, lowering overall prices and putting the squeeze on domestic companies, particularly those that continue to "play the commodity game," as Throneburg puts it.

In traditional hosiery companies, says Throneburg, "people sat in a meeting and they talked about four things: How many dozens did we ship today? What can we do to please the largest national chain stores because they're the biggest distributors of socks? How can we be the low-cost provider? And what's in fashion? And that's still their strategy, which is why they have to go to China and Mexico to manufacture."

But Throneburg plays by a different set of rules. He wants every sock designed for function, not fashion; he insists on the highest-quality raw materials and construction; he puts customers, not retailers, first; and he cares far less about volume than he does about his margins. "Revenues are important," he says, "but margins are more important." According to Dan St. Louis, director of the Hosiery Technology Center, sock industry margins vary wildly—"from 2% to 25%," he says. He's guessing that THOR·LO's margins fall toward the high end of that range. Throneburg will say only that his margins are "double the industry average." It's an enviable position to be in, and he's not about to jeopardize it by outsourcing his production overseas, where he'd lose the ability to constantly monitor the high-quality materials and production methods that justify his prices, which have remained consistently high.

In fact, he's so persnickety about quality and control that he won't even sign on an American contract manufacturer to help him make his socks. Instead, he's invested millions in his own factory, in training his employees, and in creating a company that is built on what he calls "sustainable relationships." And that has led him to turn down mass-market opportunities that would make other sock manufacturers drool. "In the last year, I turned down two or three major brands that wanted to add a sock to their lines," Throneburg says. He also rejected requests from a major U.S. retailer for a private-label sock because "they would have been just another step between me and my margin." Besides, Throneburg says, "I don't do business with anyone that I can't see a long-term sustainable relationship with. And a lot of these big retailers, if they think they need to one day, they are going to cut your throat."

And that is exactly why Throneburg has made such a significant investment in building relationships directly with the people who wear his product. "It's rare when a sock speaks to a consumer," says Marshal Cohen, an apparel industry analyst at the NPD Group, Inc., in Port Washington, New York. "Thorlos is one of those rare brands that does just that." But speaking to consumers isn't enough for Throneburg; he wants a two-way conversation.

The Consumer Is King

It is Susan Graham's job as THOR·LO's consumer advocate to listen to consumers when they decide to talk back. In a cramped office just off the shop floor, Graham spends most of her day in direct contact with customers, either on the phone or answering letters and e-mails. She hears from runners, walkers, tennis players, skiers, and hikers. But there are also a significant number of people who wear Thorlos because their jobs keep them on their feet all day. In a lilting southern accent, Graham might recommend a specific model of sock to a confused customer, take preliminary custom orders from consumers with special needs (like size 16, EEEE-width feet), suggest that a consumer send her an old sock so that she might see where it has worn down, or even have a heartfelt conversation with a mother who wants to send socks to her son in Iraq. Maternal and diplomatic, she's the antithesis of the automated help line, often punctuating her speech and her e-mails with "God bless you."

A few packages land on her desk as well. Sometimes they contain socks that have clearly been worn for years, along with letters from wearers who fret that the heels have worn out or that the elastic around the top has deteriorated. There's one from Nebraska, for instance, from a man who bought Thorlos mini crew socks and is complaining that they're sliding off his heel and are too bulky. "We'll give him a refund, and we'll send him a level-one running sock at no charge," says Graham. The level-one sock has a bit less padding in it, which should give the man's feet a little more breathing room. It'll also give THOR·LO a second shot at converting a disappointed customer into a loyal one.

The bar for customer service is now ridiculously high, and companies that expect consumers to remain committed and loyal must jump through hoops that they would have considered wholly unreasonable a decade ago. But responding to customers' complaints and needs is one thing, and using that information to inform the way you develop, innovate, and market your product or service is quite another.

Graham uses internally developed software called the Endearment Support Program to enter complaints, along with notes indicating what action was taken, into a database that now contains contact information for about 200,000 customers. That, combined with a massive physical library of customer letters, plus messages that customers send via THOR·LO's Web site, provides the company with the information it needs to change and improve its products. "One of the most frequent complaints was that the top of the sock would break down," says Rick Mende, head of new business development. "So as a result of that, we're in the process of beefing up the construction for some styles and converting to a hemmed top for others."

The customer data often leads to much more fundamental changes as well. In 2002, for instance, Throneburg made two important discoveries: a growing number of consumers were confused by the vast array of Thorlos products available at stores, and it was becoming more difficult for them to get the right fit. So he hired a market research company to do a laddering study. Laddering is a form of market research that uses in-depth customer interviews to ferret out exactly how the use of a product or service taps into feelings and attitudes. "What we found is that there are four categories of Thorlos consumers," says Throneburg. "Satisfied, delighted, bonded loyals, and role-model bonded loyals. The bonded loyals said they owned more than 10 pairs and would recommend them if a conversation about feet came up. But role-model bonded loyals were starting conversations; they were pure evangelical."

However, even some of the most enthusiastic Thorlos consumers were noticing an unpleasant change in how their socks fit. Most Thorlos devotees are aware that they'll probably need to buy a bigger shoe to accommodate the thicker padded socks, but even longtime wearers were having trouble getting the right fit. As it turned out, athletic shoes were being constructed with smaller lasts (the mold used to make the shoes), which made Thorlos seem thicker and hotter. "That gave us a whole new context," says Richard Oliver. "We'd been making a lighter-weight product, but it was always thought of as the bastard child. So we began to play around with our design criteria, and after many, many conversations with consumers in focus groups, we finally understood what people were looking for. We realized that we were in the foot-protection business, and just as with suntan lotions, people wanted varying levels of protection from their Thorlos."

The company responded by developing socks that were less thick but still wicked moisture away from the feet and cooled them down. Those slimmer Thorlos were then integrated into the traditional product line late in 2004 via a completely new merchandising strategy that assigned every sport-specific sock a protection level ranging from one (minimal padding) to three (heaviest padding).

Retail Partners

"We were one of the first retailers to have the new displays and packaging," says Jim Brown, the footwear buyer for Mast General Store, Inc., a chain of seven retail stores in North and South Carolina. "And customers have responded very well to it." It helps that Mast's employees are enthusiastic about the change. "We actually worked with THOR·LO on the new system," says Brown. "They put socks on all our staff, and we sat down with them and looked at color palettes and packaging. We also took some managers and some key staff down to tour the company for a day." The result, says Brown, is salespeople who've had a firsthand look at "what goes into making a pair of socks and what makes THOR·LO different. They came back and started spreading the word."

Throneburg knows he has work to do with retailers, particularly with the smaller, specialty outdoor stores that originally launched Thorlos into the marketplace. Since then, the competitive landscape has changed enormously. Throneburg brought that on himself, of course, because good ideas not only spawn copycats, they raise consumer expectations. Just as the athletic shoe companies taught consumers to demand "high performance" footwear, so did THOR·LO teach them to expect more from their socks.

And so today, Thorlos are not the only premium sport-specific socks on the market. There's Wigwam, Fox River, and SmartWool, the 10-year-old upstart that took the sock market by storm when it introduced the first wool sock that didn't itch or shrink in the wash. "That was one of the biggest changes in the sock industry in years," says Jim Brown. "It forced people who were making synthetic socks to step back, and they all started coming out with wool blends." That includes Throneburg, who considers SmartWool his most serious competitor, particularly in the outdoor specialty store market. "We made a tactical error," says Throneburg. "I hired two mass marketing salespeople who took us into the national chains." And while it seemed like a good thing that Thorlos were suddenly available in stores like Sports Authority and Modell's Sporting Goods, those sales efforts diverted attention from the smaller outdoor stores. "SmartWool came and took that business," says Throneburg. "But now we're going back to take that business back." And Throneburg thinks that his next big innovation will help him do just that.

Innovation 2.0

"In 20 years of consumer letters, we've only had three complaints," says Throneburg. "My sock is too thick, my shoe is too tight, and my foot is too hot. And all of this is caused by one thing: my shoe is too tight. So I decided to make the shoe so I could fit you properly." Throneburg makes it sound simple, but he's been fiddling with shoe designs for more than 15 years, wearing every prototype himself and discarding dozens of models as unworthy of the Thorlos name.

In 2003, though, he met Lou Panaccione, a dedicated runner and former senior executive at both Nike and Reebok International, Ltd. Panaccione, who is based in Boston, had been experimenting with a new design for athletic shoes that "went back to the purity of performance, designed to work with the human foot, not for fashion purposes," he says. It hadn't occurred to him to pair his technology with a sock, but he says that "the synergies between what I was doing and what Jim was thinking were very strong." So the two formed a separate research and development company, JTD, LLC, to design a high-end athletic shoe that would be sold and worn with a new patented Thorlos sock. Within months, they had developed a prototype that was not only more flexible than a traditional athletic shoe, but offered more support and was lighter weight. "It allows your foot to perform as if you were barefoot on a natural surface," says Panaccione.

As of November 2004, THOR·LO was in the last stages of field-testing its new system—a walking shoe, a removable orthotic foot bed that sits inside the shoe, and four pairs of socks—on 28 customers in Florida and Arizona. All were more than 50 years old, walked at least three times a week for 30 minutes or more, and earned over $75,000 a year. That demographic is key to Throneburg, who believes that aging baby boomers, hungry for gear that will help them stay fit and active, are his most promising market. And it's an enormous market: approximately 76 million baby boomers are now between the ages of 41 and 59; every few seconds, another one turns 50. "The major thing we learned is that this product has blown away some barriers to exercising," says Rick Mende, who watched testers being interviewed in real-time streaming video. "The testers, across the boards, felt like it was less effort for them to walk, and so they were walking more often."

Nonetheless, the new venture, in which Throneburg invested between two and three million dollars, seems like a risky business; it's fundamentally different from any kind of innovation that the company has attempted in the past. First, there's a strategic partner in the Far East that will manufacture the shoes to THOR·LO's exact specifications. For competitive reasons, Throneburg won't name the company or the country, but Panaccione, who has a long-standing relationship with the factory, assured him that it's a highly ethical business that provides all employees with medical coverage and child care. Throneburg sent his new CEO, Ron Cruickshank, to Asia to verify those claims and is satisfied that it's "a magnificent company." Still, Throneburg isn't at all accustomed to outsourcing his manufacturing, and the partnership is bound to add a more complex dimension to his business.

Second, there is the product's price to consider. The shoes, which come with four pairs of Thorlos socks, will sell for $250, a hefty amount, but not out of line for a high-quality walking shoe; mBT walking shoes, made by Swiss Masai, carry a $235 price tag, and they are considered a top-of-the-line product. Like mBTs, THOR·LO's shoes will remain a niche product since they're so expensive and require such a high level of interaction between salespeople and customers; you won't ever see them in Sports Authority. So the shoes will be launched at Foot Solutions, a franchise specialty retailer, which will test them in 10 stores and then roll them out to approximately 200 stores by the end of 2005. THOR·LO will also sell the shoes on its Web site.

The success of the product launch will depend entirely on how effective THOR·LO is in educating its retail partners on the unique features of the shoes, and on how much marketing buzz the company can generate among consumers. "The first year will be like an incubation period," says Throneburg, who thinks the product has the potential to boost revenue by "close to $20 million" in 2006 and double that revenue by 2007. But it won't be a slam dunk.

A Culture of Innovation

The single most important aspect of company ownership is probably the one that has vexed Throneburg most consistently over the past 20 years: management. "I've gone through three or four management teams," he concedes. "I see how they do, then I always come back." He has actually taken four leaves of absence from the company in order to give his CEOs breathing room and to give himself some perspective outside the hosiery world. Once, he even joined a new church in Nevada and attended its divinity school. But those self-searching sabbaticals always end up the same way: no CEO has ever lived up to Throneburg's standards; ultimately, they leave and he takes back the helm. This time, he says, he's staying put.

Throneburg, who concedes that he's devoted his life to his business, often to the detriment of his family, is twice divorced with eight children. His oldest son, Lynn Thorneburg, 46, is the company's general counsel, and son Landon Thorneburg, 42, is Throneburg's marketing consultant. Ownership of THOR·LO will not be passed down to the third generation. Upon Throneburg's death, the company will be recapitalized, with all voting stock transferred to a trust that will be controlled by key employees and advisers of the company. Preferred stock will go to the Institute of Preventive Foot Health, a not-for-profit foundation that Throneburg founded in 2003. Son Lynn is president of the foundation. THOR·LO's intellectual property, which Throneburg separated from the stock years ago, will be managed by a separate trust, and the royalties, which are paid to it by THOR·LO, will be split; half will go to the institute, and the rest will be distributed among family members and key THOR·LO employees. It may sound like a convoluted plan, but it's the best way that Throneburg can think of to insure THOR·LO's and the institute's sustainability after his death. Succession, the future of THOR·LO, and the need to foster a true culture of innovation, are now foremost in his mind.

"I had a stroke three years ago," he says. "And I reckon that gave me a change of perspective, from egocentric to humility. I changed who I was being." Today, one of his most pressing goals is to expunge what he calls "the ghost of Jim"—the ever-watchful specter that sits on everyone's shoulder, whispering, "This is what Jim would do." That's no easy task. Throneburg's presence, not to mention his opinions and his ideas, have loomed large at the company for 30 years. Now his challenge is to gradually step away from his role as innovation czar and pass the baton to employees and his hand-picked successors.

And so in 2003, he hired yet another CEO, Ron Cruickshank, a former entrepreneur who also has a PhD in social psychology, plus experience as an advertising executive who had developed global strategies for big brands such as Fujitsu and SAS. "I was on my way to California to run a small multimedia company," recalls Cruickshank. "We were looking for a house out there, and then Jim called me up." Cruickshank, who describes himself as a Thorlos "branded-loyal role model since 1982," had met Throneburg at a conference in the early 1990s and had kept in touch with him. Throneburg's impression of Cruickshank was that he was "very much like me. Our values and experience and our vision for making a difference in the world is the glue." Cruickshank says that his decision to back out of the California job in favor of THOR·LO was an easy one. "It's a company grounded in a desire for excellence and based on solid science," he says. "And I know that I can have an influence. If the job was steady-state, I wouldn't have been interested. We're a $40 million company, and I want us to be a billion-dollar company."

While Cruickshank is focused on THOR·LO's future, Richard Oliver, the company's president, attends to the existing sock business. As chairman, Throneburg sits in the middle as the hub. Both realms are critically important, and Throneburg's job is to keep them communicating to insure that the current business is not only prepared for, but will contribute to, new products and ideas that are in the works. For instance, the company plans to capitalize on its already intimate relationship with customers by adding an e-commerce element to its Web site in the summer of 2005, a project that's clearly in Cruickshank's new business domain. "But they're going to need a fulfillment center," says Richard Oliver. "So I can offer them [knitting manufacturing director] Rick Mathena for two or three hours a week to help come up with a plan."

It's Oliver, the THOR·LO veteran, who has his finger on the company's cultural pulse. While Throneburg and Cruickshank have offices in a modest trailer down the road, Oliver is positioned solidly in the main manufacturing facility, where he is visible every day to the company's plant employees. "We're in a transformation now, from a paternal business model to a participative community model," he says. "Now people come to Jim and tell him what needs to be done instead of waiting for him to come up with ideas. So people are stepping up and taking responsibility, but they're in different places on the journey."

In November 2004, for instance, THOR·LO's sales and marketing staff began hearing from various retailers that customers were asking for walking socks in gray and navy blue. Without consulting Throneburg, they got together with some folks in product development and manufacturing and began exploring the possibility of expanding the existing line of colored socks. "They built a case for it before Jim was even included in the process," says Oliver. "Then they went to him and asked if he had additional input." As it turned out, Throneburg didn't like the idea. "But they're doing it anyway," says Oliver, "because Jim told them that it was ultimately their decision. That's a huge change from three years ago, and people are just now getting used to that."

Even before Throneburg made a commitment to stop micromanaging, he had been resolute about "trying to kill hierarchical thought patterns." At THOR·LO, there are no managers or supervisors, per se. They're referred to as "resources," which Dave Varsik, who works in research and development, defines as "someone who is knowledgeable and available to help you if you need help, but not to tell you what you need to get done today." Most employees, in fact, are a bit befuddled when outsiders ask for their title since those distinctions seem to have little relevance within the company. For some, like Varsik, it's easy to create a title ("director of technology") so that the outside world can understand what he does. For others, that's not so simple. Chuck Harris, who has been with the company since 1995 and is now on his fifth job, calls himself "director of corporate evolution." A retired army sergeant major who served in Vietnam and the Gulf War, Harris's current role involves "making sure the resources (who would be called managers at most other companies) are focused on the big picture. When I see them getting too involved in the day-to-day details and losing sight of THOR·LO's mission, I try and pull them back out so they can see things from the higher perspective." Try putting that on a résumé.

Throneburg thinks that the culture he envisions may take another five to ten years to establish since it must filter down to the employees who are the heartbeat of THOR·LO—those who operate the machines on the factory floor. "Somewhere between a third and 50% of them know that we're doing something here besides socks," he says. It will be Oliver's job to make sure that passion for the product and for THOR·LO "amplifies throughout the company." In the meantime, Throneburg sits in the middle of it all, trying his best to be a font of knowledge and not just a benevolent dictator; it's not an easy task for him. THOR·LO is his baby, and he won't let it go until he absolutely must. "I just want to be used up," he says. "I don't ever want to not be totally immersed because being the best is not a static achievement. You have to work at it every day."

"Innovate the Mundane" Tips from THOR·LO

1. **Think Like an Outsider.** If Throneburg had continued to think like most other CEOs in his industry, he'd still be making low-margin goods and fretting about competition from China. Start down the innovation road by challenging every long-standing industry assumption.

2. **Get Out of the Commodity Game.** It's almost impossible for small companies to compete in the commodity world. Find a niche—or better yet, create one—that isn't being served and serve it well. Don't think volume; think margin.

3. **Identify Real Customer Needs.** Look for the trouble spots in your product or service—that's where the opportunity for innovation lies. And don't rely on customers to tell you what they want; your job as an innovator is to observe consumers' behavior and identify needs that they never even knew they had.

4. **Tweak Your Innovations.** Innovation isn't static. Throneburg knows that absolutely anything can be commoditized within two years. That's why you need to stay ahead of copycats by constantly improving and/or changing your product or service to adapt to evolving market needs.

5. **Build a Culture of Innovation.** Throneburg was the original innovator, but he knows that his growing company can't survive if others aren't innovating as well. Create a culture where communication and creativity is valued and encouraged. And don't regard failure as a mortal sin.

. . . And from Others

6. **Use Demographics to Identify New Markets.** In 1995, **Grand Circle Travel** chairman and CEO Alan Lewis identified a new microniche for his Boston-based travel agency, which had always catered to senior citizens. He knew that healthy, active people in their fifties and sixties were interested in adventure travel, but were probably not up to grueling treks with 25-year-olds carrying 40-pound backpacks. So he began offering "soft

adventure" tours to exotic locations like Vietnam, Peru, and Morocco, keeping physical activity in line with the capabilities of his older customers. In 1995, when GCT first started offering the adventure trips, 3,050 travelers signed up; by 2004, the number had exploded to 26,000.

7. **It's All in the Delivery.** Ray Kroc didn't invent the hamburger, but he did devise a way to serve it in a fast, clean, predictable, and consistent manner. You might say the same for **ZOOTS**, a chain of 60 dry-cleaning shops in the Northeast. Customers get 24-hour in-store drop-off and pickup service via an automated ZOOTS machine that recognizes customers' credit cards and sets a conveyor in motion that deposits clothes in a secure locker. The company also offers home pickup and delivery, e-mail updates, a Goodwill collection service, and an environmentally friendly cleaning system. Like all companies that seek to innovate in mundane industries, ZOOTS's founders, Tom Stemberg and Todd Krasnow (also the founders of **Staples**), took a good look at all the things that trouble the typical dry-cleaning customer and addressed them one by one. Now they're the largest dry-cleaning company on the East Coast.

8. **Democratize Innovation.** At **Amy's Ice Creams** (see chapter 5), ideas for new flavors come from, well, everywhere. Employees toss out suggestions, as do customers and restaurant clients. CEO Amy Simmons will use just about any excuse to get her ice cream machines churning out new treats for her 12 stores. Sometimes they flop (like Avocado), and sometimes they fly (like Midnight Snack—Ritz peanut butter crackers crushed into peanut butter ice cream), but Simmons's willingness to let everyone play the innovation game means that she'll never be at a loss for fresh ideas.

9. **Keep Innovation Close to Home.** Even if you're forced to move your manufacturing operation overseas, consider keeping a small percentage of it stateside. That's what Compton, California–based **Belkin Corporation** does, even though it now owns 80% of the small-office and home market for computer

cables. By keeping 20% of his manufacturing in Compton, CEO Chet Pipkin insures that his company can quickly make and seed the marketplace with newly created products. He can also respond quickly to customers' requests for special orders.

10. **Systemize Innovation. Infiltrator Systems, Inc.,** an Old Saybrook, Connecticut, maker of plastic leach-field drainage for septic systems, is known as an industry innovator because of its pioneering use of plastics. CEO and president Jim Nichols wants to keep the innovation machine well-oiled, so he uses a system called Stage-Gate to evaluate every new idea. It provides a road map that lays out several steps along the new product development road, along with criteria for moving on to the next stage. "Only half our projects make it through Stage-Gate," says Nichols. "You have to set up a culture where people are allowed to try things and make mistakes."

7 | Market Your Brand, Inside and Out

Trish Karter with Dancing Deer employees.

Company: Dancing Deer Baking Company

Business: Commercial bakery

Location: Boston, Massachusetts

Revenues: $5.8 million

Employees: 44 full-time; 2 part-time

Founders: Ayis Antoniou, Suzanne Lombardi, Trish Karter

Year Founded: 1994

Web Site: www.dancingdeer.com

Alpha Dog Credentials:

The majority of specialty food manufacturers remain small and local, unable to navigate the obstacles that lead to national distribution. But by branding her company, her products, and her mission, Trish Karter has given Dancing Deer the kind of national, cross-channel appeal that other artisanal bakeries can only hope for.

Trish Karter could be a living metaphor for her company. She's petite and lean—a compact powerhouse who runs marathons, and whose energy and passion enable her to go the distance along with the fiercest competitors. The same might be said for Dancing Deer, a $5.8 million company founded by Karter; her ex-husband, Ayis Antoniou; and baker Suzanne Lombardi. Dancing Deer started out looking a lot like just about any other small-scale commercial bakery but is now quite clearly an Alpha Dog.

Most companies like Karter's remain small and local, serving up loaves, cakes, and cookies to hometown markets. According to a recent study by the National Association for the Specialty Food Trade, Inc., median sales for specialty food manufacturers in this $22.8 billion industry is just $850,000. Dancing Deer, however, was founded in 1994 with grander intentions. Think Famous Amos and Mrs. Fields, rather than your corner bakery. "We always had in mind that we would create a national brand, because that's where you get value," says Karter.

Successful branding reaches beyond products or services to the very core of the companies that deliver them. In a February 2001 *Harvard Business Review* article, Mary Jo Hatch and Majken Schultz talk about corporate branding as "a single umbrella image that casts one glow over a panoply of products." The big-company examples are obvious and plentiful: Disney, Coca-Cola, Johnson & Johnson, Microsoft. We've come to expect a certain level of quality from products that bear their names, and those expectations drive our buying decisions; without even thinking, we separate the industry leaders from the also-rans.

And that is what Karter hopes to achieve with Dancing Deer. Up and down the supply chain, she has built a brand identity that reflects a resolute commitment to everything that makes the company distinctive. The DNA of Dancing Deer's brand: natural, kosher, baked-from-scratch goodies without preservatives; whimsical and environmentally friendly packaging; a culture that refers to its employees as "deers" and whose motto is "When people are happy, it shows in the food"; a commitment to creating jobs in Boston's economically depressed Roxbury neighborhood; and a pledge to donate 35% of one product line's revenues to charity.

It might all come off as a bit too earnest if Karter didn't keep things playful as well. In January 2005, for instance, the company's weekly e-mail to customers opened with a picture of fifteen deers contorting their bodies in the snow to spell out "Go Pats," in anticipation of the Super Bowl. The Monday after the New England Patriots' Super Bowl victory, another e-mail went out with Karter and six deers swinging from the office ceiling. The message: not only are our cookies superb, but they're baked by a spirited, fun-loving, collegial group of people.

Dancing Deer cultivates an authentic image, and in these times of extreme corporate cynicism, that's something the marketplace responds to—something that it craves, in fact. "People want a good product, but they also want a good-news story," says Karter. "And that's a key piece of how we've become a nationally recognized company."

Accidental Entrepreneur

Karter could never have predicted that the stars would align as they have. She grew up in Old Lyme, Connecticut, where she was the only girl on her high school track team. At 16, she enrolled in Wheaton College in Norton, Massachusetts, to study art history and ancient Greek, but left in the middle of her senior year to help her father, Peter Karter, shepherd his recycling company, Resource Recovery Systems, out of bankruptcy. Peter Karter had developed technology that allowed consumers to skip the tedious process of separating their recyclables for curbside pickup, and he's now widely regarded as a dean of modern recycling. Every day, Karter and her dad drove a beat-up Datsun from their home in Old Lyme to the plant in Branford, taking back roads to avoid paying the 25-cent highway toll. "It was really desperate," recalls Trish Karter. "That experience is in my veins. I don't ever want to walk that close to the edge again."

Father and daughter resurrected the company, and then 21-year-old Trish went on to become a lobbyist for the Glass Packaging Institute in Washington, DC. In 1980, she decided to continue her formal education at the Yale School of Management, and it was at Yale that she met and married Greek-born Ayis Antoniou. The couple moved to

Boston in 1987, and while Karter had high-paying finance jobs in a number of industries, including satellite television, real-estate development, and consulting, none of them "made my heart sing."

So in 1988, she and Antoniou, who was a physicist and a business consultant, decided that Karter would quit her corporate consulting job and devote herself to her first love: oil painting. A year later, their first child, Eleanna, was born. "When I moved from business to painting, it was huge," recalls Karter. "I put myself through Wheaton and Yale, and I never got a penny from anyone. But when I returned to painting, I gave up my independence and was dependent on my husband." She was content, though, spending her days in the art studio or restoring the turn-of-the-century gardens of their sprawling farmhouse in the estate section of suburban Milton, Massachusetts. In October 1993, she gave birth to a son, Dimitri. "And then," remembers Karter, "along came a baker."

Karter's house painter was married to Suzanne Lombardi, a talented baker whose all-natural pound cakes were being devoured at a Boston area coffeehouse. It was 1994—the beginning of Starbucks-induced java madness—and Lombardi was having a tough time keeping up with demand. So she baked a plateful of sticky buns and approached Karter's business consultant husband, Antoniou, for some advice. He was impressed with the offering, and with Lombardi as well. "Suzanne and I spent a lot of time talking about values and who we were," recalls Antoniou. "And we decided we'd like to go into business together. We launched the company with some really conscious principles in mind." Antoniou and Karter invested approximately $20,000 in the tiny operation. "Suzanne had been carrying her pots and pans around to rented kitchens," says Karter. "So we created a corporation and set her up in her own facility." The original plan: Lombardi would concentrate on baking, while Antoniou provided business strategy advice. Karter would continue to devote herself to painting, or so she thought.

A year or so after they had incorporated the business, though, Antoniou began spending more and more time at a consulting job in New Jersey, so Karter says she felt compelled to pick up the slack and help Lombardi run the business. It had been christened Dancing Deer, after an antiques shop in Bar Harbor, Maine, run by Lombardi's grand-mother, who had also been a masterful baker. "I was working seven days a week baking, loading stuff into my car to make deliveries, tak-ing orders, sending out invoices," recalls Lombardi. "I was so thrilled to have someone walk through the door to help me. It saved me."

Every day, Karter commuted from suburban Milton to Dancing Deer's West Roxbury headquarters. It was situated in a tiny former pizza parlor in a run-down inner-city neighborhood—1,000 square feet of space for baking, plus a cramped basement storage area that was used as an office. "There were no systems and not enough people, so I jumped in and helped do everything," says Karter. "At the very be-ginning, I thought it was temporary. Then I thought it would take two years to settle things and I'd be on my way. But then the business would take a leap forward, and we had to figure out how to do some-thing new."

Karter was genuinely excited by what she was accomplishing in the business: it was as if Dancing Deer was stimulating both her artis-tic sensibilities as well as her brain for business. But there was also a more practical reason for her continued involvement: while demand for the company's products was on the rise, Dancing Deer was still los-ing money. She and Antoniou had continued to put money into the business, and Karter felt she had to protect her family's investment, which would eventually total $180,000.

Establishing the Brand

In those early days, Karter and Lombardi were a great team. "I had all the finance and business modeling in my brain, and she had how to make cookies and cakes in her brain," says Karter. For its first two years, Dancing Deer sold delicacies such as ginger-lemon–infused pound cake and wild blueberry scones to small, upscale Boston and Cambridge area eateries. But the three partners had more ambitious plans. "We never wanted to create just a local bakery," says Antoniou. "We wanted a national brand."

A distinctive brand needed equally distinctive packaging, so the three enlisted help from Manhattan-based designer Susan Slover, a friend of Karter's. "We wanted it to be whimsical but sophisticated," recalls Antoniou. "The design was so important that in the beginning, I think we spent more on design than on equipment." Slover's firm came up with the homespun font and the winsome stick-figure deer and baker drawings that are now the company's hallmark. The drawings, like the cookies, were wholesome and homey, and the packaging itself—clear cellophane bags tied with raffia ribbon—sent the message that Dancing Deer wanted its customers to get a good look at what was inside. It was a product that busy moms, with little time to bake cookies of their own, could feel good about buying for their families.

While Dancing Deer continued to supply coffeehouses, the cakes also made inroads into several local specialty retail stores. "Marvelous treats, gingerbread in the fall, lemon-blackberry cake in the summer . . . Divine," gushed *Boston* magazine in fall 1996. By that time, the products had also attracted the attention of bigger players. Lauri Klein, then the bakery coordinator at Bread & Circus, a regional natural food store chain that had been acquired by Whole Foods Market in 1992, was just beginning to hear the buzz on Dancing Deer when she got a call from Karter. "Their products had a high degree of ingredient integrity and compelling graphics and packaging," recalls Klein. "And I liked [the owners], which is important in business."

And so Dancing Deer's cakes and cookies—all baked from scratch and delivered the following day—made their debut at Bread & Circus. The following year, 1997, Klein asked for a special holiday cookie. Lombardi's creation was so popular that Bread & Circus decided to offer it to customers year-round. Encouraged by the brand's success, Klein was keen to present Dancing Deer at a San Francisco meeting of all Whole Foods regional bakery coordinators—a pitch that would ultimately move the company's products to the West Coast for the first time and also give revenues a significant boost. For fiscal year 1998, which ended in June 1998, Dancing Deer's revenues climbed to $1.09 million, up from $690,000 the previous year. Karter and Antoniou had recouped most of their initial investment, the company was profitable, and the three partners each began drawing salaries of $20,000 each.

That initial foray into the retail market was a major turning point for the company, transforming it from a relatively anonymous supplier to coffeehouses to a branded maker of packaged goods that were featured at a major local grocery store. And it wasn't just any grocery store. Bread & Circus was one of the first local markets to catch the natural food wave. In increasing numbers, mainstream shoppers were beginning to drift to the alternative upstarts in search of the natural and organic products that were welcome antidotes to the over-processed and preservative-laden goods that dominated the big super-market chains.

It was that burgeoning demographic that drove Austin, Texas–based Whole Foods Market to acquire regional chains like Bread & Circus, as well as Fresh Fields in Rockville, Maryland; Wellspring Gro-cery in Durham, North Carolina; and Food for Thought in Sebastopol, California. Those stores embraced values and standards that were near and dear to Karter, so they were a natural home for her products. Lack of preservatives combined with relatively high prices—a bag of nine cookies costs $4—made Dancing Deer's products impractical for most supermarket chains. So early on, the partners aligned themselves with like-minded retailers. That meant forging intimate relationships with smaller chains and specialty store owners who not only understood the brand, but who pledged to closely monitor the product's short shelf life. It's a key element of branding: your customers will judge you by the company you keep. Dancing Deer's presence at Bread & Circus and Whole Foods would send a message to the marketplace that the company's products had cleared a high bar.

As so often happens, one great customer led to another. In 1997, catalogue and retail giant Williams-Sonoma, Inc., approached Karter with a lucrative request, but one that would also test Dancing Deer's brand integrity. "One of their buyers came to me and said he wanted Molasses Clove Cookies in every Williams-Sonoma store for the holi-days," recalls Karter. "They had 165 stores at the time, and I think that order might have actually doubled our revenues at that point." But Williams-Sonoma wanted the cookies to have a shelf life of four months, and Karter knew that Dancing Deer's preservative-free cook-ies would stay fresh for three weeks, tops, in the Williams-Sonoma warehouse. "It was hard to turn down," she recalls. "But we had to. There was no way I was going to put junk in the cookies."

But Williams-Sonoma was still eager to do business with the company; they came back a few days later and asked for an original gingerbread mix—a product without thorny shelf-life issues. Lombardi put her own spin on the holiday classic by developing a mix that included Chinese five-spice powder. "I figured out how to package it, and we landed it on their desk in four days," says Karter. "And that turned into a major relationship." Today, Williams-Sonoma is among Dancing Deer's top five customers.

Serendipity

At about the same time that Dancing Deer made its debut at Bread & Circus, Karter and her partners decided to open a small retail operation at their bakery. And as it turned out, one of those retail consumers would drive the next major change at the company.

In the summer of 1997, a Los Angeles writer named David Hoffman had stopped at Dancing Deer to ask for directions. Unable to resist the aroma of freshly baked goodies, he also bought a Deep Dark Gingerbread Cake. The delicacy remained so deeply etched in his taste buds that he recalled it a few months later when he was asked to contribute to a television show featuring the best holiday artisanal food in America. "So they called us and asked if we did mail order," recalls Karter. "And the answer was 'of course' even though we never had. And then they asked for our 800 number, and I said 'Well, we're just in the process of getting it up and running.' It wasn't even on my radar screen, but it was up and running in 24 hours and we were in the mail order business."

Increased retail exposure, driven largely by Whole Foods, plus the growing mail order business, boosted revenue to $1.8 million by the end of 1999—up 1,925% from the bakery's first full year. Dancing Deer had also accumulated an impressive slew of accolades: in 1998, the bakery's Molasses Clove Cookie had won a National Association for the Specialty Food Trade (NASFT) award for outstanding cookie—the specialty food industry's equivalent of an Oscar; the following year, its Chocolate Tangerine Cookie walked away with the same award, and its Deep Dark Gingerbread Cake landed the top award for outstanding baked good. Ernst & Young also recognized Karter as an Entrepreneur of the Year finalist, and the American Institute of Graphic Arts named the company a Brand Design Award Winner.

Karter had by then abandoned the idea that Dancing Deer was merely a temporary diversion from her painting; the oil portrait that she had left unfinished on an easel when she began working at the company remained neglected. But she had no regrets. With Antoniou and Lombardi, she had built a company that seemed to have taken on a life of its own, and it had become precious to her. But within the next several months, she would come dangerously close to losing it all.

Company in Crisis

The company may have been thriving, but Karter's marriage was not. The relationship had been strained for a long time, but by the end of 1999 the rift had become painfully bitter. Karter and Antoniou, who continued to live in the same house but in separate wings, decided that they could no longer work together. With Lombardi, they went into arbitration to try to restructure the company. It was obvious to the company's 30 employees that things were unraveling.

"Everyone had their résumés out," recalls controller Keith Rousseau, who was then assistant to the company's controller. "We were prepared for the possibility that we wouldn't have a job." In fact, says Karter, it was not at all certain that Dancing Deer would survive the divorce. It took seven long months of negotiating for Karter, Antoniou, and Lombardi to come to an agreement. In the meantime, the company was churning out cookies and revenues were holding steady, but the progress that Dancing Deer had made over the past two years had come to a screeching halt.

While they won't discuss the details of the deal, it was agreed in

July 2000 that Karter would buy Antoniou's shares; Lombardi would agree to sell her shares, along with the company's intellectual property (her recipes) several months later. To finance the purchase, Karter used her own capital ("pretty much everything I had"), brought in new commercial bank credit through a financial restructuring, and sold part of the company for approximately $500,000 to two investors: a married couple who were close friends and a successful food-service executive named Jim Tyson, whom Karter met through a contact at the Smaller Business Association of New England. Karter retained 51% of the company.

"The outside world didn't know what was going on, but inside, the company was a shambles," says Karter. "Our payables were mounting, and our receivables weren't being collected. People were angry and confused and anything but focused on the business." She needed help, so she turned to Jim Tyson, one of her equity investors. "He was not a warm and fuzzy guy," concedes Karter. "But he was good at efficiency and purchasing, and he did a lot to improve our margins. Our company needed to get out of crash-and-burn territory, and Jim was just the antidote." Tyson arrived in the summer of 2000 with the understanding that he would stay for a few weeks to help Karter get things in order. But he remained on staff as a full-time chief operating officer for two and a half years, drawing a salary equivalent to Karter's, which she had raised to $100,000 after nailing down the equity investments. During that time, Karter recalls, "people either loved Jim or hated him."

"I loved him," says Dancing Deer controller Keith Rousseau. "Jim was a super detail person, and he cracked the whip on the operational side, which we really needed." For instance, says Rousseau, Tyson insisted that the company start producing weekly flash reports to look at key numbers such as sales by division, sales per labor dollar, and administrative expenses. It was a weekly snap-shot that disciplined everyone at Dancing Deer to focus on efficiency and profitability and that provided an instant action plan for the following weeks. "He made us more profitable, and he did it by clamping down on every expenditure," recalls production manager Lissa McBurney. "We even had to mash down the garbage bags so we wouldn't fill up the Dumpster too fast." Tyson taught them all a critically important lesson: you can have the greatest brand in the world, but if you can't get it out the door efficiently, you're sunk.

Tyson provided the tough love that the company seemed to need so desperately after Karter and Antoniou's divorce nearly tore it apart. His presence as Karter's operating partner gave her the credibility she needed with her staff and also left her with a far more stable foundation from which to grow the Dancing Deer brand. He helped improve margins by 20% in FY 2001, and another 16.5% the following year; revenue also increased from $2.6 million to $3 million over those two years. And there was more public recognition as well: Dancing Deer had been listed by *Inc.* magazine and the Initiative for a Competitive Inner City as one of the top 100 fastest-growing inner-city companies in 2001, 2002, and 2003; NASFT dubbed the company's Lemon Coconut Pound Cake the outstanding baked good for 2002. So as the company moved into its next phase of growth, Karter stayed the course, building upon her company's brand identity, inside and out.

Holding on to Brand Integrity

As the years passed, other companies would tempt Karter to compromise her brand integrity, much as Williams-Sonoma had back in 1997. In August 2004, for example, the company was just three weeks away from shipping its first big order to Target when Tim Horton, who was Target's bakery buyer, called and asked that the cookies be shipped frozen rather than fresh. "They were pushing us hard to get the program started," recalls Dancing Deer wholesale manager Dave Lamlein. "But all of our labels said 'Baked and shipped fresh.' We had to go back and change the labels, and we had to test the packaging to make sure it would withstand freezing." Horton was not happy. "I understood that their integrity was involved," he says, "but at the same time, it was a commitment, and for us to find a replacement product at that late hour was nearly impossible."

Karter knew that delaying that initial shipment of back-to-school cookies to 116 SuperTarget stores could well jeopardize $200,000 worth of business from Target over the following months. But she felt that she had no choice. Horton made no guarantees that Target would still be interested by the time Dancing Deer was done fiddling with packaging and putting together a product offering that was suitable for the winter (the back-to-school theme was out, of course). But three months later, Karter and crew knocked on his door with every problem solved. "For a small company, they reacted very, very quickly," says Horton. A new deal was clinched, and as of October 2004, Target had ordered nearly $200,000 worth of frozen and fresh cookies from Dancing Deer.

While companies like Target might give Dancing Deer broader exposure in the marketplace, Karter is well aware that courting them could threaten relations with the specialty stores that were so instrumental in launching her brand. In fact, channel conflict is a common problem for every entrepreneur whose product suddenly migrates from the corner store to the superstore. How do you grow your company on a bigger playing field and still remain loyal to the customers who knew you when? "The specialty food stores will complain as you move to the supermarkets, and the supermarkets complain as you move to the big-box stores," says John Roberts, president of the National Association for the Specialty Food Trade. "And the big-box stores have been known to complain if you move to the Web. Everyone is saying, 'Protect me from the big guy next door.' "

Karter has hit upon several solutions to the "protect me" plea. For the past year, for example, Dancing Deer has been developing special products exclusively for Whole Foods. There's Black-and-White Sesame Seed Shortbread, plus a biscuit made with rice grown by Indonesian family farmers and purchased via fair trade programs, which negotiate directly with farmer cooperatives and guarantee growers fair market prices. The exclusive products single out Whole Foods as a valued Dancing Deer customer, while solidifying Dancing Deer's brand identity as an innovator. "It's a direct response to the stress everyone feels from competition and channel conflict," says Karter. "So you do something different to accommodate, and before long you have to do something else, so we're constantly dealing with that."

The company's Web site, ramped up in fall 2001 with an

e-commerce engine to sell directly to consumers, is also a source of potential channel conflict. So Karter makes sure that her product offerings and pricing structure don't compete with valued retailers. On the Web, for instance, consumers will pay $14.50 plus shipping for 18 artfully gift-packaged Cherry Almond Ginger Chew Cookies. At Whole Foods, they could buy the exact same cookies in two packs of nine for a total of $8. "So Whole Foods doesn't mind at all that we sell on the Web because we're making them look better," says Karter.

In fact, the Web site, which now accounts for more than $1 million in sales, is more of a threat to customers like Williams-Sonoma, whose catalogue customers may see a particular Dancing Deer product, then attempt to order directly through Dancing Deer. That's verboten, says Karter, whose staff always bounces those customers back to Williams-Sonoma. "We have a contract that says we'll never touch their customer list," says Karter. Frequently, she says, companies like Williams-Sonoma will call Dancing Deer with a "ghost" order just to check up.

It may sound like a high-maintenance relationship, but it's one that pays off. Williams-Sonoma mails out 55 million catalogues 4 times a year, and Dancing Deer's presence in them strengthens the company's brand. The resellers are also a great place to test-market new products that are offered exclusively for a specific period of time, then brought back into the Dancing Deer stable for broader distribution. In 1998, for instance, Karter offered William-Sonoma a one-year exclusive on a set of all-natural food coloring. "It proved itself so well in their catalogue that when the year was up, we had the confidence to build inventory with it," says Karter.

Branding the Workplace

"Don't bake angry—it'll ruin the cake." It was one of Suzanne Lombardi's most frequently uttered directives, and it stuck to Dancing Deer like icing on a cookie. "When the kitchen was working well and people were enjoying each other, everything went smoothly," says Karter. "But when there was stress and conflict, we'd have a production failure. So we needed a happy company because when people are happy, it shows in the food."

Karter and her partners knew how important it was to have a reliable, steady workforce, so they went to great lengths to distinguish their company in an industry that's notorious for poor working conditions and high turnover. All full-time employees were provided with health insurance before Antoniou and Karter took a penny of compensation for themselves. In 1996, they made an outright stock grant to all employees, giving away 1% to 2% of the company. In fact, 10 original employees have stock, including the bakery manager and a dishwasher. When it was no longer practical to give away stock, Karter began granting options to all new hires, with the qualification that all vested options be cashed in when the employee leaves the company. As of summer 2005, 13% of the company's stock was held by employees. Annual bonuses are based on a formula that includes not only the company's top- and bottom-line performance but personal goals as well. "There's a nice bonus structure at the company," says bakery manager Robert McLeod, who has been with Dancing Deer since 1997. "And that's really rare for a bakery."

Word has spread in Dancing Deer's inner-city neighborhood that the company is a good place to work, so Karter has never been at a loss for applicants. Adelina Bano, an Albanian immigrant with an economics degree, recalls the day in 1996 when she first knocked on the company's door looking for work with just a few English phrases scrawled on a scrap of paper: "I am looking for a job," "I will start today." Karter hired her immediately, and Bano began as a packer, stacking freshly baked cookies into cellophane bags and tying them up with raffia ribbon. She kept an Albanian-English dictionary by her side at all times and tried to learn a few new words every day. Before long, her husband, Ilir, also landed a job at Dancing Deer. "I worked the morning shift and he worked in the afternoon," says Bano. "Sometimes our kids were even in the bakery."

Bano, who is now fluent in English and was promoted to packing room supervisor, left the company in 2004 for a job with an education finance company; her husband has opened his own pizza parlor. But there are six more Albanian immigrants at Dancing Deer, where signs in the break room are printed not only in English and Albanian, but also in Spanish and Cape Verdean Creole, a dialect spoken in the West African archipelago of Cape Verde. To help break down the language barriers, Karter offers English as a second language classes on company time, rewarding employees with an hourly wage increase when they complete the course. Thirty-four employees have taken her up on the offer.

Karter also reimburses employees up to $500 a year for job-related education expenses. Diana Betancur, for instance, has been with the company since 1999 and has attended two management classes at the University of Massachusetts—training that helped her become a supervisor in the packing room. Other trainees include Jesus, Betancur's husband, who started out in the packing room and is now a lead baker; and Milton Torres, who was a packer and is now the head development test baker.

Having invested so much in their success, Karter is determined to retain her employees. The company's busiest time is October to December, when Dancing Deer might churn out 110,000 goodies a day. Things slow down in the spring and summer, but Karter won't lay off her employees seasonally. "Right now it's so slow, we're sucking up labor," Karter told me when I visited her in spring 2004. "But we're keeping people's jobs for them."

In 1998, when the company outgrew its cramped West Roxbury quarters, Karter chose to remain in the inner city rather than move to a tidy office park in suburban Canton. In the Newmarket section of Roxbury, she found an old brick fish-processing plant, built in the early 1900s and sorely in need of renovation. "Our employees come from the inner city, and we didn't want to lose them," Karter says. "We calculated the cost of running a bus back and forth but realized that with staggered shifts, it could never work, especially in the busy season when we'd most need transportation at odd hours." She also didn't want to lose her "group of hip, ambitious, smart young managers who were a long way from suburban life. Staying in the city made us more attractive to them as well." And so Newmarket was the obvious choice.

Today, Dancing Deer occupies two stories of the former fish plant at 77 Shirley Street. The bakery and packing room are down-

stairs, while "management" occupies the second floor. Everyone—
even Karter—stakes out territory in one big, open space that's divided
by a double row of black metal filing cabinets and is filled with art ta-
bles disguised as desks, which are often scattered with cookies or
packing material. The concrete walls and floor are painted a creamy
yellow, matchstick blinds hang cockeyed on the windows, and a dusty
potted plant languishes in the corner. The only door in the place is the
one to the conference room, and that's enclosed mostly by glass. It
looks and feels a bit like a big college dorm room, and it offers about as
much privacy. But that work environment—open, communicative,
transparent, and sometimes noisy—fits the company perfectly and
sends a message to job applicants: if you want a traditional corporate
environment, you'd better look elsewhere. "You either love the place
or you crash and burn quickly," says production manager McBurney.

Deers are a loyal, hard-working bunch, but they have fun too. On
opening day 2004 at Fenway Park, home of the perennial underdog
Boston Red Sox, deers gave away 5,000 individually wrapped Break
the Curse Cookies to fans, hoping to send the Red Sox some desperately needed good karma. The cookies were later sold at local retail
outlets and on the company's Web site. And lest the stunt be perceived
as merely a revenue-boosting publicity ploy, Karter donated five cents
from every Break the Curse Cookie sale to a local nonprofit project
called the Kids Can Dream Fund; $1,800 went to buy bats and gloves
for homeless children. When the Sox won the Series, Dancing Deer
got plenty of local and national publicity. Karter was interviewed on
the *Today* show and also appeared on Japanese television.

Branding the Cause

Of course, marketing and publicity efforts such as the Break the Curse
campaign *do* result in commercial gain for the company. A growing
number of companies now engage in cause-related marketing, wrapping their products or services around philanthropic causes that make
customers feel good about their purchases, and perhaps a little less
guilty about paying premium prices. In the food industry, the most vis-

ible example is probably Newman's Own, co-founded by actor Paul Newman and his buddy A. E. Hotchner in 1982. The company donates 100% of its profits to educational and charitable organizations—a practice that has generated more than $150 million for philanthropic causes, and that probably drives revenue growth as much as Newman's name and likeness on the labels.

Carol Cone, CEO of a Boston-based cause-related marketing company called Cone, Inc., says that cause branding is on the rise. "Businesses are taking a cause and deeply infusing it into their brand so that the brand equity goes beyond the product," she says. "And there are more and more companies doing it than I have ever seen before. Our own business is up considerably because of cause branding." Why? In the wake of 9-11 and an onslaught of corporate scandals, consumers are more eager than ever to embrace and reward good corporate citizenship, and employees are demanding more meaning from work. The confluence of those two trends makes cause branding a particularly effective way for companies to differentiate themselves.

Karter's own cause-branding efforts evolved organically. Over the years, she earned a reputation among local charities as a CEO who always seemed willing to donate cash or cookies to worthy causes. Then, in July 2001, she was approached by Melinda Marble, executive director of the Paul and Phyllis Fireman Charitable Foundation, a Boston-based nonprofit whose efforts include raising money for the homeless. "They wanted a cookie shaped like a house that could be sold to raise money," says Karter. "It was insane to think of launching a product by the holiday," recalls Marble. "But we did it, and Trish [Karter] plunged in with all of her ideas." The cookie was sold on Dancing Deer's Web site, with the company pledging to donate 35% of the proceeds to the foundation's One Family initiative. And the foundation, says Marble, pledged that 100% of those funds would go directly to homeless families. "That first year, the cookie generated $20,000 to $25,000 [for the One Family initiative]," says Marble. "It was amazing, because we thought we'd be lucky to break even."

"I loved the idea that this was a chance for us to focus on a cause and make a difference," says Karter. So she deepened Dancing Deer's relationship with the One Family initiative by creating a separate Web page that would be devoted to a special line of products that were labeled "Sweet Home." They included the house cookies, cake and cookie packages, and a gingerbread house kit. Like the house cookie project, 35% of the retail price would go directly to the One Family initiative. In three years, Sweet Home has raised approximately $100,000 for One Family; last year alone, the contribution was $40,000, which amounted to approximately 0.8% of Dancing Deer's $4.8 million in revenue.

"I cared about homelessness, and there was a logical connection between baking and home," says Karter. "Plus, it's smart marketing. People see that it's not fluff and they respect us for it. It's consistent with our brand and what we stand for." From Marble's perspective, the joint venture makes good business sense because Dancing Deer's brand is associated with "the high-quality, innovative packaging, and playful spirit that especially appeals to women who are affluent, creative, and intelligent." And that's exactly the donor base that the foundation hopes to educate and engage.

It's tough to measure the real bottom-line effects of cause branding, but cause-marketing consultant Carol Cone offers some revealing statistics. In her 2004 Cone Corporate Citizenship Study, 80% of 1,033 adults surveyed said that a company's support of social causes wins their trust; in 1997 the percentage was just 59%. And 86% said they'd be likely to switch to a brand associated with a good cause if price and quality were similar. "There are a lot of great bakeries out there," says Cone. "When you do cause branding well, it's a distinct competitive advantage."

Getting the Word Out

Karter's biggest coup, perhaps, is the way is which she has successfully branded herself as leader of Dancing Deer. She is a high profile CEO, a virtual public relations machine who seizes every opportunity to put Dancing Deer in the spotlight. Last year, for example, she held a Blessing of the Batter ceremony at Fenway Park, where she gathered interfaith spiritual leaders (including a rabbi, a minister, and a holistic healer) around a giant mixer to bless the batter for her Break the Curse Cookie. She got press coverage in both Boston and New York.

Those kinds of antics typically generate lots of attention that evolves into other opportunities for Dancing Deer. "Branding involves making connections between what you're doing so that you can leverage one activity on behalf of another," says Karter. "And a lot of it is about relationships." The highly publicized Break the Curse Cookie, for instance, caught the eye of an executive at Boston-based John Hancock. Before Karter knew it, Dancing Deer was baking chocolate chip cookies for John Hancock to include in goodie bags for Boston school children who were studying electoral politics. Chalk one up for Dancing Deer's corporate sales department.

While opportunities like that appear serendipitous, they're actually a direct result of tireless, pavement-pounding brand promotion. And that can come in many forms. Take Dancing Deer's Web site, for instance, which effectively mimics the product packaging—it's uncluttered, playful, and filled with stick-figure deer and bakers holding cakes as big as their heads. But more importantly, it's loaded with information that familiarizes consumers with Dancing Deer's spirit and culture—its commitment to all natural ingredients, environmentally sound packaging, philanthropy, and a great work environment. Customers who order online receive a newsletter 24 times a year, and it includes not only the predictable product pitches but an inside peek at the company's culture.

At Easter, for instance, there were pictures of the company's international potluck feast; employees, many still wearing their bakery-mandated hair nets, smiled and waved at the camera before tucking into such delicacies as Albanian cheese pie, Vietnamese egg rolls, empanadas, stuffed grape leaves, and knishes. Over the summer 2004, there were pictures of deers at a company outing on a 125-foot schooner, and during the Olympics, the site featured a winning picture of Karter on her racing bike, surrounded by a half-dozen other "deerthletes." The message is crystal clear: we're a happy, collegial company filled with diverse, fun, active people. And Karter, who hopes to grow her Web-driven direct-to-consumer division by 50% this year, most definitely thinks that makes a difference to customers. The proof: orders typically quadruple for a day or two right after the newsletter lands in customers' e-mailboxes.

While some of Karter's efforts may seem over the top, consider that she hopes to grow Dancing Deer into a $20 million company by 2008; she's shooting for $9 million by FY 06. The first half of FY 05, which ended in December 2004, was promising; sales were up 27% and EBITDA was up 65%. But to achieve her long-term goals, Karter will have to pull out all the stops. And she knows that she must continue to professionalize Dancing Deer so that sales are driven by solid strategies, and not merely by the power of her own formidable personality. On her radar screen: landing big corporate clients who will buy Dancing Deer products all year round to give away to loyal customers; beefing up sales to food service companies who buy frozen baked goods that can be inventoried; increasing direct sales to consumers via the Web; and a second facility on the West Coast if revenues spike according to plan. With such ambitious plans, it would be tempting, understandable even, for a company like Dancing Deer to gradually drift away from the principles that drove its initial success.

At several points in Dancing Deer's 10-year history, it would have been easy for Karter to build revenue and profitability by cutting corners. She might have used cheaper, artificial flavoring, cut back on her charitable donations, or laid off staff when business slowed down. All of those things would have added a temporary glow to the balance sheet, but they would have compromised the brand integrity and Dancing Deer's ability to differentiate itself going forward. And it would have made Karter miserable. "Back when I was in desperate straits," she recalls, referring to the dark days after the breakup of her marriage and business partnerships, "the things that carried me through were my instincts for what's right and ethical, and I didn't lower myself to anything less than that. And that's what enabled me— and the company—to survive."

"Market Your Brand" Tips from Dancing Deer

1. **Tap into Your Customers' Emotions.** The essence of branding is the emotional connection you make with your customers. Are you saving them time? Catering to their desire for affordable luxury? Appealing to conservatives—or contrarians? From its humble beginnings, Dancing Deer's brand spoke to consumers who were yearning for preservative-free, homemade-style baked goods with natural ingredients that they could feel good about serving to their families. The company hasn't wavered from those values, so consumers have come to trust the brand message.

2. **Choose the Right Partners.** You will be judged by the company you keep. Dancing Deer pursued Whole Foods and smaller high-end specialty stores to launch its brand because those retailers reflected the bakery's values. Consumers rely on retailers like Whole Foods and resellers like Williams-Sonoma to set a high bar for the products they offer. Establish great relationships with esteemed partners, and their sheen will rub off on your brand.

3. **Sell Your Brand to Employees.** "When people are happy, it shows in the food" has been Dancing Deer's motto for years. In its inner-city neighborhood, the company has a solid reputation for paying well, training and advancing its employees, and offering a cooperative and nontraditional work environment that's diverse, vibrant, and fun. In fact, Dancing Deer was one of just five Boston companies chosen by the *Boston Globe* to participate in a contest called the Big Gig. Young people competed for coveted internships at Staples; ad agency Hill, Holiday; radio station KISS 108; television station WB56; and Dancing Deer.

4. **Publicize the Brand.** Karter is a public relations maven. Last fall, she even asked her assistant to track down a police officer who had given her a traffic ticket so that she could send him some cookies. But whether she's gathering spiritual leaders to

bless the batter for a promotional cookie or publicizing her company's "kosherization" (the process of making a business kosher), her efforts to promote Dancing Deer are always consistent with her brand identity.

5. **Brand Your Values.** More and more consumers care about good citizenship. Dancing Deer gives away 35% of revenues generated by its Sweet Home product line to the One Family initiative, which works to end homelessness in Massachusetts. While Karter's own pet causes are the arts, women's issues, and the environment, she felt that any effective cause-branding effort should relate directly to the company. "There was a natural connection between baking and home," she says.

. . . And from Others

6. **Outbrand Your Competitors.** What town really needs another pizza parlor? To Todd Parent, CEO of **Extreme Pizza** in San Francisco, that's a silly question. He turned a mom-and-pop operation into a $12 million franchise company by focusing on not one but two branding strategies that differentiated Extreme Pizza from the pack. First, he offered fresh, innovative ingredients, like hummus, toasted walnuts, baby spinach, and barbecued chicken, which gave his pizzas a trendy, gourmet patina. Secondly, he incorporated his love of extreme sports into the philosophy and design of his stores. The company, whose motto is "Life is too short for mediocrity," was one of the first sponsors of the X Games. The stores are filled with pictures of surfers, snowboarders, skiers, and mountain bikers pushing the limits of their endurance; television monitors play extreme sports videos; and patrons might park themselves on benches made of snowboards. The brand strategy must be working: Extreme Pizza now has 25 locations, and Parent is opening, on average, one new store a month.

7. **Respond to Customer Demographic Changes.** Harley-Davidson has had bad-boy cult appeal for years. Think James Dean and Elvis. But now the iconic motorcycle company has a new kind of

consumer—affluent, aging baby boomers longing for a ride on the wild side. So Harley dealers, like **Mike's Famous Harley-Davidson** (see chapter 9), are making sure the brand is responding to the needs of this new market. At Mike's, an on-site restaurant, museum, and glove-clean restrooms appeal to families with kids. And along with the leather jackets and boots, you'll also find Harley-branded baby clothes.

8. **Guerrilla Market Your Brand.** Several years ago, Bret Lamperes, CEO of Fort Collins, Colorado–based **Dandelion Moving & Storage,** expanded his tiny company into the nearby town of Greeley with just $2,000 earmarked for marketing. "We had no market presence there, and people thought we were crazy," says Lamperes. So he dispatched four trucks, all sporting Dandelion's distinctive flower logo, to the north and west of town. Drivers were instructed to spend all day on the road, crisscrossing the city as many times as possible. The trucks were empty, but Greeley's residents had no way of knowing that. "People started calling us up and saying, 'You must be the busiest moving company around because we're seeing your truck all over the city,' " recalls Lamperes. He stayed in budget, and the new office broke even within two months.

9. **Brand Your Culture. Southwest Airlines** customers love the cheap fares, but they also genuinely enjoy doing business with a company with such a distinctive culture. Chairman Herb Kelleher created a corporate culture based on fun that borders on zaniness, teamwork, value, and great service. The result: the airline gets consistently high marks for top-quality customer service, for being a great place to work, and for being a good corporate citizen. Southwest also has 32 consecutive years of profitability under its belt.

10. **Be the Contrarian Brand.** "We made Bills better by not changing a thing" is the company motto at **Bills Khakis.** CEO Bill Thomas started the company in 1990 because he couldn't find a replacement for his favorite pair of World War II khakis. The world of men's pants had become, well, trendy, and Thomas didn't like that one bit. "The world changes every day," he

poses, "but there are things that are worth preserving—things that are good and reliable." So Thomas used his World War II khakis as a model, signed on only U.S. manufacturing firms to make them, and sold them to high-end independent clothiers. The pants, which are now also available in Nordstrom, sell for about $100. "I would describe us as a cult brand," says Thomas. While the company's product line is spare—mostly plain-front and pleated pants in regular and full fit—Bills is now a $7.5 million company. Thomas's brand strategy is ridiculously simple: "Once a guy gets into a pair of khakis he loves, he just wants to go back and get them again. He doesn't want you to move his cheese."

8 | Build a Village

PRConsultants Group founders Barb Harris, Solveig Thorsrud-Allen, and Marisa Vallbona-Freeman (second from right) with Dallas anchorwoman Gloria Campos (center) and PRCG member Lisa Faulkner-Dunne (far right). Photograph: Julie Dennehy

Company: PRConsultants Group, Inc.

Business: Alliance of 34 independent public relations firms

Location: Nationwide

Revenues: $5 million to $8 million, collectively

Founders: Marisa Vallbona-Freeman (president of CIM Incorporated), Solveig Thorsrud-Allen (president of The Firm Public Relations & Marketing), Barb Harris (president of teamworks public relations & marketing communications)

Year Founded: 2000

Web Site: www.prconsultantsgroup.com

Alpha Dog Credentials:

PRConsultants Group is a formal alliance of small public relations companies and solo public relations practitioners. Each retains its independence, yet the group leverages its combined expertise and contacts to land and serve clients that would have been out of reach for any one of them working alone.

Marisa Vallbona-Freeman typically rises at 5:30 a.m. and sips the cup of green tea with cream delivered to her by her husband, Roger Freeman, while she reads the *Wall Street Journal* and two local San Diego newspapers. She then reviews East Coast e-mails before driving ten-year-old Timothy to a before-school program at the La Jolla YMCA.

On the days she isn't marathon training (which means she'll run anywhere from three to ten miles along the coast), she'll stay at the Y to swim laps, spin, or lift weights. Back at her home office, a room wedged between her bedroom and the family fun room, she'll get in a solid few hours of work before she needs to run out to collect Timothy and 15-year-old Donald at school. Once in a while, she can't avoid a client conference call during pickup time, so she listens in with her cell phone on mute while her boys and their noisy pals pile into her Mercedes sedan. Then it's back to her desk until dinnertime. Such is the life of a home-based soloist.

"It's a great life," says the 41-year-old Vallbona-Freeman, a petite, meticulously coifed blonde who could pass for a young Joan Rivers. But when you hear her talk about her day, you find yourself assuming that this 20-year veteran of the public relations industry must have paid a steep price for the balance she seems to have achieved. How can she possibly serve high-paying clients on her own? Wouldn't she make more money and enjoy more prestige if she had a "real" company?

Don't be fooled. Vallbona-Freeman is a high wage earner with companies like Blockbuster, Inc., Union Bank of California, and 7-Eleven, Inc., on her client roster; she's been on teams that have won three Silver Anvil Awards (the Oscar of the public relations world), and she's got a slew of local business and public relations awards to her credit. But although she's a soloist, she didn't achieve all that on her own. She's had a little help from her friends.

Vallbona-Freeman is a co-founder, along with Solveig Thorsrud-Allen in Las Vegas and Barb Harris in Phoenix, of PRConsultants Group (PRCG), a network of 34 independent public relations consultants (PRCs) whose collective reach extends to every state. Many, like Vallbona-Freeman, are soloists, but some, such as Thorsrud-Allen, also have a handful of employees. Members of the group, all of whom have had at least 15 years of public relations experience with large agencies or with corporations, were originally assembled in 1992 by a client, Karen Raskopf, who then worked with 7-Eleven. Seven years later, the network took on a life of its own when the three founders formed PRCG.

The companies work with one another on national accounts; the person who lands the account acts as the manager du jour by providing the client with a single point of contact and hiring other PRCs as needed. PRCG members might work directly for a client, such as Blockbuster, or act as subcontractors to larger public relations companies that need broader reach. For instance, the group worked for Irvine, California–based PainePR, a public relations firm with 50 full-time employees, to help launch XM Satellite Radio in 2001. The campaign won the coveted Best of Silver Anvil Award from the Public Relations Society of America. "They're a seamlessly integrated extension of our team, and they're an asset when it comes to pitching business," says PainePR president Daryl McCullough. "We think the world of many of them."

For network members, 26 of whom are women, the affiliation typically yields increased revenues, lower overhead, a steadier flow of work, and the less quantifiable benefit of having 33 other trusted colleagues who are just a phone call or an e-mail away. "People ask me if it drives me crazy to work alone," says co-founder Barb Harris. "But I don't feel like I'm alone—I've got four of our PRCs [public relations consultants] on instant messaging."

Network Power

Networks and alliances such as PRCG are an increasingly popular tool among entrepreneurial companies that want to stay small but occasionally need to look and act big. And why not? By banding together to secure a marketplace advantage, they're merely following the examples of their behemoth brethren. Consider that in the years when Vallbona-Freeman and her partners were beginning to formalize their network—1999 and 2000—there were $2.8 trillion in mergers and acquisitions. But most entrepreneurs don't play the traditional consolidation game.

Typically, small business alliances find ways for their member companies to come together to achieve specific goals while maintaining the independent ownership they value so deeply. Call it virtual M & A. "There's been a wonderful increase in the number of small businesses being able to link up with each other to serve big companies," says Jessica Lipnack, co-author with Jeffrey Stamps, PhD, of *Virtual Teams: People Working Across Boundaries with Technology*. "Incredible things are happening on the Web; freelancers are working together in ways that they never could before. What's rare now is to find people still working on their own."

But networks and alliances were around long before the Internet. Take, for example, Harry Brown, an Erie, Pennsylvania, entrepreneur whose name is known to anyone who is even vaguely interested in networks. Back in 1986, Brown bought Erie Bolt Corporation (which he renamed EBC Industries), the kind of old-economy, rust-belt company that we've all come to think of as obsolete. But Brown was convinced that even a lowly manufacturer of industrial fasteners could thrive if it partnered selectively with neighboring small companies that could provide complementary skills and resources.

Ultimately, he assembled 50 or so companies in Pennsylvania, New York, and Ohio, and created one of the most successful flexible manufacturing networks in the country. Some members are even competitors, but they market their combined capabilities to big companies, use one another's sales representatives, and recommend each other to customers. And they still compete when that makes sense. EBC, says Brown, is now a $9 million company—twice the size it was in 1986. "If you look at the last two years, especially after 9-11, without having the flexibility of the alliance, we probably would not have survived," says Brown. "But in fact, during that period, we were able to add equipment and maintain our customer base so that when the economy picked up, we were ready to go again." Sometimes, it really does take a village to build—and sustain—a company.

Manufacturing companies like Brown's pioneered the concept of alliances largely as a survival tool. Big clients were beginning to cut back on their number of vendors, seeking out subcontractors with broad capabilities. Smaller manufacturers just couldn't meet those demands on their own, so they gathered together like the Lilliputians, whose collective strength and spirit of cooperation ultimately earned Gulliver's attention and respect.

But while alliances may be born out of need, good ones almost always go on the offensive. For instance, in "The Declaration of Independents," a September 2001 *Inc.* magazine cover story, author Susan Greco profiled a Phoenix-based alliance of 115 independent dry-wall contractors, who use their combined purchasing power to nail down competitive pricing on goods and services, as well as to buy health insurance; a Louisville, Kentucky, group of independent insurance agents that aggregates premiums for its members and offers mentorship and technology training; a cooperative group of funeral homes in New Jersey that pools their resources to create a collective human resources department; and the Independent Booksellers Consortium, a nationwide group of 25 bookstore owners who buy products collectively at discounted prices and give one another advice on best business practices. Whatever their raison d'être, alliances not only give muscle and staying power to small businesses that might otherwise be steamrollered by larger competitors, but they provide those businesses with an innovative path to growth and prosperity.

That doesn't mean they're easy to manage, though. The prospect of sharing information—and sometimes clients—can make even the most forward-thinking entrepreneur feel protective and vulnerable. It's risky business to disclose your most effective business strategy or reveal your most vexing weakness to someone who has the power to use that information against you. But entrepreneurs who are sold on alliances will tell you that it's riskier still to remain an island in a sea of fierce competitors. There's safety in numbers; little fish swimming together can often outsmart the big ones. As Vallbona-Freeman and her colleagues will tell you, it all boils down to trust—and a very solid set of operating principles.

Who's the Champion?

Every network needs a champion—someone who first steps up to the plate to assemble a group, then acts as a referee to make sure everyone plays fair. For PRCG, that person was Karen Raskopf, who, as a publicity manager for 7-Eleven in 1992, took a rather unconventional approach to her job and unwittingly breathed life into the network. "7-Eleven was trying to revamp its image," recalls Raskopf, whom one PRCG member described as a "five-foot-one human dynamo." "They wanted people to know that it wasn't just beef jerky and beer—that the stores carried healthy products with good prices." The campaign, called "The Comedians," featured television commercials in which up-and-coming stand-up comics, such as Brett Butler, made fun of the old 7-Eleven, then touted the company's new image.

Raskopf wanted her public relations efforts to include more than just press releases about the commercials, and she knew she didn't want a large firm to handle the job. "I have typically found that they would send in their big guns to make the pitch, but when it came to doing the actual work, you'd get the guy straight out of college," she says. She wanted experienced, senior-level people with local roots, so she proposed a big-company alternative to her boss, Jim Notarnicola. "I went to him and said, 'Let's target a handful of key markets and hire local public relations people who know the local media and can work with local radio stations to do promotions. I really think I can show you that it will have more impact than hiring a large agency. Let me start off with six.' "

Notarnicola agreed and Raskopf pulled out her Public Relations Society of America (PRSA) handbook and began calling members who were clearly soloists. "I wanted people who had at least 10 years of experience, who had worked in big agencies, and who had lived in their communities for a while," recalls Raskopf. "And I wanted to like them." With help from Lisa Faulkner-Dunne, a Dallas solo public relations practitioner who was already doing work for 7-Eleven, Raskopf narrowed down her prospects and ultimately signed on Vallbona-Freeman in San Diego, Thorsrud-Allen in Las Vegas, Toni Antonetti in Chicago,

Bob Schiers in Hainesport, New Jersey, Linda Little in Denver, and Susan Hamburg in Orlando. "I had one meeting with them, and two months later FedEx rang the doorbell and the contract was on my doorstep," recalls Vallbona-Freeman. For all of them, the 7-Eleven account dropped out of the sky like pennies from heaven—a gift that turned out to be more valuable than any of them could have predicted.

"Over the course of a year, we grew from five markets to twenty," recalls Raskopf. "The campaign worked so well that the marketing people kept giving me money, and that's really unusual." Raskopf never met most of the consultants, but she introduced them to one another via conference calls, where she'd lay out 7-Eleven's objectives in particular markets. "At first, you could tell that they held back," she says. "And then they got more comfortable, and they'd call each other after the conference call." And as Raskopf brought on new consultants, many of them recommended by her core group, she'd typically ask a veteran to mentor a newbie. She was creating a tightly knit community. "We began asking each other about business issues," says Vallbona-Freeman. "And when clients other than 7-Eleven needed help, we would recommend each other."

By 1997, the group was working so effectively for Raskopf that she was lured away from 7-Eleven by her former boss, Notarnicola, who had by then moved to Blockbuster. "He called me up and said, 'Come here and do what you did with the PR consultants at 7-Eleven.' I got promoted at 7-Eleven and I got my job here at Blockbuster because of the network," says Raskopf. "It wasn't just a press release machine; they became part of the fiber of who we were."

So while the network members continued to work for 7-Eleven, they put their collective creativity and PR savvy to work for Blockbuster as well. Bob Schiers, owner of RAS Associates in Hainesport, New Jersey, commissioned a giant ice sculpture of the *Titanic* to promote the movie's video release. And in Milwaukee, Brian Knox of Zeppos & Associates, booked three skydivers dressed as characters from *Austin Powers, The Spy Who Shagged Me* to parachute onto a square of green shag carpeting in a Blockbuster parking lot. There were also Spider-Man promotions with costumed characters rappelling down buildings and wielding "web shooters"; Harry Potter parties with local magicians and broomstick-riding contests; Pokémon events where parents and kids did the Hokey Pokey Pokémon. Raskopf was thrilled. "They went crazy," she says.

Formalizing the Network

In April 1999, Marisa Vallbona-Freeman and Solveig Thorsrud-Allen, who had worked together on the Blockbuster and 7-Eleven accounts for years, had their second face-to-face meeting at an industry conference in Tucson. A few years earlier, they had met in San Diego, where they had first discussed turning their client-driven network into an independent entity. "I was noticing a trend," recalls Thorsrud-Allen. "Clients were needing more and more work done nationally, and they wanted people on the ground to make events happen. So I saw the network as a really good resource."

It wasn't a new idea. Public relations networks such as the Worldcom Public Relations Group, Pinnacle Worldwide, and IPREX had been up and running for years. But for the most part, those organizations were made up of larger public relations companies, and their reach spanned the globe. Smaller networks were emerging as well, but many of them were comprised of freelancers who were between jobs or younger professionals just starting out; they seemed to lack structure or purpose.

What Vallbona-Freeman and Thorsrud-Allen had in mind was fundamentally different. "We didn't want to be a big formal network," says Vallbona-Freeman. "We wanted to offer power to the little guy." Their existing network was made up entirely of little guys, but they were all professionals who had paid their dues in the corporate world and had made a conscious choice to go it alone. And while few of them had actually met one another face-to-face, they were an intimate group who understood one another's capabilities. That combination would provide potential clients with the kind of senior-level counsel that so often eluded them at bigger firms, as well as the ability to reach multiple markets via a highly organized group of people with strong local ties and a national reach.

As appealing as the idea was, the more Thorsrud-Allen and Vallbona-Freeman talked, the more they realized that organizing the group would be an enormous job. "At the time, I had just had my second child, and I thought, 'I'd like to do this, but I just can't handle it right now,' " recalls Vallbona-Freeman. "We decided we really needed a third person to help us organize the network, so we just let it slide."

But the idea came up again in Tucson, and this time it took flight. Vallbona-Freeman and Thorsrud-Allen invited the network's Tucson consultant, Barb Harris, to meet them at their hotel. The three gathered for drinks, hit it off immediately, and under the palm trees on the patio of the the Westin La Paloma Resort & Spa, Vallbona-Freeman and Thorsrud-Allen enlisted Harris's help. The three stayed up until midnight, using cocktail napkins to sketch out plans for a Web site and to jot down the criteria they thought were most important for network members.

The first hurdle: "We wanted to like them," says Vallbona-Freeman. They also wanted everyone to have a minimum of 10 years traditional public relations experience and a highly professional image. "We didn't want to hear their dog in the background during a conference call with Blockbuster," says Vallbona-Freeman.

Ego came into play as well, since a network member might be a team leader for one project and a minor player on another, depending on who brought the client to the table and what markets were being targeted. "They were all used to running their own shows," says Vallbona-Freeman, "but they had to be willing to relinquish control." It was important, however, that network members retain as much independence as possible. For instance, they wouldn't be asked to disclose financial information, nor would they be required to use other network consultants if they didn't want to. And they'd never be compelled to work for clients with whom they felt uncomfortable.

As for the founders' roles, they agreed to take turns running the network, with each playing the key administrative role for four months at a time. If a major decision was on the table and all three were not available, two were free to act on their own. They agreed to set up the network as a not-for-profit entity, which would collect dues ("Less than $1,000 a year," says Vallbona-Freeman) from its members to cover the cost of a Web site, advertising, and any network-related business travel. But no client fees would pass through the network; while members would work together on projects, each would be responsible for billing clients, contracting work out to others, and negotiating fees.

With the ground rules laid out, Vallbona-Freeman, Thorsrud-Allen, and Harris decided to extend 27 invitations to join their new network, which they christened PRConsultants Group (not all of the consultants assembled by Raskopf were included). By July of the following year, the original group of 30, including the three founders, was up and running. Karen Raskopf gave them her blessing. "I thought it was great when they decided to formalize," she says. "I told them, 'As long as you guys are giving me the service I want, go for it.' "

Putting the Network to the Test

Just a few months after PRCG was formed, the group landed its first major client. Barb Harris got a call from a business associate who worked for an events planning company that specialized in traveling exhibit trucks. Barnes & Noble had signed the company to manage a nationwide tour of a traveling interactive truck that featured Web-based technology to promote Barnes & Noble's online store, barnes andnoble.com. "We had worked with her in the past for Blockbuster," recalls Harris. "She thought we would be perfect for bn.com so they could get local market coverage for their traveling exhibit."

So Harris and Sharon Kreher, her business partner in St. Louis, pitched the network to Barnes & Noble executives and landed the account. For nine months, Harris coordinated publicity events in 29 markets, served as the liaison with Barnes & Noble, and handled all billing. She managed the network much as Raskopf did for Blockbuster. "This was a literacy initiative–book drive," says Harris, "and many of our consultants had contact with local literacy groups and, because so many of us are parents, with schools and groups of kids. That local touch really warmed up the events and made them hometown events, not just something directed from New York."

The project was PRCG's first official gig, and it gave the partners a reality check on the intricacies of managing a network. It was a task that would take more time and effort than they originally anticipated. "The first two years, we were spending 20% to 30% of our time just on administration," recalls Vallbona-Freeman. They had to iron out turf issues, coordinate the logistics for multicity events and campaigns, and cope with unexpected legal problems. At one point, a woman in Colorado became so intrigued with the idea of a public relations alliance that she formed her own and registered a URL that was suspiciously similar to PRCG's. "She even had the nerve to go after some of our members," says Vallbona-Freeman. "So Barb and I hired an attorney in San Diego and filed cease-and-desist papers against her." The legal action cost several thousand dollars, which came out of PRCG's bank account.

The Payoff

Five years after its formal conception, PRCG is still going strong; 28 out of the 34 current members have been with the group since its inception. Over the years, they've become intimately familiar with one another's strengths and weaknesses, often forming tightly knit satellite groups within the larger group but remaining flexible enough to enlist help from others in the network.

For many of them, those relationships have been extraordinarily fruitful, both financially and strategically. Boston PRC Julie Dennehy, who succeeded Thorsrud-Allen as a managing partner in December 2004, says that more than half of her billings now come from PRCG work. "I've grown sales 40% since joining the network, and my profitability has increased 40% because we're getting bigger and better projects," she says. While the members are sensitive about income figures, Vallbona-Freeman estimates that the majority of soloists in the network make six-figure incomes, while larger firms with a few employees are posting revenues in the low millions. "Almost everyone has nearly doubled their income," she says. The network's benefits include:

Playing on a Bigger Field

New Orleans PRC John Deveney says his network affiliation has enabled him to take on national work from at least two major clients in the past five years—the Pharmaceutical Research and Manufacturers of America (PhRMA), which represents major pharmaceutical companies, and Oceana, an environmental advocacy nonprofit organization. Deveney had been working for PhRMA for less than a year when the client asked him to take on more territory. "It was an easy decision," says Deveney. "I knew we could do it because of the network." For the past two years, he's been subcontracting to as many as 30 PRCs to get national media coverage for information on new drugs, the industry's response to state of the union addresses, and health issues affecting minorities.

For Oceana, he's used 18 PRCs to help the organization put pressure on the cruise ship industry to use the best available technology to treat waste on their ships. In 2003 and 2004, he paid out more than $500,000 to network members who have helped on those accounts and others. "It taps me into a national network of expertise that is really unparalleled," he says. "It's a very generous fraternity."

Omaha-based Deborah J. Trivitt, who works regularly for Deveney on the PhRMA account, may have an opportunity to return the favor this year. She's been working with an Omaha start-up called HDC 4Point Dynamics to publicize the company's new emergency medical smart card, which allows patients to carry their personal health history on what looks like a credit card. According to HDC sales manager Keith Clark, 10,000 of the cards, along with the proprietary software needed to read them, are currently being used by several Nebraska hospitals and ambulance and rescue companies, but the technology has attracted national attention.

"We've already been contacted by 35 states and several foreign countries," says Clark. In 2005, he says, the company plans a national rollout of the product in 22 different sales territories, and Trivitt, with help from the PRCG network, will lead the publicity charge. "We considered a larger firm," he says, "but we like the hands-on regional closeness of Deb's network. They're specialists on their own turf, and they're all seasoned professionals." Trivitt will be the lead consultant on the account, providing HDC with a single point of contact while she farms out the work as needed. "It's a company with huge potential, and I never would have gotten the business without the network," she says. "I may have to expand into the second bedroom." Many PRCs, in fact, work out of home offices and can continue to do so even as their revenues grow.

Growth Without Overhead

"Even in the early stages, I realized what a powerful group of people we were, both individually and as a group," says Margaret Nathan, a Park City, Utah, consultant who runs her business with her husband, Kevin Kruke. Nathan was part of the original Blockbuster group and began using others in the network even before it was formalized.

Back in 1996, she had been hired by Norwalk, Connecticut-based Labatt USA, now InBev USA, after a September 2004 merger with Beck's North America; the company is a subsidiary of the Belgian company InBev. Labatt asked Nathan to help the company hire a public relations firm, but, she recalls, "at one point, the vice president of marketing said to me, 'We love the way you think, so would you take on our business?' " Nathan demurred at first, but ultimately took on the business and immediately started enlisting her colleagues' help. "I picked up Julie Dennehy out of Boston, Susan Hamburg in Orlando, Melissa Libby in Atlanta, and Jack Maddigan in Pittsburgh," she recalls. "We used network members to build a senior-level public relations firm specifically for Labatt USA."

Nathan still has the account, and she uses up to 10 PRCG members to help her in local markets. InBev gives her a budget, and her company, Strategic Communication, Inc., pays the PRCs as subcontractors, negotiating rates with each of them confidentially. One of the network's most important tenets is that consultants don't compare fees with one another; typically, they sign confidentiality agreements. "The network allows me to have people in the field without having to build a huge base of employees, so it keeps my overhead down by

100%," says Nathan. It also allows her to serve her clients quickly and more effectively.

Two years ago, for instance, there was legislation in the works to change the container law in Florida—a law that, if passed, would have allowed InBev broader distribution of its Stella Artois beer. So Utah-based Nathan alerted Orlando-based Susan Hamburg, who contacted the National Association of Beer Importers to help get press in Florida. "Susan knew the beer industry really well by then," says Nathan. As it turned out, the legislation passed, despite grumbling from the domestic beer industry.

Nathan's experience is fairly typical. Stacia Kirby, who is based in Seattle, landed a job with the Alaska Seafood Marketing Institute to promote the health benefits of Alaska salmon and used PRCG consultants in 19 different markets. "They did a better job in their individual markets than I could have," says Kirby. "So for the client, I was able to deliver much better results."

New Business from Out of the Blue

Clearly, it's great to be on the receiving end as well. The consultants that Kirby hired had business handed to them without having to spend time and money on marketing and new business development. And that's exactly what happened with XM Satellite Radio, which in 2001 was searching for public relations counsel to help publicize the September launch of its new product.

Twenty public relations firms competed for the coveted XM account, and it was finally awarded to Irvine, California–based PainePR. President Daryl McCullough, who had worked with PRCG consultants for years on the Blockbuster account, had pitched the network as "an extension of our team." That sounded good to Melissa Andrews, who was the senior communications consultant at Washington, DC–based XM at the time of the company's official launch. "I chose Paine based on their entire capability, and PRConsultants Group was a very critical part of that," says Andrews, who is president of her own communications firm, the Andrews Group. It turned out to be a fortuitous decision.

The advertising campaign for the XM launch was developed by

creative powerhouse TBWA\Chiat\Day, an agency known for its unconventional thinking. They didn't disappoint. The broadcast ads featured musical celebrities like David Bowie, B.B. King, and Snoop Dogg, falling from the sky with musical instruments and bursting into people's lives at home, in the office, and on the highway. It was a sleek campaign that XM planned to combine with national press outreach in Dallas, San Diego, and Washington, DC, on the day of the launch, September 12, 2001. Press reports estimated XM's budget for the campaign at $100 million.

But the ads, which had been running in movie theaters since August and on television since the beginning of September, were abruptly pulled off the air after the 9-11 terrorist attacks. Overnight, a campaign that had seemed so clever and edgy suddenly became jarring and inappropriate.

"I think it was the biggest challenge of our careers for all of us," recalls Melissa Andrews. "We put the launch on hold and we completely changed our plan. After 9-11, I didn't think it would be likely that we would get national press coverage, so we switched to regional and local outreach, and that's where the network came into play."

Working with McCullough and Vallbona-Freeman, Andrews made plans to cover 50 markets in 60 days—"a punishing schedule" that was arranged in just two to three weeks. There were press conferences, special events, and demonstrations of XM's product in cars outfitted with the satellite radios. Chicago consultant Toni Antonetti, for instance, covered Indianapolis, Dayton, Columbus, and Louisville, where she chauffeured local reporters in an XM-equipped Saab, maneuvering the unfamiliar stick shift through tunnels and city streets while demonstrating the radio.

"The launch was entirely PR driven since the ad campaign had been put on hold," says Andrews. "And it was hugely successful." She estimates that the launch generated 90 million media impressions, a number that's calculated using circulation figures for print media and the number of viewers and listeners for broadcast media. At XM's Washington, DC, headquarters, the walls of the lengthy hallway that runs from the employee parking lot to the main building were covered with press clippings from all over the country—a testament to

PainePR's and PRCG's dogged media outreach. "The coverage was extraordinary," says Andrews. The Public Relations Society of America (PRSA) thought so too. In the spring of 2002, the organization awarded PainePR, along with Andrews and PRConsultants Group, its Best of Silver Anvil Award.

Information Sharing

Even soloists who wouldn't dream of working any other way can become weary of the isolation that working alone imposes upon them. The Internet is an antidote, of course, for anyone willing to reach out into cyberspace to find like-minded colleagues. But for PRCG, technology is more than just a convenient way to keep in touch—it's a strategic tool that network members use to share best practices, business advice, and to avoid reinventing the wheel.

Susan Hamburg, for example, came up with a clever promotion idea for Blockbuster during the Super Bowl—a pitch to reporters for chick flicks that women could cozy up to while their men were watching the game. So she fired off an e-mail to her colleagues, sharing the idea with the entire network. What goes around comes around. Several weeks later, she received an e-mail from a network member in Ohio, with an idea for a Blockbuster holiday media pitch—a reminder to buyers of video game systems to pick up an extra controller so that Dad wouldn't be excluded from all the fun. "He'd gotten good media response from it, so he sent it out to the rest of the network for us to use," she says.

That kind of give-and-take happens almost daily. "It's tough when you're a solo practitioner because you work in a vacuum," says Toni Antonetti, the PRC in Chicago. "So we trade a lot of information, and we use the network to work faster and smarter." One consultant might write a pitch letter for a radio station promotion and send it out over the transom for her colleagues in different markets to use as well; someone who's not quite up to speed on the latest technology might enlist the brainpower of a more tech-savvy network member willing to help solve the problem remotely; or the consultants might brainstorm together via conference call to come up with creative publicity stunts for clients.

Even when they're not working together for clients, the network members call upon one another for advice. For instance, when Deb Trivitt was hired to do publicity for an Omaha shopping center, she e-mailed her colleagues for help and heard back from several, including John Deveney, who had done similar work for a number of different clients. Deveney, in turn, might turn to the network's food industry expert, Atlanta's Melissa Libby, when he's brainstorming ideas for a local steakhouse. But the network offers less tangible benefits as well. "Sometimes when I'm feeling overwhelmed—like when it's the middle of the summer and the kids are starting to drive me crazy—I can just call Stacia and know that I'm not alone," says Marisa Vallbona-Freeman.

Trouble Spots

Of course, things don't always go smoothly in a network. Entrepreneurs are independent souls by nature, and it can be tough to share a treasured possession, whether it's a client or credit for a job well done. "Where things get messy is when people stop cooperating and start competing," says network expert Jessica Lipnack. "But networks are very self-correcting. When that happens, then the network exiles that person. Without trust, you don't have anything."

While PRCG has operated relatively smoothly for the past five years, the network has had its share of growing pains. Sometimes, there's a communications breakdown, such as when a single PRC unintentionally started pitching an account against a larger agency that had already arranged to use the network. "It was just the most embarrassing situation," recalls Vallbona-Freeman. "I got a call from the PR firm, and they said, 'What the hell are you doing? One of your consultants is pitching against us!' " The unsuspecting PRC quickly bowed out. Then there was the time when an East Coast consultant tried to steal a client from a network member on the West Coast. She was found out and immediately expelled. The same goes for a Midwest consultant who breached client confidentiality. "You can have a loose cannon in the network," says Vallbona-Freeman. "For example, after we won the Silver Anvil with PainePR, one of our PRCs sent out a postcard saying that his firm had won the award, and he made no mention of PainePR. It created such a problem that we ended up asking him to leave the network."

Incidents like that are few and far between, but when they do occur, the partners act swiftly and decisively to nip conflict in the bud. The best way to prevent discord is open communication and guidelines that are made clear up front. "There were some territorial boundary issues," says New Jersey–based Bob Schiers, who has grown his business from three to six employees on network projects. "For example, I cover Philadelphia and the tristate area, and I used to handle Pittsburgh. Now, though, we have a Pittsburgh PRC, but when he came on, the agreement was that I would continue to handle my long-term client in Pittsburgh and hands off. That kind of thing happened all around the country."

Another effective way to avoid conflict is to give network members as much flexibility as possible. PRCG's consultants aren't ever compelled to take jobs that they feel are either beyond their expertise or that grate against their personal values. "For instance," says John Deveney in New Orleans, "if you were a PRC and you said to me, 'I really need to do some outdoor advertising in your market,' I don't do that, but I'd tell you where to go."

Marisa Vallbona-Freeman, who is politically conservative, tends to stay away from projects that smack of liberal causes, and she also refuses to promote the gaming industry. So if Las Vegas–based Solveig Thorsrud-Allen has a casino client who needs public relations work in San Diego, Vallbona-Freeman will pass, but she'll help Thorsrud-Allen find someone else to do the job. Harris, who is less conservative in her social and political views, started doing work on a big corporate account run by another PRC but says she "stepped down because I didn't feel comfortable" with the client's message. "I can only promote and do media relations for something I believe in," she says.

With 34 people in the network, such differences of opinion are inevitable, and within a less professional group, they might be a serious impediment to delivering high-quality results to clients. But PRCG's diversity is also its strength; the network can split up into smaller like-minded groups that come together to serve specific client needs, then break apart to move on to the next project.

The Network Grows Up

In 2003, Vallbona-Freeman, Thorsrud-Allen, and Harris began hearing from several PRCs that they were champing at the bit for face-to-face meetings with their fellow network members. It seemed like a natural next step, so the founders organized their first conference, held in Dallas in February 2004 and hosted by PRC Lisa Faulkner-Dunne. "That first national meeting really pulled things together," says Bob Schiers. "We're now functioning more collectively." For many, it further solidified the relationships they had been building for years.

Margaret Nathan, for example, met Vallbona-Freeman for the first time in Dallas and is now confident that she's the right person to bring on board for a new product rollout she'll be working on in the coming months. "Now that I've met her, I know that the client will love her," says Nathan.

In January 2005, the group held its second conference on John Deveney's home turf in New Orleans. They kicked off the gathering on his apartment's wraparound gallery, where they had a great view of the Krewe du Vieux Mardi Gras parade—a colorful introduction to life in the Big Easy. For the next three days, however, they got down to business. They organized workshops on marketing the network, gave one another updates on new technology, and discussed operational issues, like how to handle clients who won't pay. And Boston-based PRC Julie Dennehy taught her colleagues a new method for creative brainstorming.

"Everyone decided that we definitely need to do this once a year," says Vallbona-Freeman. The meetings, which the PRCs will take turns hosting, give the consultants face time with one another, but they also provide a venue for serious strategic planning. In 2005, for instance, each PRC came away from the meeting with a hit list of public relations firms, advertising companies, corporations, and radio stations to pitch in their local markets. "We've got FedEx, JCPenney, Xbox, Aveda,

JetBlue, Quiznos," says Vallbona-Freeman, rattling off just a few of the companies that the network will pitch. "We're such a diverse group— we can do anything."

But even as the network moves on to the next level of sophistication, it remains true to its origins. "I'm surprised after all these years they haven't gotten tired," says Blockbuster's Karen Raskopf. In December 2004, when Blockbuster announced that it would no longer charge late fees for video rentals, PRCG was asked to help get the word out. Thirty network members organized New Year's Eve promotions to give away gift baskets to the second baby born in each of 40 Blockbuster markets because "it's okay to be a little late." The baskets, valued at approximately $1,000 each, included goodies like DVD players, baby clothes and paraphernalia, a red wagon, movies, and free Blockbuster rentals for a year.

"Logistically, it was a nightmare," recalls Vallbona-Freeman. "We had to call the media on New Year's Eve, and then we were up all night, calling hospitals and waiting for babies to be born." It paid off, though. The baby stunt generated nationwide publicity, including a mention on CNN. "Absolutely, we could not have done the second-baby promotion without them," says Karen Raskopf. "Usually, if you stay with an agency this long, things start getting stale," she says of PRCG. "But they still approach everything as if it's fresh and new."

"Build a Village" Tips from PRConsultants Group

1. **Appoint a Leader or Leaders.** Whether you're putting together a formal alliance or merely forming a network of companies for a one-time project, someone has to be in charge. An alliance without a leader is a recipe for chaos. Consider rotating the leadership role periodically among a limited group of participants.

2. **Articulate Purpose and Principles.** Be clear about what your alliance will accomplish. Is the goal to increase revenues and/or lower overhead? Give members access to a diverse range of expertise? Beef up your roster with more impressive clients? How are territories divided up? Are members permitted to compete with one another outside the network? What happens when there's a breach of trust? How is information shared? Are members required to farm out work only to other members, or can they go outside the network? Make sure everyone knows the rules of engagement from the outset.

3. **Choose Members Carefully.** It'll be easier to market your alliance to potential customers if you can rattle off a set of criteria that apply to all of your members. At PRCG, for example, everyone has at least 15 years of industry experience, a stint at a large company, and solid ties to the community. And don't underrate your initial personal impression of prospective members: these are people who have the potential to make or break your own business, so you must like and trust them.

4. **Designate Project Managers.** Customers typically want one point of contact with a vendor. So even if you've landed business using your network's joint capabilities, assign just one lead person to serve as the customer's liaison and to coordinate network members.

5. **Demand Loyalty.** Take a no-tolerance approach to breaches of trust. If a network member unintentionally steps on the toes of another, cut her some slack. But an offender who, say,

poaches another member's customer, should be voted off the island for good.

. . . And from Others

6.   **Leverage Combined Purchasing Power.** Ten years ago, David Bolduc, owner of **Boulder Book Store,** helped start the Independent Booksellers Consortium, a group of approximately 25 nationwide independent book stores. The group gathers three times a year to exchange ideas and business advice, often bringing in outside speakers from publishing companies. The group also leverages its combined buying power. "We've bought wrapping paper and bags together to get better rates from vendors," says Bolduc. "And we just negotiated a better rate with American Express."

7.   **Befriend Your Competitors.** Sometimes you've got to cooperate to compete. In 2004, ten Maine boat-building companies joined together to form **Maine Built Boats Organization** (MBBO) to jointly promote their industry. "We will have a Maine presence at major national and international boat shows . . . bring designers and journalists into the state and provide tours of yards, and develop a Maine-built boat brand image," says Steve VonVogt, manager of special projects at Hodgdon Yachts, an MBBO member. The goal: to convince wealthy East Coast customers who might be tempted to buy their boats abroad that Maine builders offer superior quality and craftsmanship.

8.   **Employ a Network of Freelancers.** Cheryl Osborn, owner of **Casco Contractors** in Irvine, California, has eight full-time employees, but she credits five regular freelancers with a significant percentage of her growth. Osborn, who provides architecture, engineering, construction, and construction management services to commercial clients, has steady relationships with five women—all moms with young children, who are also architects and designers. "People let me know what their schedules are and when they're going on vacation," says Osborn. "And if we need them, they work, and if we don't,

they play with their kids." The arrangement has allowed her to keep her overhead low and to pass on those savings to customers. "I'm competing with standard design firms," she says, "and I'm told all the time that my clients save upward of 60% by working with us."

9. **Form a Peer Group.** "We have 190 locations, sell 2.5 million tires a year, employ 2,000 people, and have revenues of $275 million," says Barry Steinberg, CEO of **Direct Tire & Auto Service.** But here's the catch: Steinberg isn't talking about his own business, but rather a nationwide group of 14 independent companies that calls itself the National Retail Tire Network. Steinberg and Craig Sumerel, owner of **Bob Sumerel Tire & Service** in Cincinnati, Ohio, founded the network about five years ago. The purpose: to meet three times a year to share information in a no-holds-barred, feet-to-the-fire forum where everyone comes away with fresh new ideas to bring home to their own companies. The group's geographic diversity means that members can share information—even financials—without worrying that the disclosure will come back to bite them.

10. **Pool Administrative Resources.** No one relishes spending time on back-office administrative tasks. **Thanexus, Inc.,** a Wall Township, New Jersey, cooperative of over 60 small independent New Jersey funeral homes, helps ease that pain for its members, who each hold stock in the co-op but operate as separate entities. Thanexus runs its members' human resources departments, offers marketing and training support, and provides insurance and risk management services.

9 | Embrace Reinvention

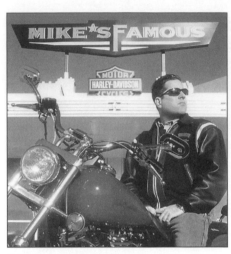

Mike Schwartz on a low-rider.

Company: Mike's Famous Harley-Davidson, Inc.

Business: Harley-Davidson dealership

Location: New Castle, Delaware; Smyrna, Delaware; Groton, Connecticut

Revenues: $47.8 million

Employees: 196 full-time; 80 part-time

Founder: Mike Schwartz

Year Founded: 1994

Web Site: www.mikesfamous.com

Alpha Dog Credentials:

Mike Schwartz bought a lackluster Harley-Davidson dealership on the wrong side of the tracks and transformed it into a major roadside attraction. But reinventing his business just once wasn't enough; to keep several steps ahead of his competition, he does it every day. In 2004, his New Castle, Delaware, facility sold more new Harley motorcycles than any other U.S. Harley dealership.

Spend a few hours at Mike's Famous Harley-Davidson dealership in New Castle, Delaware, and chances are you will witness someone's moment of consummate joy. You'll be wandering around the massive, warehouse-like building, constructed in the late 1990s with reclaimed brick, pine floors, and antique factory fittings. You might be admiring the supple leather jackets or running your covetous hand along the gleaming fuel tank of a Sportster while grooving to the classic rock that plays constantly in the background on Mike's Famous Radio. And then you'll hear the riotous clanging of a bell. Mike's salespeople, clean-shaven and dressed in chambray shirts and blue jeans, will whoop and give one another high fives; the mechanics will lay down their wrenches for a moment; and browsing customers will applaud and grin broadly and maybe even dream a little about the day the bell might ring for them. Someone has just bought a Harley, and the good vibes reverberate like the revving engine of a Fat Boy. The bell rings more than 1,700 times a year, which makes Mike's Famous one of the largest Harley dealers in the world. The average dealer sells 400 to 500 bikes a year. And that makes CEO Mike Schwartz very happy—but not complacent. He remembers too well what his business looked like 10 years ago.

Ever since Schwartz acquired a run-down Harley dealership in 1994, he has been incessantly restless. For an entrepreneur, that's a good thing. In "The Quest for Resilience," a September 2003 *Harvard Business Review* article by Gary Hamel and Liisa Välikangas, the authors argue that in an increasingly turbulent world, the continued success of businesses relies on resilience, or "the ability to dynamically reinvent business models and strategies as circumstances change . . . The goal is a strategy that is forever morphing, forever conforming itself to emerging opportunities and incipient trends."

The changing demographics and emerging industry trends that Schwartz saw coming down the road made him realize that his small business could either hunker down and run with the pack or break out and lead it. He chose the latter. But that meant that he would need to "morph," not just once but continually. He turned a hole-in-the-wall dealership into a major tourist attraction, professionalized his company, scrapped programs that didn't work, and expanded ones that were successful. And just when he felt "done," he opted to do it all again, with a new satellite dealership in Smyrna, Delaware, and a third one in Connecticut. Schwartz lives in the future, and he reinvents his company according to the landscape he envisions. It's what we'd expect of an Alpha Dog CEO.

Humble Beginnings

Schwartz does not project the image of a stereotypical Harley dealer or rider. He doesn't favor chains, piercings, or tattoos, and although he's at ease in black leather, he looks a lot more comfortable in jeans and a denim shirt with "Voted #1 Dealer Worldwide" embroidered above the pocket. His closely cropped hair, slightly flipped up in front, and his black-framed glasses bring to mind a 1950s soda jerk. And while he exudes self-confidence and an air of authority, he's nonetheless soft-spoken. But don't be fooled. These days, guys like Schwartz are more typical of Harley's customers than you'd think.

Schwartz grew up in the suburbs of Philadelphia and studied economics at the University of Delaware. That's when he bought his first motorcycle. It was a practical purchase, not a passionate one: he and a roommate cashed in their meal tickets to buy a $1,200 Kawasaki street-legal dirt bike to get around campus. As a young adult, Schwartz was never a motorcycle enthusiast; he was too busy thinking about how and when he'd start his own company. He worked in retail, at a small restaurant, and as a salesman of tanning beds until he built up enough knowledge and confidence to strike out on his own.

By the time he was 33, in 1992, he had founded two small and profitable companies: Apple Paging and Communications, which sold cell phones and pagers, and ABC Ticket Company, a sporting events ticket vendor. He had a wife and a son; he was successful but perhaps a little restless. And that's when he wandered into a Harley dealership in Wilmington. "There was this buzz around Harley," he recalls. "It was the intrigue that brought me there." Suddenly, he had a powerful jones for a Harley.

The dealership's neighborhood had seen better days. Northeast Boulevard, once the major traveling route between Philadelphia and

Washington, DC, suffered a rapid decline when the Interstate 95 corridor was built in the 1950s. The Harley dealership—a 29-year-old, $1.8 million business selling 153 bikes per year when Schwartz first walked through the door to buy his motorcycle—was surviving on the momentum of consistent demand for the iconic motorcycles; Schwartz was told he'd have to wait a year and a half for his $13,000 Heritage Softail cruiser, which was not an excessive lead time back then.

"Every couple of months, I'd go back there to check on the status of the bike," recalls Schwartz. And every time he returned, he'd shake his head a little. "You could tell the business hadn't changed in years," he recalls. Schwartz knew that the place was a diamond in the rough, just waiting for someone with a little business know-how to make it shine. He mulled that over for about a year, and then he finally got the word that his bike had arrived. "He came home from picking up the bike, and he told me, 'I'm going to buy that place,' " recalls his wife, Debbie, a slender, pretty blonde who sometimes helps out at the dealership. "And knowing Mike, I knew he meant business." And he did. In February 1994, he bought the dealership, which was then losing money, for $325,000. He financed the sale with earnings from his other businesses and with the dealership's current owner.

What did Schwartz see in this distressed business on the wrong side of the tracks? The roof leaked, the financials were sketchy, the employees were unmotivated, and the customers were disgruntled. But it wasn't the business he *bought* that sparked his imagination: it was the business he planned to *create*.

History Lessons

Harley-Davidson Motor Co.'s own long and colorful history was a textbook tale of reinvention. The company was founded in 1903 in a Milwaukee shed by William Harley and Arthur Davidson, whose brothers Walter and William would later join the fledgling company. Like all great entrepreneurs, they owed their success to a fortuitous combination of innovation, guts, and dumb luck.

For decades, the U.S. government was Harley's biggest customer.

Rural mail carriers rode the company's motorcycles; General John J. Pershing used one to chase the elusive revolutionary Pancho Villa; and a total of more than 100,000 Harleys were shipped to allied forces in both world wars. GIs rode them fast and furiously—a habit many found hard to break when they returned home. And so Harley, by then an American icon, also earned a bad-boy reputation. High-profile riders like Elvis, Steve McQueen, James Dean, and Marlon Brando fueled the brand's rebel image and drew in everyday consumers eager to buy into the fantasy. By 1953, says Harley-Davidson's Web site, the company was the sole U.S. motorcycle manufacturer and would remain so for 46 years. It was a nice ride, but the smooth sailing didn't last.

Cheaper and relatively high-quality Japanese imports steamrollered the company so effectively that it nearly collapsed in 1969, when it was sold to the American Machine and Foundry Co. (AMF). Back then, writes retired Harley-Davidson CEO Richard Teerlink in the July-August 2000 issue of *Harvard Business Review,* Harley "had a poor reputation for quality and reliability, and it was behind the curve on product design and development. Breakeven points were high and, not surprisingly, market share was falling . . . It's no wonder that in 1980, when AMF engaged an investment bank to sell the division, it found no takers."

Thirteen Harley executives stepped up to the plate in June 1981 and bought the company back from AMF via leveraged buyout. They walked through fire for the next few years, cutting the company's workforce by 40%, restructuring finances, tweaking product design, and struggling to restore dealers' faith in the company and the brand. But Harley remained plagued by a boatload of debt and increasing overseas competition. At the end of 1985, Harley's bankers jumped ship.

"It was New Year's Eve of 1985," says Bob Simonson, a leisure industry analyst with William Blair & Co., "and Harley's executives sat in front of a fax machine with two stacks of papers—one stack was the paperwork trying to get a new banking relationship, and the other was the bankruptcy filing." Twenty minutes before midnight, Merrill Lynch signed on as Harley's new lead bank, rescuing the company from bankruptcy.

A little more than a year later, in July 1986, Harley-Davidson went public on the New York Stock Exchange with a flourish, selling two million shares of stock at $11 a share and raising $25 million more than its underwriters expected, according to Teerlink. At this writing, in February 2005, the stock, which subsequently split, was at $61, and Harley had just announced its 19th consecutive year of record revenue ($5.02 billion) and net income ($890 million).

But things could have turned out quite differently. Harley's resurrection is really a story of reinvention. Sure, the company improved quality, but it also changed its manufacturing processes, its management philosophy, the way it marketed products, and its relationships with dealers and customers. It's not the same company it was in the mid-1980s, and it will probably look considerably different in another 10 years.

On a much smaller scale, the same is true for Mike Schwartz. When he bought his dealership, called Harley-Davidson of Wilmington, steady consumer demand was keeping the company afloat. But he knew that the industry had a long history of being cyclical. What would happen if demand fell off? If the economy softened? He knew that he needed to insulate himself from the vagaries of the marketplace and to do that, he'd have to completely change the way he operated. And so he gave up the idea that the dealership was merely a hobby and took the first step toward reinventing his business, rechristening it Mike's Famous Harley-Davidson.

If You Build It . . .

Famous? Not back then. But the name was like a gauntlet that Schwartz flung at his own feet; if he didn't live up to his own boast, he knew the name had the power to make a mockery of him. "Mike speaks his life into existence every day," says Otis Hackett, a sales consultant who has worked with Schwartz. "It's almost as if he says, 'This is what I'm going to do,' and then it happens."

It's not that easy, of course. What lay ahead for Schwartz was in many ways more difficult than starting from scratch, because he had bought a company based on a business model that was quickly becoming irrelevant. "The dealers were mostly developed by a cadre of enthusiasts," one Harley dealer told me. "It was kind of like a club, and it wasn't customer focused. You'd hear stories of customers who rode up on a competing brand of motorcycle and were snubbed." But by the early 1990s, a new kind of Harley customer had surfaced, and he was a lot less likely to put up with that kind of treatment. He was in his late thirties, educated, demanding, sophisticated, and while he may have watched *Easy Rider,* chances were he had also read *In Search of Excellence: Lessons from America's Best-Run Companies.* If he didn't like the way he was treated when he walked into a dealership, he would not think twice about walking out. And in the coming decade, "he" was increasingly likely to be "she."

As Schwartz saw it, there was a huge opportunity in the disconnect between the typical Harley dealer and the new breed of Harley customer. He knew his business would always attract leather-clad bikers with tattoos and chains, but he also wanted the clean-cut baby boomers with lifelong dreams or midlife crises—consumers who might be tempted to buy a ride on the wild side, but who might just as easily decide on a home theater system or a sailboat. He knew the demographic because he *was* the demographic.

"From the very beginning, I was thinking restaurant," recalls Schwartz. "If I was pitching to families, was a Harley place an acceptable place to stop? Maybe," he poses. "If it also had a restaurant, would that make it better? Probably. And if there was also a museum? There's no way you'd ever associate a museum with someplace dangerous."

It was an ambitious plan, but everywhere Schwartz looked, businesses were creating more enticing environments for consumers. Bookstores were serving up lattes and live music, department stores were building cafés, and stadiums were constructing museum-caliber tributes to their teams, sometimes with interactive exhibits. Schwartz wasn't thinking of his business as just a Harley dealership anymore. It would be a tourist destination, like Hershey's Chocolate World or Legoland.

"In the retail world, the big shift in the 1990s was from selling a product to selling an experience," says Mike Rubin, president of MRA

International, Inc., a Philadelphia consulting firm that helps clients develop leisure, sports, and retail projects. "Mike needed to create a draw so that people were motivated to get off the highway. It had to feel like a place that a motorcycle caravan might pull up to, but that was still family friendly. The goal was to create something that really broke out of the box." Rubin, along with a small cadre of other experts, helped Schwartz turn his vision into bricks and mortar.

Restaurants and museums were far removed from Schwartz's realm of expertise, but that didn't stop him. He was prepared, in fact, for the restaurant to be a loss leader—an attraction that may not be profitable on its own, but that would beckon travelers off the highway for a snack and ultimately lead them into the dealership. But could he draw enough customers? "I went to the rest stop five miles down the road, and I also counted the cars that stopped at Cracker Barrel," he recalls. "These people might wait an hour for a seat on Sunday—for ordinary food and to buy a trinket." Schwartz did the math. He reckoned that if he could snag 0.5% of those customers, sell each one of them $6 worth of food, and entice 10% of them to buy a t-shirt, he'd have a sustainable business.

Schwartz's plans for a reinvented business cried out for a new location, and he had his heart set on the most heavily traveled road in Delaware: I-95, an eight-lane highway traveled by 30 million vehicles a year, many of them making long-distance trips. Directly to the south, roadside restaurants are few and far between; to the north lie two and a half hours of New Jersey Turnpike rest stops. Schwartz thought he could offer an attractive alternative to weary travelers.

He searched for several months for the perfect site, until his dream location finally became available in February 1996, nearly a year after he started looking. Just south of the Delaware Memorial Bridge, on I-295, was a 5.8-acre tract of land that had been home to one of the first Howard Johnson's Motor Lodges, built in 1957. The ramshackle buildings, including the original orange-roofed HoJo's reception hut, were highly visible from I-95 and had been abandoned for years. The site had become "a blight to the local community," according to Judy McKinney-Cherry, who had worked for the Delaware Economic Development Office and is now its director.

"You'd come over the bridge and it was the first thing you'd see; it wasn't something the state was proud of."

With traditional financing from a local bank, plus cash from his newly profitable dealership, Schwartz signed an option to buy the land for $1.36 million. But before he could develop it, he'd have to clear several hurdles. The surrounding community had already nixed several projects—including a halfway house for recovering drug addicts and an auto repair company—and Schwartz wondered how they'd feel about having a motorcycle dealership in their backyard. He also needed to nail down Harley's approval to move the business, conduct the required environmental impact studies, and slog through a host of zoning issues. Schwartz needed help, and lots of it.

No Man Is an Island

Growing a business requires a steadfast commitment to enlisting the proper reinforcements—people to fill in the knowledge gaps so many entrepreneurs find it difficult to acknowledge that they even have. Schwartz knew what he knew, but he was also keenly aware of what he didn't know. And he wasn't shy about asking for help. He hired Wendie Stabler, a prominent land-use attorney; signed on Mark Kleinschmidt, a former New Castle County economic development director to help him with the land use and development process; retained retail consultant Mike Rubin for guidance on the overall concept and the mixed-use elements of the dealership; and hired Jack Rouse Associates, a Cincinnati designer of themed entertainment attractions. And to communicate his vision to his new neighbors, he approached Bill Houghton, a Delaware state representative who happened to live in the neighborhood, and Rev. Wendell Hall, head of the neighborhood civic association. "Our people were afraid of what motorcycles tend to bring to a neighborhood—motorcycle gangs," says Hall. "But Mike told us his clientele was quite different, and he told us that noise wouldn't be a factor because the operation would be totally inside."

Over the next year and a half, Schwartz would have benefited greatly from cloning technology. He was still running the dealership out of its original location, and he had grown it to just about $8 million in revenue and $700,000 in profit. But the place was bursting at the seams. By the fall of 1997, he had all his ducks in a row. He had nailed down all the proper permits and had presented his plan to Harley, securing not only their approval, but also a commitment for a $6 million loan from the company's financing division. He had also spoken to local community groups, conducted noise studies in the neighborhood, and agreed to put his repair shop on the side of the building that faced the road, not the residential area. "It wasn't the best situation because we should have had bikes facing the road," says Schwartz. "But it was about doing the right thing for the neighbors."

In November 1997, the wrecking ball finally came down on what was left of the old HoJo's. A dozen or so customers and employees even attached chains to their Harleys and helped pull down the dilapidated buildings. A few weeks later, a construction trailer was hauled to the site. There would come a time, says Debbie Schwartz, when "Mike sat in that trailer and literally watched every brick go up." At night, she recalls, "we would take the blueprints down to our basement, because that's where we had the most floor space." The two spent hours studying and tweaking the architects' drawings. Schwartz's attention to the details seemed, at times, almost compulsive. At one point, though, it became an absolute necessity.

In March 1998, the design firm that was responsible for the building's interior suddenly went out of business. So Schwartz and his architect, Joe Chickadel, picked up the slack themselves. They rummaged around abandoned warehouses, collecting the old screws, bolts, molds, and lighting fixtures—the "found objects" that would be an integral part of the building's design. Schwartz even instructed the bricklayers to crack the bricks and leave the mortar dripping because he thought it looked more authentic that way. And he found an antique map store, where he chose the maps that he wanted laminated on the restaurant's tabletops.

Schwartz also had ambitious plans for his Museum of the American Road. He had heard motorcycle legend Dave Barr speak at a Harley-Davidson conference, and he became intrigued with the idea of featuring Barr in the museum. Barr had earned a place in the *Guinness Book of World Records* by riding a Harley from the coast of France, through Northern Europe, and across Russia (in the winter) to the Pacific Ocean. It was the ultimate motorcycle adventure, made even more awe-inspiring by his disability; he has two prosthetic legs.

"Mike called me and asked me if I'd like to have a look at the dealership he was building," recalls Barr, who is now a public speaker and has also done occasional training programs for Harley. "So I met with him in New Castle, and what I saw was a man who wasn't afraid of risk, who had a sense of destiny and vision, and wasn't going to give up, no matter what. I get approached by dealers all the time, and I get a lot of offers and a lot of it is just rubbish. But Mike was the guy." So Barr agreed to send Schwartz the bike he'd ridden into the Guinness record. Later, he would also donate his Sportster—the bike that had taken him around the world and upon which he had viewed every ocean on the planet. He also pledged to hand over his medals, pictures, and other memorabilia that Schwartz would use to create an interactive exhibit and tribute to Barr. In return, Schwartz would give Barr a modified Sportster (with a Mike's logo on the fuel tank) to ride on his Southern Cross journey, a 45-day trip between the four extreme geographical corners of Australia. It was a marketing coup.

At about the same time, Schwartz enlisted his golf buddy, Mitch Hill, to build a sound system for his new facility. Hill, a television and radio advertising producer, had designed a software program that was essentially "a radio station in a box." While all the content—music, commercials, even DJ patter—was prerecorded, customers would actually get the impression that a radio station was being broadcast live from the dealership. Schwartz loved the idea, and he and Hill went to work immediately, digitizing more than 5,000 classic rock songs, plus jingles and commercials for the dealership. Customers would hear Mike's Famous Radio when they pulled into the parking lot, in the restaurant, in the restroom, in the dealership, and in the service department. "It became a very important part of the facility," says Hill. "It was a natural extension of the brand." Not the Harley brand, the Mike's Famous brand.

Going Live

It was December 18, 1998, when Schwartz first opened the doors to his new dealership so he decided to be somewhat low-key; he would save the real fanfare for the spring when his potential customers were more likely to be dreaming of the open road. Nonetheless, the dealership was packed. "I remember thinking that we did more business in one day than in any single week at our old place," Schwartz recalls. The building itself seemed to generate as much buzz as the motorcycles in it. From the road, the 40,000-square-foot complex was reminiscent of Harley's early redbrick manufacturing plants, while its back entrance mimicked a post–World War II service station. Inside, the theme was an eclectic combination of Route 66, art deco, and turn-of-the-century warehouse. The restaurant, called Mike's Warehouse Grill, was about as different from a New Jersey Turnpike Roy Rogers as a Harley was from a moped. It was designed to resemble a manufacturing plant cafeteria with steel conveyors, cogs and wheels on the walls, and even a faux boiler furnace that seats six.

When the weather warmed up, in June 1999, Schwartz planned a proper grand opening, Harley-style. It began in York, Pennsylvania, home of the factory that had built the 1972 WideGlide that Dave Barr would later retire to its final resting place at Mike's Museum of the American Road. Barr and Schwartz rode their motorcycles side by side—with 500 pumped-up Harley devotees following behind. "We rode with a police escort," Schwartz recalls. "It was a beautiful summer day, and I was riding right out in front with Dave—a living legend. I'll never forget it."

That first year at the new dealership would be as memorable as that ride: Schwartz's revenues rose to $13 million, and he earned Harley's coveted Gold Bar & Shield Award, which recognizes the top 4% of dealerships in the country for outstanding customer service and sales performance. And in 2000, *Dealernews* magazine, a respected trade publication, named him dealer of the year. It must have seemed as if nothing could go wrong.

Beware the Comfort Zone

"When you're comfortable, you're never performing at 100%," says Dave Barr. It might be Schwartz's mantra. Mike's Roadside Rest had earned him press accolades, respect from Harley, and a combination of admiration and envy from other dealers. Still, he found it difficult to rest easy.

The restaurant, as it turned out, was a blessing and a curse. Customers loved the homemade coleslaw and salsa that Mike's kitchen staff spent hours chopping and seasoning. And everyone raved about the meatloaf and freshly baked apple pie. Nonetheless, the restaurant's balance sheet was dismal. "We were so focused on our unique products that we didn't realize we had to keep an eye on our food costs," says Schwartz. "It became pretty obvious that something was wrong when the restaurant manager kept coming to me asking for a check to cover payroll." The operation was bleeding cash because Schwartz had insisted on creating a restaurant to satisfy his own tastes, rather than one tailored to market needs. It's a common mistake among business owners, but Schwartz could have kicked himself. "I was no different from those old-school Harley dealers who don't understand customer services," he admits. The restaurant would lose approximately $200,000 in 1999.

Schwartz realized he needed to rethink at least part of his reinvented company. Tired and hungry customers, he reckoned, would be content with a simpler menu—good, basic roadside food that was still several cuts above turnpike fare. "We could either continue to labor over all this high-quality food," he says, "or we could get lean and mean and still give customers what they wanted." So he scaled back the menu, favoring foods that required little preparation time and that could be easily inventoried. Both the chef, who was a master baker, and the restaurant manager left the company, and Schwartz brought in a no-nonsense cook and an accountant to "tear apart the business." It took two years, but the restaurant finally turned a small profit.

But it wasn't just the restaurant that was troubling Schwartz. "The first two years were spent just screaming about the business," he recalls. "We really didn't know how to sell motorcycles; they had been selling themselves. What we failed to realize was that it wasn't about getting the customer in the door, it was about how we treated them once they were here."

In the process of reinventing his business, he had overlooked a critically important element of growth—one that countless entrepreneurs are guilty of neglecting. Revenues had increased from $8 million in 1998 to $13 million in 1999, his first year at the new location, and margins were healthy (close to 8%), but his organization was still in its infancy. In the frenzy to staff up, he had hired haphazardly; there was no selling system on the retail floor, and his own vision of how big he wanted the company to be did not seem to resonate with some of his most trusted managers. Revenues for 2000 would be $17 million, but Schwartz noticed that when he compared August with December revenues for 1999 and 2000, they were nearly identical. The number of motorcycle sales was also stagnant for that period. Schwartz was not happy, but his efforts to persuade his staff of his own gut conviction that "we could be a $20 to $25 million business" were thwarted by employees who were more comfortable with the status quo. "Sometimes feeling the wall at your back is what gets you going again," he says.

It was January 2001, and Schwartz had just taken courses in profitability and change management at a Harley-Davidson University (HDU) dealer operations training seminar in Fort Lauderdale. He had always looked forward to the three-day annual retreat. "Mike is a big player in all of our training," says former HDU director Benny Suggs. "We like to think that's one of the reasons he's doing so well." As usual, Schwartz came home with some ideas that he was eager to implement at his company. But his employees were unmotivated. In comparison with his own lofty thoughts, the concerns of his staff seemed petty and shortsighted, but Schwartz realized that he was partly to blame for that. "After those two courses, I knew I had to develop an organization that was change oriented," he says. "But if I was going to ask my people to change, then I had to change first."

Reinventing the Reinvention

Schwartz's business was suffering from a classic case of prolonged adolescence—it was a like teenager who looks deceptively grown-up but who is still wildly immature. It's a phase that every growing business experiences, and one that a company can remain in indefinitely unless its owner helps it to grow up. And that almost always involves stepping away from the product or service that the business is selling and attending to the business itself. It means professionalizing your company in a way that will grate on some of your most veteran and loyal employees.

For Schwartz, the first step was a hard-nosed assessment of his own strengths and weaknesses. "I live in the future," he concedes. "I'm very imaginative; I create the messes." In their marriage, Debbie was always the pragmatist, creating order out of his chaos. "Most of us don't like to step out of the box," says Debbie. "But Mike lives out of the box." At his company, though, Schwartz was spending a little too much time out of the box, and there was no Debbie to clean up his proverbial messes.

He thought he had surrounded himself with people who complemented his strong entrepreneurial bent, but he was beginning to realize that his company was quickly outgrowing some of those home-grown employees. "It's difficult to try to evaluate longtime employees," Schwartz says. "Your heart tells you to do one thing, but your best judgment tells you what you have to do. I knew I had to rip the business apart down to its core in order to build it back up again."

So shortly after he returned from Fort Lauderdale, Schwartz says, he "parted ways" with his sales manager, his general manager, and his personnel manager. And he placed two ads on Monster.com—one for a human resources manager and another for a CFO. Within a month, he had signed on Mark Hollinger as CFO and Kelly Haines as HR manager. Neither had motorcycle dealership experience; Hollinger had been the number two man at a staffing company, and Haines had worked at a long-term care facility. But Schwartz didn't care. Hollinger, he says, was "a solid operator—a nuts-and-bolts guy and a great complement to me." And Haines, although just 24 years old, had "a sunny disposition but at the same time, she's not going to be rolled over," he recalls.

Next, Schwartz signed on Otis Hackett, a LaPorte, Indiana, consultant who specializes in motorcycle dealerships. Schwartz had read an industry newsletter article that Hackett had written about sales systems, and it resonated with him. "He called me and said he needed to make some changes," recalls Hackett. "To reinvent, you have to reevaluate, and the clarity of reevaluation comes with being totally truthful. And Mike is not afraid of the truth."

Professionalizing the Business

That year, 2001, was turbulent and often chaotic. "The biggest problem was knowing where to start," says Hollinger. "Mike had built a $17 million company, but there were cracks in the foundation." Haines beefed up the company's employee handbook, which laid out everything from a new and more generous benefits plan (predictably popular) to a formal dress code (not so popular). "We had a lot of turnover that first year," says Haines. "We were trying to create structure and accountability." But it was sometimes tough, she admits, "for a 24-year-old girl who didn't know anything about bikes to correct a technician about not wearing the right shirt."

Schwartz, Hollinger, and Hackett zeroed in on the sales department, which had dwindled to one full-time salesperson, one part-timer, a full-time finance manager, and Schwartz, because "I had to run into the burning building." Getting himself off the sales floor—and putting the right people with the right tools in place—was a top priority. To help lead the charge, he hired two new sales managers, both from nearby automobile dealerships, and then he turned Hackett loose on the business.

On the day that Hackett first began evaluating the dealership, he sat at the front door and counted customers. "I've never seen so much traffic in my life," he told Schwartz. But what happened after that shocked him. The customers weren't greeted when they walked through the door, and those who were lucky enough to strike up a conversation with a salesperson were often interrupted when the main office sent telephone calls down to the sales floor. To Hackett, that was double trouble. The conversation on the retail floor was being interrupted, and the potential customer on the phone was given short shrift since the salespeople were too distracted to get their names and numbers. "It was a waste of a Yellow Pages ad," grouses Hackett.

"We didn't really understand how to sell motorcycles," concedes Schwartz, who worked 30 days with Hackett "from bell to bell" to analyze what was happening on the sales floor and devise a system to fix it. "We started to look at every customer as an opportunity, talking to them about why they were there and what their needs were. And when we did that, we went from selling clothes and parts and service and motorcycles along the way to *really* selling motorcycles."

And it all began with answering the phone. Schwartz created a business development center, staffed with employees whose sole responsibility was to take calls from prospective customers. "My main job is to set up appointments and get them in the building," says Jane Spoerl, who is one of three operators in the center. Spoerl has an inventory of every bike in the store so that she can instantly tell customers if Mike's has what they're looking for. She can rattle off information on warranties, insurance, and financing, and she'll even promise callers a free lunch at the restaurant if they come in for an appointment. But she never, ever, transfers calls to the retail floor. "Last month, 80% of the people who set up appointments showed up at the dealership and 50% bought bikes," she says. Everyone—even those who don't make an appointment—goes into Mike's database along with Spoerl's notes. If they do wander in at some point, salespeople can pull up their information right on the sales floor.

Next, the sales force needed to be whipped into shape. Schwartz and his team created a new sales training program, which starts with an ad in the local newspaper inviting prospective hires to apply for a free three-day training course. Acceptance into the program doesn't guarantee anyone a job, and being an avid Harley rider doesn't give you a leg up. Typically, nine out of ten participants stay the full three days and Schwartz hires one-third of the class. He runs the class four or five times a year, usually in the winter, so that he can hire approximately 10 new salespeople for the spring peak selling season.

Mike's organizational reinvention extended to virtually every department at the company. The delivery department—previously called "finance and insurance"—where customers go to fill out the paperwork that completes their motorcycle purchase, was completely overhauled to shorten the process to just 45 minutes. "Before, it took up to two hours," says Hollinger. "And it just wasn't consistent." Now customers are treated to a meal at Mike's Warehouse Grill if there's a wait for their turn in the delivery department. And because the experience of buying warranties and insurance pales in comparison to buying a bike, Hollinger standardized the selling process and moved it from the noisy showroom up to the museum's more private second floor, where customers are surrounded by eye-catching memorabilia. "After we improved the process, bike sales increased from 800 to more than 1,700, and delivery department profits quadrupled," says Hollinger. He says that Harley-Davidson actually filmed Mike's delivery process and has used it as a training tool for other dealers.

Hollinger also introduced a program called Famous for Service, a focus group that's comprised of six employees from different departments. They meet once a week to hash out any current problems the company might be having and brainstorm new ideas. "You get a service person sitting there with a salesperson, and the barriers start breaking down," says Hollinger, who was promoted to general manager in April 2001. Employees in the group might also shadow one another for a day so that, say, a parts department employee gets a taste of what it might be like to work as a service technician or as a salesperson. A new group of employees rotates into the group every six months.

Schwartz's changes yielded impressive rewards. By the end of 2002, sales were $33 million, up from $22 million the year before. The growth continued through 2003 ($38 million) and 2004 ($47.8 million, which included sales from the new dealership in Connecticut). "Before we had these systems, there was always some problem that had nothing to do with the business and everything to do with the people," says Schwartz. "There was always another fire to put out. But after we reinvented ourselves again, it was about the systems and finding the right people to run them, and then improving the systems." In fact, Schwartz is so confident of his systems that he's opened a new satellite dealership 40 miles away in Smyrna, Delaware; he also bought another Harley dealership in Groton, Connecticut. He's bringing his Mike's Famous brand to both new facilities, which open in 2005; his projected revenues for that year are $60.6 million.

"I always set my sights on being the best Harley dealership in the world," he says. But that's a tricky distinction. Harley, while it hands out annual awards such as the Gold Bar & Shield to approximately 25 of its 650 dealers, is like a parent with hundreds of children: the company just won't name a number one. But the more you talk to Schwartz, the more you come to realize that "best" is merely how he hopes to define his business to himself. It's a quest for perfection that's never quite over. Like a road trip on a Harley, it's not the destination that's appealing. It's the journey.

"Embrace Reinvention" Tips from Mike's Famous Harley-Davidson

1. **Don't Let Past Success Make You Complacent.** Mike's original dealership was growing in revenue and profits, but he realized that industry trends, like the growing number of older, more affluent, and demanding customers, would soon make his business model obsolete. Before his business could begin to suffer, he reinvented the dealership so that it would be prepared to ride that trend. He created a retail environment that focused not just on products and the Harley iconography, but on family entertainment.

2. **Be Your Own Critic.** When you try new things, you're going to make mistakes. Learn to recognize and correct them before they steamroller you. Schwartz, for instance, realized that his restaurant was bleeding cash because his menu offerings were too complex and labor intensive. After he scaled back and simplified the operation, it finally began to post a small profit.

3. **Enlist Reinforcements.** When you reconceive your business, it's likely that you'll step out of your comfort zone. Enlist the help of experts whose knowledge and networks will help you avoid costly mistakes. Schwartz called on community leaders, the city government, a retail consultant, and other real-estate developers to help him conceive and build his new facility.

4. **Hire Managers Who Complement Your Own Skills.** When Schwartz's company began to grow exponentially, he acknowledged that he didn't possess all the skills needed to manage the business. Hiring a new general manager, CFO, sales managers, and human resource manager—people whose skills complemented his own—gave him the confidence to delegate tasks so that he could devote himself to big-picture strategizing.

5. **Anticipate the Domino Effect.** Every time you reinvent your company, whether that involves pursuing a new market or developing new products, you'll create stress on your organization. As Schwartz discovered, employees may balk and move

on, and you'll be faced with the task of bringing on new people who are up to more demanding tasks. Anticipate that every deliberately executed change is likely to precipitate more unexpected and sometimes unpleasant ones as well.

. . . And from Others

6. **Listen to the Market.** In 1995, **Inspiration Software** CEO Don Helfgott noticed that an increasing number of elementary school teachers were using the visual mapping software that he was selling to the corporate market. Back then, educators represented just 5% to 10% of his company's revenues, but Helfgott saw huge growth potential in that small niche, which was using his product in a way he had never imagined. So he "reoriented everyone in the company to switch over to the kid's mind-set," retooling the software and abandoning the corporate market almost completely. "It was a pretty wrenching change," he admits. But it was worth it. Inspiration has grown from $2 million to $19 million in revenues since its reinvention.

7. **Evaluate Your Resources.** When Adam Kamens took the helm of his family's $4 million magnetic shield manufacturing company in 1999, he evaluated not just the company's products but the machines and people making them. By closely examining **Amuneal Manufacturing**'s capabilities and its skill base, Kamens determined that he could also manufacture custom metal furniture with very little additional investment in machinery. Now he makes high-end retail fixtures, like clothing racks, for companies like Barneys and Abercrombie & Fitch, and custom architectural fabrications, like steel staircases and railings, for casinos, shopping malls, and sports arenas. The strategy, says Kamens, "has allowed us to more than double our sales to $9 million in the past five years."

8. **Reinvent on the Inside Too.** Steve McDonnell, CEO of **Applegate Farms,** had solidly established his Bridgewater, New Jersey, organic lunch meat company as "a brand that soccer moms could trust." But he wanted Applegate to look as good to his em-

ployees as it did to his customers. So he started by completely redesigning his building to reflect the company's image. He outfitted his headquarters with new Herman Miller open-plan furniture and built rooms that he says "embody 90% of the nature of most business engagement." For instance, there's a meditation-yoga room, a vision room, a play room, a boat room (the team-building room), and a project room. "Finally, I have a physical manifestation of my business ideology," says McDonnell. "The key is to have your internal profile mirror your external profile."

9. **Respond to Demographic Changes. La-Z-Boy, Inc.,** the company whose name is virtually synonymous with "recliner," understood that it would forfeit an enormous segment of the market if it just continued to manufacture the kind of chair that Frasier Crane's dad lived in. Instead, says Greg White, the company's vice president of merchandising, "we wanted to provide recliners to the style-conscious market . . . by designing a chair that looks stationary but has the hidden function of reclining comfort." Enter fashion designer Todd Oldham, whom La-Z-Boy signed on to create a hip line of contemporary furniture geared toward younger consumers, because aging baby boomers may have inherited Dad's aching back and feet, but they don't particularly want his recliner.

10. **Don't Stop Reinventing.** Who's more successful than **Starbucks** chairman and "chief global strategist," Howard Schultz? And yet, at this writing, Schultz was in the process of launching a chain of coffeehouse–music stores through a wholly owned subsidiary called Hear Music. The concept: when customers walk into the Hear Music coffeehouse, they'll not only be able to order up a tall latte, but they'll also have the opportunity to a burn a CD, choosing from more than 150,000 songs. By the end of 2005, Schultz is hoping that upward of 1,000 of his music coffeehouses will be giving music downloading sites and traditional retailers a run for their money, proving once again that even extraordinarily effective formulas for success can always be improved upon.

10 | Alpha Dog DNA

Between February and September 2004, I spent a few days with almost every Alpha Dog CEO on his or her home turf; they welcomed me into their companies and their lives with sincere generosity of spirit, allowing me to learn more about them and their companies than I could even dream of chronicling in one book. And I had a great time with them.

At Mike's Famous Harley-Davidson, Mike Schwartz gave me a true insider's look at a business I've admired for years, and one that I frequently visit when I travel from New York to Washington, DC; Steve Simmons took me on a tour of nearly every Amy's Ice Creams in Austin and left me longing for an Amy's in New York; I saw champion auctioneer Levi Jordan in action at two of Deb Weidenhamer's auctions in Phoenix; I watched Dancing Deer Baking Company's director of product development, Chris Gagnon, test the batter for a new pumpkin spice pancake and waffle mix; in North Carolina, Jim Throneburg gave me a sneak peak at THOR·LO's new walking shoes and treated me to crab legs at Big Daddy's, along with half a dozen employees who hung on his every word; back in New York, public relations consultant Marisa Vallbona-Freeman carved time out of a short business trip to meet me at the Marriott Financial Center, where we compared notes on our lives as soloists; at Dorothy Lane Markets in Dayton, Norman Mayne shopped for lamb chops, mâche, black rice, and a bottle of Darioush cabernet, then whisked me back to his stunning Frank Lloyd Wright–style home, where his wife, Terry, cooked and served a meal I still can't replicate; and I went to a business conference with bike shop owner Chris Zane and listened in awe as he imparted his wisdom to a room full of senior executives from companies like American Express and Pitney Bowes.

The better I came to know them, the clearer it became that each of these Alpha Dog entrepreneurs was living the kind of life that their peers might only dream of. And yet, their businesses started out looking a lot like most young companies. Their founders focused on the fundamentals: gaining acceptance in the marketplace, growing sales, managing cash flow, and becoming profitable. They were proprietors, not CEOs. But at some point, all of them had what THOR·LO's Jim Throneburg would call "an 'aha' moment." Trish Karter nearly lost her company in the throes of divorce; Norman Mayne could have been crushed by competition from big supermarket chains; Chris Zane was overwhelmed by premature success; Deb Weidenhamer's entire industry was disrupted by eBay; Mike Schwartz realized that his company had grown but not grown up.

They responded by changing not what they do, but how they do it: they held fast to the core strategies that had fueled their growth, but at the same time, they created company architectures of systems and procedures that would help them execute those strategies with consistency and predictability. Karter sums it up perfectly: "Many people call me for advice on how to start or run a food company. I always try to talk them out of it because it's so often the case that they pursue the business for the love of food, but are wiped out by the business reality of producing and selling it. Anyone can make a great cookie. It's all the rest of what it takes to build a team and deliver a great quality product 52 weeks a year while staying profitable that's challenging." In other words, what really makes an Alpha Dog isn't just its stock in trade; it's the company itself. Companies make the leap from ordinary to extraordinary when their leaders step back from what they do and focus on how they're doing it. And so it should come as no surprise that these companies, as different as they may seem, have more in common than you might think. They:

- **Beat Goliath.** Zane's Cycles competes against Wal-Mart and the category killers by providing the kind of customer service and product guarantees that big companies can't or won't offer.

Amy's Ice Creams goes head-to-head with national chains because its local identity resonates with consumers in a way that cookie-cutter companies don't. THOR·LO doesn't worry about sock imports from China because the company's innovative products appeal to a much different kind of consumer. And PRConsultants Group leverages the united power of small, local companies to compete against much bigger public relations firms.

- **Forge strong community connections.** Even though it's a commercial bakery with national distribution, Dancing Deer has a strong inner-city Boston identity. The company is known for its multicultural workforce, its ties to local not-for-profit organizations, and its manic support of Boston's sports teams. Amy's Ice Creams founder Amy Simmons spearheaded a small business coalition, Choose Austin First, that promotes local companies and raises funds for community charities. The group helps identify Austin companies as homegrown so that consumers who want to keep their dollars local know which businesses to patronize. But community isn't just about geography. THOR·LO has ongoing relationships with over 30 outdoor-related organizations, which the company often supports with sock donations. And both THOR·LO and Mike's Famous Harley-Davidson are sending goods to U.S. troops in Iraq; THOR·LO is sending socks, and Mike's is shipping boxes of boots. Why does any of this matter? Because in this age of corporate cynicism, consumers want to feel good about the companies they do business with and employees want to be proud of the companies where they work.

- **Build closer, more direct relationships with customers.** That's easy to discern at companies like Zane's Cycles, Mike's Famous Harley-Davidson, Amy's Ice Creams, and Dorothy Lane—companies that have direct relationships with the end users of their products. But even companies like Dancing Deer and THOR·LO, which sell mainly through retailers or resellers, are working hard to establish more personal connections with their consumers. Both companies, for example, are beefing up their Web sites so that customers can order directly from them. And those Web sites aren't just e-commerce tools. They reflect company culture in a way that helps brand the companies and create stronger bonds with consumers.

- **Commit to employee development.** For every Alpha Dog CEO, employee recruitment, training, and advancement are high priorities. Amy Simmons (Amy's Ice Creams) has sent her managers to training seminars at Disney Institute and Franklin-Covey; Mike Schwartz (Mike's Famous Harley-Davidson) sends his employees to Harley-Davidson University; Deb Weidenhamer (Auction Systems) and Trish Karter (Dancing Deer) also pay for their employees to attend training courses. That kind of continuous learning brings new ideas and best practices into companies, and it can also trigger promotions or job changes. The result: employees at Alpha Dog companies are highly engaged, and turnover is typically lower than industry average. If a labor shortage does materialize within the next several years, Alpha Dogs will be prepared for it.

- **Focus on experiences, not just transactions.** Mike's Famous Harley-Davidson isn't just a motorcycle dealership. It's a high-concept highway destination where families can stop to grab a bite to eat, stroll through the Museum of the American Road, or just use the impeccably tidy restrooms. At Amy's Ice Creams, you don't just get a scoop, you get entertainment as well—Amy's employees might sing, dance, and toss scoops up in the air and catch them behind their backs. Her goal: "To make your day." Deb Weidenhamer knows that Internet auctions are infinitely more fun if participants can listen to the auction live, so she added a real-time audio component to her simulcast auctions and increased participation by 416%. Alpha Dog CEOs know that business is a stage and that customers will always come back for more if they enjoy the show.

- **Leverage new technology creatively.** THOR·LO uses technology to train new employees on knitting machines, develop new products, and manage a huge customer database; Chris Zane has a webcam in his warehouse that allows customers to watch his technicians assemble bikes in real time; Norman Mayne's intranet is also an open-book management tool; Mike Schwartz's computerized inventory system rivals the one at Hertz. And Deb Weidenhamer of Auction Systems brought an ancient industry into the 21st century by combining live auctions with an Internet marketplace. Alpha Dog CEOs make investments in technology that help them streamline their businesses, serve their customers, and stay connected to their employees. And they generally do it well before their competitors.

- **Reject the commodity game.** Alpha Dogs rarely compete on price. THOR·LO's socks, Dancing Deer's cookies, Amy's ice cream, Zane's bicycles, Auction Systems' commissions—none of these products or services distinguish themselves through low cost. Instead, they're positioned as affordable luxuries with a little something extra: a sock with special padding; a bike that comes with lifetime free service; a kosher, baked-from-scratch cookie; ice cream that's customized with your choice of crushed-in treat. Even middle- and lower-income consumers want to splurge once in a while, and these Alpha Dogs satisfy such cravings for "new luxuries."

My Alpha Dog entrepreneurs had other traits in common as well. They were all, for example, perennially restless. While I chose them for the success they had already achieved, I discovered that not a single one of them was complacent. All of them felt an urgency to continually reinvent and grow their businesses not just because the competition was nipping at their heels but because, well, it's pretty good fun. Amy Simmons was building a new production facility, store, and restaurant; Jim Throneburg was preparing to launch a new walking shoe; Mike Schwartz had bought another Harley-Davidson dealership in Connecticut and had built a new satellite location to his existing business in Delaware; Chris Zane was negotiating to buy Huffy Bicycle Company, which filed for Chapter 11 in November 2004; Deb Weidenhamer was making new inroads into the real-estate auction business; PRConsultants Group had begun to actively market its alliance to new customers; Trish Karter was ramping up to quadruple her bakery's revenues in three years; Norman Mayne had already made his big leap by opening a third store.

When I was growing up in western Massachusetts, back when there were no Wal-Marts or Targets, my dad had a way of referring to the small, local businesses that he admired: "It's a good outfit," he'd declare. The expression was clearly a throwback from his military days when he was with "an outfit" in Korea, and it always seemed to me an odd way to describe a gas station, a coffee shop, or a hardware store. But now I think the description makes perfect sense. He wasn't really commenting specifically on what he was buying, whether it was a cup of coffee or a socket wrench; a business was "a good outfit" if you walked away feeling that you had not only been well taken care of, but that your expectations had in some way been exceeded. Good outfits had a way of expertly executing the task at hand and of taking pride in even the most humble kind of work.

It strikes me that Alpha Dogs and good outfits have a lot in common. The business itself—not the product, the service, or even the entrepreneur—is the Alpha Dog. It's responsive, dynamic, and takes nothing for granted; it's resilient and sustainable. And it refuses to accept the conventional wisdom that size is limiting. It knows that even a very small dog, when it stands in the proper light, can cast an awesome shadow.

ACKNOWLEDGMENTS

I am extraordinarily fortunate to have spent the bulk of my career as a business journalist within a community of smart, generous, and passionate writers and editors—my former and current colleagues at *Inc.* magazine. George Gendron, editor-in-chief of *Inc.* for more than 20 years, is a brilliant big-picture thinker, and he spent hours helping me work through the framework for this book. George not only has spot-on instincts about business, but he also had a gift for hiring great people. Many of them contributed mightily to my growth as a writer and to my education as a journalist: Nancy Lyons, John Case, Bo Burlingham, the late Tom Richman, Elyse Friedman, Bruce Posner, Steve Soloman, Karen Dillon, Evelyn Roth, Michael Hopkins, Leigh Buchanan, Josh Hyatt, Joe Rosenbloom, Martha Mangelsdorf, Elaine Appleton Grant, Susan Donovan, and Mike Hofman. *Inc.*'s current editor-in-chief, John Koten, sent more wonderful editors my way: Jane Berentson, Loren Feldman, and Larry Kanter. You are cherished friends as well as respected colleagues, and I'm most grateful to all of you.

For this book specifically, I owe a huge debt of gratitude to my fantastic agent, Esmond Harmsworth, who coaxed the idea from me over drinks on a snowy February night at the Gotham Bar in Manhattan, then shepherded its development with painstaking devotion. I could not have asked for a better partner on that journey.

To Collins Business editorial director, Marion Maneker: it's a rare and wonderful thing when an author finds an editor who so thoroughly believes in her project; from the day we first met, I knew that my book had found the perfect home. And to my editor, Leah Spiro: your years of experience as a first-class business journalist, your candor, your no-nonsense advice, and your unflagging enthusiasm for the book guided me expertly through the process of writing (and rewriting). The author genie must have been looking out for me. Thanks, darlin'. Larry Hughes, Tony Valado, Tara Cibelli, and Alexandra Kaufman worked tirelessly to help me get the word out on *Alpha Dogs*.

I would never have been able to write *Alpha Dogs* without the generous cooperation of Trish Karter, Norman and Calvin Mayne, Mike Schwartz, Amy and Steve Simmons, Jim Throneburg and Lynn Thorneburg, Marisa Vallbona-Freeman and the PRCG network, Deb Weidenhamer, and Chris Zane. They hosted me at their companies, introduced me to their employees and customers, and endured hours of phone interviews and slews of e-mails (all beginning with "just a few more questions"). Moreover, all of them knew that while the book would be independently fact-checked, they would not have the opportunity to physically review the manuscript before publication. They placed an enormous amount of trust in me, and I can only hope that, in balance, the experience was as rewarding for them as it was for me.

Michael Kempner was a steady source of wisdom and great advice. Rob Lederer understood my idea immediately and promptly introduced me to an Alpha Dog. Chris Heintzen put his considerable design skills to work for me to create a spectacular logo.

Kascha Piotrzkowski, my czarina of fact-checking, not only committed herself to the accuracy of every fact in this book with exhaustive attention to detail, but was a wise and trusted sounding board. Any remaining errors in the book are due to my own foolish disregard of her expert counsel.

Most importantly, I want to thank my husband, Guian Heintzen, and my children, Ariana and Erich Heintzen. They endured my frequent absences, my preoccupation, and many, many "survival of the hungriest" nights with loving tolerance and good humor. They're the best people I know, and I'm lucky to be in their pack.

SOURCES

The following books, articles, organizations, and people helped me develop and support the ideas in *Alpha Dogs*.

Introduction

Don Peppers and Martha Rogers, PhD, *The One to One Future: Building Relationships One Customer at a Time* (New York: Doubleday Currency, 1993).

To read my first story about Chris Zane, "Leader of the Pack," see *Inc.,* February 1996, available at www.inc.com.

John Case, "The Gazelle Theory: Are Some Small Companies More Equal Than Others," *Inc.,* May 2001.

Amar V. Bhidé, *The Origin and Evolution of New Businesses* (New York: Oxford University Press, 2000).

The Family Firm Institute (www.ffi.org) is a great source of information on family businesses.

Center for Women's Business Research (www.womensbusinessresearch .org) provides the best research on women-owned companies.

Chapter One

For statistics on small businesses, go to the United States Small Business Administration's Office of Advocacy (www.sba.gov/advo/).

For research on entrepreneurial activity in the United States, see "2003 Global Entrepreneurship Monitor," available at www.gemconsor tium.org.

Sam Dolnick, "Developer Drops Plan for NYC Wal-Mart," Associated Press, February 24, 2005.

Sprawl-Busters (www.sprawl-busters.com) is a clearinghouse for information on the anti-big-box retailer movement.

Both the American Independent Business Alliance (www.aimba.net) and the Business Alliance for Living Economies (www.living economies.org) are wonderful resources for small business owners who want to join or start a local alliance.

For more information on the National Customer Rage Study, visit the Customer Care Alliance's Web site (www.ccareall.org) and Arizona State University's W. P. Carey School of Business Web site (www.wpcarey.asu.edu).

"Time to Switch Drugstores?" *Consumer Reports,* October 2003.

Information on the projected labor shortage came from *The American Workplace 2003: Realities, Challenges and Opportunities* (Employment Policy Foundation, 1015 Fifteenth Street, NW, Washington, DC 20005; www.epf.org) and from Jay Jamrog, "The Perfect Storm: The Future of Retention and Engagement," available on the Human Resource Institute's Web site (www.hrinstitute.info).

B. Joseph Pine II and James H. Gilmore, *The Experience Economy: Work Is Theatre & Every Business a Stage* (Boston: Harvard Business School Press, 1999).

U.S. Census Bureau, *Income, Poverty, and Health Insurance Coverage in the United States: 2003.* Available at www.census.gov.

Michael J. Silverstein and Neil Fiske, *Trading Up: The New American Luxury* (New York: Portfolio, 2003).

Michael E. Gerber, *The E-Myth Revisited: Why Most Small Businesses Don't Work and What to Do About It* (New York: HarperBusiness, updated edition, 1995).

Chapter Two

Bicycle industry statistics came from the National Bicycle Dealers Association (www.nbda.com). Executive director Fred Clements helped me make sense of the data.

Bryan Miller, "In Norwalk, A 'Disneyland' Dairy Store," *New York Times,* June 22, 1983.

To read a detailed account of Chris Zane's entry into the premiums and incentives industry, read my article "A Bigger Wheel," *Inc.,* November 2000, available on www.inc.com.

Jack Mitchell, *Hug Your Customers: The Proven Way to Personalize Sales and Achieve Astounding Results* (New York: Hyperion, 2003).

Chapter Three

Eric Klein and John B. Izzo, PhD, *Awakening Corporate Soul: Four Paths to Unleash the Power of People at Work* (Vancouver, BC: Fairwinds Press, 1998).

For more information on the Great Place to Work Institute, as well as the companies on their annual lists, go to www.greatplaceto work.com.

Supermarket industry statistics are available at the *Supermarket News* Web site (www.supermarketnews.com), as well as from the Food Marketing Institute (www.fmi.org/facts). Industry consultant Howard Solganik (www.solganik.com) also provided valuable perspective.

To read about Dorothy Lane Market and other top specialty food retailers, see "Important Specialty Food Retailers," September 1, 2004, available at www.gourmetretailer.com.

Chapter Four

For more information on the Initiative for a Competitive Inner City, go to www.icic.org.

Auction industry information came from the National Auctioneers Association (www.auctioneers.org).

Deb Weidenhamer's columns for *Auction World* not only give insight into her industry, but are also a great source of general business advice. They are available on her Web site, www.auctionand appraise.com.

Chapter Five

For more information on Austin's "weird" movement, read "Keep Austin Weird?" by Alexis Kanter in the *Daily Texan,* September 9, 2005, available at www.dailytexanonline.com. And to read about how the idea has spread to other cities, read "Small Merchants Adopt 'Weird' PR Campaign" by Brett Barrouquere, Associated Press, March 22, 2005.

To read about Reuben Mattus and the founding of Häagen-Dazs, go to www.mattusicecream.com. For historical perspective, I also relied on my own childhood memories and a conversation with Ed Marks, an ice cream historian (www.icecreamhistorian.info).

"Austin Disregards Its Dungarees," *Economist,* May 26, 1984, was the article that sent Amy Miller and Scott Shaw to Austin.

For more information on Choose Austin First, go to www.choose austinfirst.com.

For great pictures that chronicle the restoration of Mangiasaurus rex, go to the Texas Memorial Museum's Web site, http://www.tmm .utexas.edu/education/mangia/.

Chapter Six

Sally Kay, president of The Hosiery Association in Charlotte, NC (www.nahm.com); Dan St. Louis, director of the Hosiery Technology Center in Hickory, NC (www.hosetech.com); and Marshal Cohen at the NPD Group in Port Washington, NY (www.npd .com), provided me with statistics and general information about the state of the U.S. hosiery industry.

Peter F. Drucker, *Innovation and Entrepreneurship* (New York: Harper & Row, 1985).

Tom Kelley, *The Art of Innovation: Lessons in Creativity from IDEO,*

America's Leading Design Firm (New York: Random House, 2001).

Summaries of the medical research sponsored by THOR·LO can be found on the company's Web site (www.thorlo.com). A partial list of the studies includes:

Aritidis Veves, E. M. Hay, Andrew J. M. Boulton, "The Use of Specially Padded Hosiery in the Painful Rheumatoid Foot," Boulton University Departments of Medicine and Rheumatology, Manchester Royal Infirmary, Manchester, UK.

"Test Report: Improved Sock System Customer Test." United States Army Test and Experimentation Command Experimentation Center, Fort Liggett, CA 93928-5000, January 1994.

Aritidis Veves, MD; Ewan Masson, MRCP; Devaka Fernando, MRCP; Andrew J. M. Boulton, MD; "Studies of Experimental Hosiery in Diabetic Neuropathic Patients with High Foot Pressures," *Diabetic Medicine* 7 (January 1990): 324–326.

Kirk M. Herring, DPM; Douglas H. Richie Jr., DPM; "Friction Blisters and Sock Fiber Composition, a Single Blind Study (Part 2)," presented at 75th Annual Meeting of the American Podiatric Medical Association, Las Vegas, NV, August 1990, published as "Comparison of Cotton and Acrylic Socks Using a Generic Cushion Sole Design for Runners," *Journal of the American Podiatric Medical Association* 83 no. 9 (September 1993).

Chapter Seven

Ron Tanner, "The State of the Specialty Food Industry," *Specialty Food,* April 2005. For more industry information, go to the National Association for the Specialty Food Trade Web site, www.nasft.com.

Mary Jo Hatch and Majken Schultz, "Are the Strategic Stars Aligned for Your Corporate Brand?" *Harvard Business Review,* February 2001.

Colin Mitchell, "Selling the Brand Inside," *Harvard Business Review,* January 2002.

To read more about the history of Newman's Own and its social mission, go to the company's Web site, www.newmansown.com.

For more information on the 2004 Cone Corporate Citizenship Study, go to Cone, Inc.'s Web site, www.coneinc.com.

For more information on the Paul and Phyllis Fireman Charitable Foundation's One Family Initiative and the Sweet Home project, go to www.onefamilycampaign.org.

Chapter Eight

Jessica Lipnack and Jeffrey Stamps, *Virtual Teams: People Working Across Boundaries with Technology* (New York: John Wiley & Sons, second edition, 2000).

To read more about Harry Brown and alliances in general, see my article "Sleeping with the Enemy," *Inc.,* November 1997. Available at www.inc.com.

Susan Greco, "The Declaration of Independents," *Inc.,* September 2001. Available at www.inc.com.

Chapter Nine

Gary Hamel and Liisa Välikangas, "The Quest for Resilience," *Harvard Business Review,* September 2003.

The historical information on Harley-Davidson came from these sources:

Rich Teerlink and Lee Ozley, *More Than a Motorcycle: The Leadership Journey at Harley-Davidson* (Boston: Harvard Business School Press, 2000).

Rich Teerlink, "Harley's Leadership U-Turn," *Harvard Business Review,* July-August 2000.

Hog Heaven: The Story of the Harley-Davidson Empire, A & E Entertainment, 1998.

The Harley-Davidson Web site (www.harley-davidson.com)

For more information on Dave Barr, go to www.davebarr.com.

INDEX